Fathers on Film

Library of Gender and Popular Culture

From *Mad Men* to gaming culture, performance art to steam-punk fashion, the presentation and representation of gender continues to saturate popular media. This new series seeks to explore the intersection of gender and popular culture, engaging with a variety of texts – drawn primarily from Art, Fashion, TV, Cinema, Cultural Studies and Media Studies – as a way of considering various models for understanding the complementary relationship between 'gender identities' and 'popular culture'. By considering race, ethnicity, class, and sexual identities across a range of cultural forms, each book in the series will adopt a critical stance towards issues surrounding the development of gender identities and popular and mass cultural 'products'.

For further information or enquiries, please contact the library

Claire Nally: claire.nally@northumbria.ac.uk
Angela Smith: angela.smith@sunderland.ac.uk

Advisory Board

Dr Kate Ames, Central Queensland University, Australia

Prof Leslie Heywood, Binghampton University, USA

Dr Michael Higgins, Strathclyde University, UK

Prof Åsa Kroon, Örebro University, Sweden

Dr Niall Richardson, Sussex University, UK

Dr Jacki Willson, Central St Martins, University of Arts London, UK

Published and forthcoming titles

The Aesthetics of Camp: Post-Queer Gender and Popular Culture
By Anna Malinowska

Ageing Femininity on Screen: The Older Woman in Contemporary Cinema
By Niall Richardson

All-American TV Crime Drama: Feminism and Identity Politics in Law and Order: Special Victims Unit
By Sujata Moorti and Lisa Cuklanz

Bad Girls, Dirty Bodies: Sex, Performance and Safe Femininity
By Gemma Commane

Beyoncé: Celebrity Feminism in the Age of Social Media
By Kirsty Fairclough-Isaacs

Conflicting Masculinities: Men in Television Period Drama
By Katherine Byrne, Julie Anne Taddeo and James Leggott (Eds)

Fat on Film: Gender, Race and Body Size in in Contemporary Hollywood Cinema
By Barbara Plotz

Fathers on Film: Paternity and Masculinity in 1990s Hollywood
By Katie Barnett

Film Bodies: Queer Feminist Encounters with Gender and Sexuality in Cinema
By Katharina Lindner

Gay Pornography: Representations of Sexuality and Masculinity
By John Mercer

Gender and Austerity in Popular Culture: Femininity, Masculinity and Recession in Film and Television
By Helen Davies and Claire O'Callaghan (Eds)

The Gendered Motorcycle: Representations in Society, Media and Popular Culture
By Esperanza Miyake

Gendering History on Screen: Women Filmmakers and Historical Films
By Julia Erhart

Girls Like This, Boys Like That: The Reproduction of Gender in Contemporary Youth Cultures
By Victoria Cann

The Gypsy Woman: Representations in Literature and Visual Culture
By Jodie Matthews

Love Wars: Television Romantic Comedy
By Mary Irwin

Masculinity in Contemporary Science Fiction Cinema: Cyborgs, Troopers and Other Men of the Future
By Marianne Kac-Vergne

Moving to the Mainstream: Women On and Off Screen in Television and Film
By Marianne Kac-Vergne and Julie Assouly (Eds)

Paradoxical Pleasures: Female Submission in Popular and Erotic Fiction
By Anna Watz

Positive Images: Gay Men and HIV/AIDS in the Culture of 'Post-Crisis'
By Dion Kagan

Queer Horror Film and Television: Sexuality and Masculinity at the Margins
By Darren Elliott-Smith

Queer Sexualities in Early Film: Cinema and Male-Male Intimacy
By Shane Brown

Steampunk: Gender and the Neo-Victorian
By Claire Nally

Television Comedy and Femininity: Queering Gender
By Rosie White

Gender and Early Television: Mapping Women's Role in Emerging US and British Media, 1850–1950
By Sarah Arnold

Tweenhood: Femininity and Celebrity in Tween Popular Culture
By Melanie Kennedy

Women Who Kill: Gender and Sexuality in Film and Series of the Post-Feminist Era
By David Roche and Cristelle Maury (Eds)

Wonder Woman: Feminism, Culture and the Body
By Joan Ormrod

Young Women in Contemporary Cinema: Gender and Post-Feminism in British Film
By Sarah Hill

Fathers on Film

Paternity and Masculinity in 1990s Hollywood

Katie Barnett

BLOOMSBURY ACADEMIC
LONDON • NEW YORK • OXFORD • NEW DELHI • SYDNEY

BLOOMSBURY ACADEMIC
Bloomsbury Publishing Plc
50 Bedford Square, London, WC1B 3DP, UK
1385 Broadway, New York, NY 10018, USA
29 Earlsfort Terrace, Dublin 2, Ireland

BLOOMSBURY, BLOOMSBURY ACADEMIC and the Diana logo are trademarks of Bloomsbury Publishing Plc

First published in Great Britain 2020
This paperback edition published in 2021

Copyright © Katie Barnett, 2020

Katie Barnett has asserted her right under the Copyright, Designs and Patents Act, 1988, to be identified as Author of this work.

For legal purposes the Acknowledgements on p. xiii constitute an extension of this copyright page.

Cover design: Charlotte Daniels
Cover image © John Pankow, Jennifer Aniston and Paul Rudd in *The Object of My Affection* (1998) (© 20th Century Fox / Courtesy Everett Collection / Mary Evans)

All rights reserved. No part of this publication may be reproduced or transmitted in any form or by any means, electronic or mechanical, including photocopying, recording, or any information storage or retrieval system, without prior permission in writing from the publishers.

Bloomsbury Publishing Plc does not have any control over, or responsibility for, any third-party websites referred to or in this book. All internet addresses given in this book were correct at the time of going to press. The author and publisher regret any inconvenience caused if addresses have changed or sites have ceased to exist, but can accept no responsibility for any such changes.

A catalogue record for this book is available from the British Library.

A catalog record for this book is available from the Library of Congress.

ISBN: HB: 978-1-3501-2088-4
PB: 978-1-3501-9160-0
ePDF: 978-1-3501-2086-0
eBook: 978-1-3501-2087-7

Typeset by Newgen KnowledgeWorks Pvt. Ltd., Chennai, India

To find out more about our authors and books visit www.bloomsbury.com and sign up for our newsletters

For Jon

Contents

List of Figures	x
Series Editors' Foreword	xi
Acknowledgements	xiii
Introduction	1
1 Fathers of the future: Extinction, survival and apocalyptic narratives	37
2 Dad versus the state: Hollywood's courtroom battles	65
3 Boys, interrupted: Fathers, sons and loss	97
4 Return of the (lion) king: Fatherhood beyond death	131
5 Guys that say goodnight: Gay fatherhood and the quest for legitimacy	161
Conclusion	195
Notes	209
Bibliography	233
Index	249

Figures

1. Kimble wins the adoration of his young pupils in *Kindergarten Cop* — 18
2. *Jurassic Park*'s hastily created nuclear family in peril — 40
3. Harry protects A.J. and sacrifices himself in *Armageddon* — 57
4. Daniel is reunited with his children at the end of *Mrs. Doubtfire* — 73
5. Scott and Charlie bond after Scott's transformation in *The Santa Clause* — 87
6. Macaulay Culkin as the epitome of innocent childhood in *My Girl* — 109
7. The Hoods reunite the morning after Mikey's death in *The Ice Storm* — 127
8. Resurrected as a snowman, Jack makes amends in *Jack Frost* — 145
9. In *Contact*, Ellie encounters an alien manifestation of her father — 156
10. Nina and George discuss parenthood in *The Object of My Affection* — 173
11. The Goldmans reinvent themselves as the Colemans in *The Birdcage* — 183

Series Editors' Foreword

Many of the books in this library chart changes in gender and sexuality representations in popular culture. In the contemporary world, these changes often directly spring from the civil rights movement of the 1960s, with particular emphasis on feminism and sexuality. However, a more recent development, largely as a result of gender equality successes, has been a change in how fatherhood comes to be formed in society and in the case of Barnett's study, how this is reflected in film.

The so-called crisis in masculinity that emerged as a result of the successes of feminism in the 1970s and 1980s saw more employment opportunities for women to enter paid employment in the public domain, and consequential changes in the domestic sphere saw men turn to the apparent constancy of fatherhood. Barnett refers to this as a 'saving mechanism' and draws on Hollywood films from the 1990s to explore how this is represented in popular culture as a remedy for the crisis in masculinity of this decade. While traditionally it is a female character who 'saves' the troubled male lead, what Barnett explores in this study is how the child takes on this role in many films, thus reflecting the uneasiness with the strides in female empowerment that second-wave feminism had achieved. While the films discussed in the book cover mostly one decade, Barnett reveals that the figure of the father is often shown to be one that invests in, and thus is part of, a discourse of reproductive futurism. As Barnett shows, this is played out across a range of genres: romcoms, fantasy, sci-fi, drama and disaster. Although these films are analysed in terms of 'the family', they are not necessarily family films, and thus this book intersects with others in the library that explore gender and sexuality across specific genres, while also forming links with studies that deal with gender more broadly in popular culture of this period.

By exploring both blockbuster and more low-budget films of this period, Barnett is able to explore the figure of the father against the crisis of masculinity in the United States, and indeed more globally, at this time. While issues of sexuality and race increasingly appear in such films, Barnett shows the primacy of the white, American, heteronormative family reasserting itself and thus underlines the point made in many of the books in this library that gender in popular culture is changing, but only slowly.

Angela Smith and Claire Nally

Acknowledgements

This book began life as part of my doctoral research at the University of Birmingham, and I remain grateful to Michele Aaron, whose guidance was instrumental as I developed many of the ideas that remain intact here. Since then, my colleagues at the University of Chester and University of Worcester have been a valuable source of encouragement and advice. In particular, I would like to thank the fellow survivors of Bredon 202 – Sharon Young, Katy Wareham Morris, Ruth Stacey and Whitney Standlee – whose friendship and collegiality have greatly enriched my academic life. Thanks for letting me use the good computer for those early drafts. Thanks, too, to Andreas Mueller for reminding me it was probably time to write a book; to Paul Elliott for the initial publishing advice (and for pretending not to notice when Spielberg kept appearing on the syllabus); and to Mark Duffett for answering a multitude of research-related questions. I am also grateful to the many students, past and present, who have both indulged and enhanced discussions of various films explored here, and I hope I haven't ruined *Mrs. Doubtfire* for too many of you.

Thank you to Lisa Goodrum for her initial enthusiasm for the project and to all the people at Bloomsbury who have helped shepherd it to completion, particularly Anna Coatman, who has been diligent and supportive throughout the process.

Thanks to my friends, who developed a sixth sense about when it was okay to ask how it was going (and when it wasn't) and who have cooked me dinner, given me a place to stay and provided distraction and encouragement in equal measure, not least Kim Loynes, Tom Stone and Ed Mushett Cole. And thanks, especially, to Becca Stone and Jenny Palmer, who over the years have been great readers, great cheerleaders and, most importantly, great friends. You are the Goldie and Diane to my Bette.

Thank you to my family: first, to my mum and dad, Jacqueline Lawrence and John Barnett, without whose love and encouragement this book, and much else, would not be possible. To my grandparents, Shirley and Albert Barnett, for their generosity of support; to Jayne Barnett for frequently steering me back on course; and to Thomas Barnett, my first cinema buddy, my first collaborator and always *mi hermano favorito*.

And finally to Jon, whose unfailing belief and enthusiasm are this book's secret ingredients. You are my favourite person. Thanks for telling me I could do it. I did it. Let's see the whole world.

Introduction

'Who is my daddy and what does he do?'

This is the question that John Kimble (Arnold Schwarzenegger), undercover police officer turned small-town kindergarten teacher, poses to his class in *Kindergarten Cop* (Ivan Reitman, 1990) after discovering that he is living in the 'single parent capital of America'. In the ensuing montage the children give an account of their fathers. These accounts range from matter-of-fact ('My dad works on computers'; 'My dad watches TV all day long') to faintly disturbing ('My dad doesn't live with us anymore ... my mom hopes he's gonna die real soon') and forlorn ('I don't know what my dad does. I haven't seen him in a long time'). Few are flattering.

In this scene, no more than a few minutes long, the anxieties are revealed that would shape Hollywood throughout the 1990s. These anxieties centred on the role of the father, his absence and his enduring importance: just who *was* he, and what *did* he do? In *Kindergarten Cop*'s conclusion, as Kimble returns to claim his second chance at fatherhood, the answer to these questions becomes clear. The best daddies were playful, emotional and dedicated to their children. What they did – a question traditionally associated with work and breadwinning, that most ingrained of paternal duties – was reclaim their fatherhood, not just as provider but protector, playmate and ally. As the millennium approached with all its attendant uncertainties, Hollywood embarked on a project of rehabilitation and restoration, determinedly shaping its troubled men into dedicated, engaged fathers. It would be Dad who led the way into the new millennium, as the United States contemplated the end of the so-called American century.

This book explores Hollywood's enduring preoccupation with the father during this *fin-de-siècle* moment. It contests that fatherhood is repurposed as a powerful tool able to save the men that, as the world changed around them, were struggling to make sense of a modern masculine identity. As many of the traditional markers of American masculinity stuttered or crumbled, fatherhood represented a life raft, capable of stabilizing these uncertainties. With a desire for paternal restoration permeating the political, cultural and social rhetoric of the United States, Hollywood began its own interrogation of the father. As the scene in *Kindergarten Cop* reveals, the image is not universally complimentary. The emphasis remains, however, on rehabilitating the father and cementing his continued relevance. In fatherhood, an apparently uncertain future could be transcended. It becomes what I term a 'saving mechanism', capable of delivering men from the widely discussed yet contentious crisis of masculinity and restoring their sense of worth and dominance. Throughout 1990s Hollywood, from action films to romantic comedies, animated films to family dramas, fatherhood is constructed as the answer to a much masculinized sense of uncertainty and feared loss of purpose.

On the surface, the decade preceding the millennium is one of progress and optimism. A sense of cultural crisis is more commonly attributed to the 1970s, as a post-Watergate, post-Vietnam pessimism descended across the country, leading President Jimmy Carter to lament the nation's 'crisis of confidence' and its loss of unity and purpose. In the so-called Malaise Speech of July 1979, Carter admitted his own 'mixed success' in office and appealed directly to the American public, telling them, 'I need your help'.[1] This admission, interpreted as weakness, helped seal Carter's fate as a one-term president. It serves as an indicator of the precarious and dissatisfied cultural mood that encompassed a nation suddenly unsure of itself, bruised from war and struggling with an energy crisis and a stagnant economy. In contrast, the 1990s are generally heralded as a period of relative peace and prosperity, following a fleeting recession under President George H. W. Bush and the brief conflict of the First Gulf War. On the surface, confidence prevailed. President Bill Clinton, the first Democrat in office since Carter, approached the millennial moment with a persistent rhetorical image of crossing a bridge into the twenty-first century, embracing a sense of hope and opportunity. In his 1997 State of the Union address he declared, 'We don't have a moment to waste. Tomorrow there will be just over 1,000 days until the year 2000; 1,000 days to prepare our people; 1,000 days to work together; 1,000 days to build a bridge to a land of new promise.'[2] He returned to this image frequently. Two years later, he talked not only of building the bridge but also of crossing it: 'The promise of our future is limitless,' he told the nation, evoking the now-familiar countdown: 'Barely more than 300 days from now, we will cross that bridge into the new millennium.'[3] This futuristic vision is typical of Clinton's optimistic oratory, and entirely expected in a decade that marked not only the end of the century but also the end of a millennium. Such a unique temporal occasion provides an unparalleled opportunity for presidents and citizens alike to stake a claim on their place in history as engineers of the future, and Clinton was no exception.

Just below the surface, however, bubbled tensions, anxieties and potential crises that complicate this cultural moment. Change and challenge characterized the decade, offering progress for some and uncertainty for others. On a grand scale, technological and environmental change promised a lasting impact on home, work and leisure, not only nationally but also globally. Meanwhile, challenges to the established order continued with demands for overdue equality for women and minorities, whose historical marginalization persisted, if not always in law then in practice. Second-wave feminism had brought debate and change to the ways in which society perceived gender and gender relations in the 1970s and 1980s. By the early 1990s, third-wave feminism continued these debates, expanding and diversifying discussions of gender equality and raising consciousness for a generation of American women who had grown up with the gains of feminism. Racial tensions were exacerbated by the videotaped beating of Rodney King by Los Angeles police officers, leading to the LA Riots in 1992. Gay rights campaigns coalesced around issues of marriage, parenting and kinship rights, while AIDS activism continued to draw attention to the devastation caused by the virus and push for increased research, funding and political recognition.

Economically, the United States experienced an extended period of growth and a rise in GDP under Clinton, but on the ground the effects of deindustrialization were reshaping local communities. Traditional blue-collar industries – logging in the Pacific Northwest, coal mining in Appalachia, textile industries in the Southeast and the steel, iron and manufacturing works across the Rust Belt – disappeared or relocated overseas. Job security was increasingly precarious. The diminished viability of the single-breadwinner household was just one factor contributing to the changing shape and face of the American family. As more women obtained college degrees and entered the workforce, they tended to marry and have children later, if at all.[4] The number of same-sex couples parenting children increased as laws began to change and reproductive technologies became more widely available. Meanwhile, divorce rates rose, the number of children living with one parent increased and the spectre of the 'deadbeat dad' attracted the ire of journalists, politicians and the president himself.

Amidst all this social and economic uncertainty, a presidential sex scandal and high-profile acts of domestic terrorism – including the FBI siege in Waco, Texas (1993), the Oklahoma City bombing (1995) and the Columbine school shooting (1999) – occupied the media, while another source of existential anxiety shimmered in the background.

In 1941, *Time* publisher Henry Luce declared the twentieth century to be the 'American century', based on the economic, political and cultural dominance of the nation and the potential for the global spread of American ideals and values. As the end of the century loomed, the United States would look over the horizon and wonder how long its status as a single superpower could continue.

This landscape forms the backdrop to that persistent claim mentioned above, that America's men were in crisis.[5] To be clear, such men – whether explicitly or not – were largely perceived as being white and straight. These were the men who expected to inherit a future of promise and certainty, only to find that promise eroded by the shifting terrain of late-twentieth-century America. To use Clinton's bridge metaphor, these were the men who had expected to 'cross the bridge' with ease, only to find the way more precarious than they had imagined. The lynchpin of the crisis of masculinity is a sense of insecurity, rooted in the erosion of 'the structural foundations of traditional manhood' that contributes to a perception of disenfranchisement and a loss of faith in what it means to be a man.[6] Expectations are disrupted: company loyalty goes unrewarded, the family splinters, male social communities fracture.[7] In short, the landscape of American manhood was mutating, as those structuring forces – work, family, home and community – underwent inevitable change.

The extent to which this state of affairs is legitimately characterized as a 'crisis' is now as much a part of the discussion as the crisis itself. The notion of a crisis of masculinity presupposes prior stability, a period during which masculine identity was both established and infallible; it also presumes an end point by which the crisis can be said to have passed. In reality, gender is perpetually in flux. Masculinity, like femininity, is a construction, not natural but socially determined and culturally performed.[8] Neither is masculinity a singular notion. Hegemonic masculinity describes the normative, dominant construction of masculinity underpinned by ideological power, against which femininities and subordinate masculinities are measured; inevitably, the parameters of hegemonic masculinity, as with any gender constructions, shift over time.[9] Masculinity routinely intersects with other factors, including race, ethnicity, sexuality, class and disability, and as such not all masculinities share the same inherent privilege. Therefore, the assumption that masculinity can ever be definitively determined, that there is an ideal or mythic masculinity to which the cessation of crisis would return men, is to deny its inherent constructedness.

Furthermore, as noted above, the crisis of masculinity is generally associated with those men – straight, white, able-bodied, often middle class – who have, historically, been afforded great advantages in American society. As such, though this hegemonic form of masculinity was under considerable scrutiny during the 1990s, this in itself does not qualify it for crisis status. Nor should scrutiny be misread as a loss of privilege. Indeed, the frequency with which crises of masculinity have been posited, including during the postwar era and again in the 1970s, suggests that 'crisis' may be better understood as an inevitable ebb and flow of anxiety over men's roles and status, rather than something that can ever be decisively resolved. Michael Kimmel's contention that the masculine crisis is cyclical is helpful in emphasizing the more perpetual anxiety surrounding American masculinity and its relationship to shifting perceptions of power and status.[10] In its hyperbolic nature, the notion of crisis also risks obscuring the continued discrimination and hardship faced by historically marginalized identities. Donna Peberdy's substitution of 'angst' for 'crisis' is likewise a useful intervention in this sense, exchanging the drama of the latter for the anxious apprehension of the former.[11] Sons had inherited the peaceful, prosperous world of their fathers only to find their grasp on it less secure than they would like; all of a sudden, that which had been assured was 'under siege'.[12] Facing the millennium, American men – much like the nation – were forced to consider how they would remain both relevant and dominant. In the 1990s, this anxiety was magnified by the cultural conditions outlined above, many of which saw the parameters of the traditional male role – husband, father, breadwinner – shift. Straight white masculinity became increasingly negatively associated: the corrupt cop, the school shooter, the homegrown terrorist, the libidinous president. Alternative models of masculinity, most prominently the emotional, nurturing 'new man'[13] and the image-conscious, urban-dwelling 'metrosexual',[14] offered conflicting accounts of what the men of the future could or should be, while the burgeoning men's movement channelled masculine panic into evocations of a return to mythic wilderness-infused manhood. While the veracity of the 'crisis' remains a lively discussion, the conflicts and concerns around American masculinity during this period cannot be dismissed. Crucially, for the focus of this book, it is imperative to understand that Hollywood invests fully in this troubled image of white masculinity. Anxious men abound, their fears and fallibility writ large on the big screen. These are the heroes who were struggling to lay claim to that same secure status. The films discussed in the following chapters internalize the masculine crisis, and it is through this prism that the determined focus on fatherhood is read. Amidst all this uncertainty, blame and confusion, fatherhood remains a perennial role. Done right, it connotes strength, loyalty and commitment. It is, critically, a status that can only be bestowed on men.

The looming shift in the calendar lends an apocalyptic edge to this sense of crisis, in which the fear of becoming obsolete intertwines with the figurative threat of erasure. Against this threat, fatherhood is deployed as the aforementioned saving mechanism, a form of specifically masculine survival. These threads of masculinity, fatherhood, erasure and survival are woven together in a wide variety of Hollywood's output between 1990 and 2000, crossing genres, budgets and audiences. Taken together, the films that form the case studies within this book reveal a persistent project of masculine redemption anchored to fatherhood. The survival of America's men – maligned, uncertain, apparently in crisis – depended on their full and committed embrace of the paternal role. Schwarzenegger's Kimble is an instructive example. Patrolling a derelict, faded neon version of LA reminiscent of a distinctly 1980s Hollywood aesthetic, he is in danger of becoming an anachronism. His nemesis Crisp (Richard Tyson) aptly reminds him of his tenuous grasp on existence when he observes, 'Without me, you wouldn't even have a life.' Kimble eventually sidesteps the limitations of his unemotional, lonely performance of 'hard-bodied' masculinity by committing himself to Crisp's ex-wife Joyce (Penelope Ann Miller) and her son Dominic (Joseph & Christian Cousins), not only as their protector but as an emotionally invested part of their family.[15] Crisp, the bad father, perishes; Kimble embraces his second chance and transcends the dead end of his former life, trading obsolescence for purpose. For the United States and its citizens, whether the year 2000 promised a beginning or an end remained undetermined. One thing, however, is certain. At the end of the twentieth century America's concerns, as filtered through the machinery of Hollywood, boiled down to three things: What it meant to be a man, what it meant to be a father, and what it meant to survive.

Future-proof: Hollywood, masculinity and fatherhood in the 1990s

This book interrogates these questions through an examination of a range of Hollywood films made during the 1990s, from blockbuster hits such as *Jurassic Park* (Steven Spielberg, 1993) and *Armageddon* (Michael Bay, 1998) to more modestly budgeted fare such as *Paradise*

(Mary Agnes Donoghue, 1991) and *The Ice Storm* (Ang Lee, 1997). It includes a number of films whose critical discussion has previously been limited. To demonstrate Hollywood's evident preoccupation with its fathers, a multitude of genres are covered, including comedy (*Mrs. Doubtfire* [Chris Columbus, 1993]), romance (*The Object of My Affection* [Nicholas Hytner, 1998]), fantasy (*Jack Frost* [Troy Miller, 1998]), science fiction (*A.I. Artificial Intelligence* [Spielberg, 2001]), drama (*Falling Down* [Joel Schumacher, 1993]), disaster (*Dante's Peak* [Roger Donaldson, 1997]) and animation (*The Lion King* [Roger Allers and Rob Minkoff, 1994]). It draws on a range of theories and disciplines, including gender theory, queer theory, sociology, psychoanalysis and American cultural history, to illuminate the depth and breadth of Hollywood's mission to rehabilitate the father. This interdisciplinary approach combines textual analysis of the case study films with social, political and cultural context to demonstrate how and why saving the father was of such primary concern on- and off-screen during the 1990s. Many of these films are aimed at the lucrative family audience market, the pursuit of which shaped a significant portion of Hollywood's output during the decade.[16] This is not a prerequisite for inclusion, however. Rather, these films are best characterized as being *about* the family in its various forms. As 'a cultural dream obsession to which we return and return',[17] by the 1990s the family was a subject of 'obsessive speculation' in Hollywood.[18] In these films, whether directly or indirectly, the family remains prominent as a source of both anxiety and comfort.

The films discussed are all products of a Hollywood undergoing significant industrial and technological change. The new wave of mergers that began in the 1980s when News Corp. acquired 20th Century Fox continued, as Viacom acquired Paramount Communications and Blockbuster Entertainment in 1993. In 1995, Time Warner, already the result of a significant merger between Time Inc. and Warner

Communications in 1989, acquired Turner Broadcasting System, which included New Line Cinema. The same year, Disney bought the ABC television network.[19] The line between mainstream cinema and independent cinema blurred as major studios partnered with independent producers (such as Castle Rock, New Line, Carolco and Imagine Entertainment), broadening their market appeal and diversifying their production content.[20] VCRs became widely available in the 1980s and by the 1990s were a feature of two-thirds of households.[21] The rise of home entertainment benefited from a ready pool of family-friendly films available on videocassette, and the promise of this secondary market ensured that such films proliferated in Hollywood. Accordingly, discussions of 1990s Hollywood have often taken an industrial or technical approach,[22] while others have explicitly focused on the construction of the family audience.[23] Though these aspects of filmmaking, production and distribution are inevitably reflected in many films chosen for discussion, this does not form a significant aspect of the case studies presented here. Rather, I am interested in the unifying thread that binds together these otherwise apparently disparate films, namely, the ways in which fatherhood is reconstructed, rehabilitated and restored in a bid to save the anxious and unfulfilled men populating Hollywood in the run-up to the millennium.

The seeds of this argument are sown in Amy Aronson and Michael Kimmel's essay 'The Saviors and the Saved', in which they suggest that traditionally, men have been cast as saviours within Hollywood cinema, reinforcing the ideological construction of a traditionally masculine hero. However, more recently men have been the ones in need of saving. While a female romantic interest was once charged with fulfilling this function, increasingly it has passed to a child. Aronson and Kimmel attribute this shift to a wariness surrounding feminism. Traditionally, it was the 'transformative power of women's pure love' capable of rescuing the troubled detective, the lone cowboy, the flawed hero.²⁴ However, in an era when feminism was perceived to have replaced this amorphous 'transformative power' with a more concrete power that served women as well as men, women were no longer 'pure' enough to act as saviour. The child, then, must provide deliverance. Only the child who has yet to be besmirched by the adult world is innocent enough to save the man from destruction.

This book's central argument cleaves to a similar line, although with one crucial difference. Aronson and Kimmel mark out the child as saviour, but this obscures the true survival mechanism being advanced. The real saviour is fatherhood or, more accurately, the act of being a father. While the child is a prerequisite for fatherhood to be realized, she or (most often) he is merely the catalyst. It is the fathering that ensures the man's survival, allowing him to envisage a future into which he survives intact, secure in his status and contributing to future generations. In a period characterized by masculine crisis, rooting the male self within the role of father promises a stake in the very future that the president's millennial rhetoric conjured up in the American imagination, a way of crossing that elusive bridge.

The father is a ubiquitous figure in Hollywood, although there remains a limited amount of scholarship specifically discussing his representation on screen; notable exceptions include Stella Bruzzi's 2005 survey of fatherhood and masculinity in post-war Hollywood, and Hannah Hamad's work on post-feminist fatherhood in twenty-first-century American cinema.²⁵ Work on representations of motherhood²⁶ and the family more generally has, however, proliferated more widely.²⁷ Discussions of fatherhood in cinema have most often focused on the relationship between fathers and feminism (or, increasingly, post-feminism), including how representations of the father may be understood as products of domesticated 'new man' masculinity²⁸ and, latterly, how fatherhood has become the 'ideal masculinity' of post-feminism.²⁹ Feminist criticism of the newly domesticated father has frequently focused on his appropriative function and the attendant marginalization of the mother, particularly the image of what Lynne Joyrich calls the 'fathered-only child'.[30] These accounts point to an on-screen desire to prove the father's worth, revealing his necessity through the anxious usurping of the maternal role. This desire is further observed in Bruzzi's suggestion that from the 1990s onwards fatherhood underwent a process of 'pluralisation' as Hollywood devoted attention to numerous and diverse images of the father. Though Bruzzi reads this pluralization as a positive fragmentation of 'the traditional paternal role model that has hitherto underpinned Hollywood's preoccupation with the father', this diversification of the father image reveals a persistent anxiety as much as a broadening of the terms of family and fatherhood.[31]

The theme of masculine anxiety ameliorated through fatherhood is an important facet of this existing scholarship and my own analysis builds on this. However, the tension frequently observed between the roles of 'father' and 'mother' is reoriented here to consider an alternative binary: that of 'father' and 'non-father'. To be denied his fatherhood, or to realize too late its importance, is the biggest threat to Hollywood's troubled men. The non-father is at risk of erasure. Therefore, any tension between father and mother – which, to be clear, remains a common feature – is secondary to the more pressing concern of becoming, and remaining, a father. Furthermore, in focusing specifically on the 1990s I hope to illuminate a period of mainstream cinema that has been relatively under-discussed as a whole. Given the unique cultural moment that the 1990s provided, this *fin-de-siècle* characterized in equal part by futuristic hope and considerable trepidation, it is worth investigating in more depth. After the events of 11 September 2001, a number of scholars have understandably taken as their focus the post-9/11 milieu of Hollywood.[32] The 1990s, as a result, have often gone under-evaluated or serve only as a symbol of the last years of Hollywood before 9/11 reshaped both the cultural consciousness and the cinema that it produced. Here, I consider the decade to be significant in and of itself, not least in its construction and reconstruction of masculinity and fatherhood, a process of representation that cannot be untangled from the temporal period in which it emerges.

To lay claim to fatherhood is to lay claim to a future. This is the underlying, yet unexplored, premise of Aronson and Kimmel's argument, in which the focus is on the act of being saved. It is this link between fatherhood and survival – so crucial in a decade of uncertainty about the very real future on the horizon – that is the common link between the films discussed here. The belief that there is immortality to be found after death has its original roots in religious doctrine. In 'The Future of an Illusion', Freud interrogates the allure of religious belief, including the promise that 'death itself is not an extinction' because the afterlife contains the promise of fulfilment not found in mortal existence.[33] It is this same desire to believe that one may not only live beyond oneself but also find a kind of 'perfection' in this latter existence, that similarly shapes Freud's imagining of parental narcissism, in which the child fulfils the 'wishful dreams' of its thwarted parents.[34] This assumption of immortality thus survives in contemporary culture in the secularized guise of generational succession – what Peter Blos terms the 'generational continuum' – which suggests that even beyond death, a part of the self survives in the memories, habits and genes of its descendants.[35] The child becomes symbolic of continuation, a living embodiment of the future.

Freudian psychoanalysis, and psychoanalytic theory more generally, remains a crucial aspect of film analysis, not least when considering the family and, in this case, the father, who looms as large in psychoanalysis as he does in Hollywood. As such, Freud's work on narcissism, grief and the death drive form a significant part of the interdisciplinary intervention this book makes. In cleaving to Freudian psychoanalysis I recognize that this approach necessarily curtails other potential readings, which may equally and differently illuminate Hollywood's father fixation during this period. For example, Hannah Hamad's work on postmillennial fatherhood examines the dominance of idealized paternal masculinity through a post-feminist lens. As noted above, such an approach is adopted in other work on fatherhood; equally, recent work on motherhood has utilized sociocultural and narrative analysis alongside psychoanalysis.[36] To read these films through a Freudian lens is to approach them on their own terms, given Hollywood's own persistent recycling of Oedipal myths and tropes of familial dysfunction, particularly when representing masculinity and fatherhood. This, of course, brings limitations as well as opportunity. Freud's work predates the advancements and debates of feminist theories, masculinity studies and queer theory, all of which illuminate discussions of men, fatherhood and masculinity in the late twentieth century. It can, therefore, only account so far for the representations seen on screen during this period, which emerge as much from contemporary fears and issues as from Hollywood's own Oedipal complex. In attempting to mitigate against some of these limitations, the discussions that form the following chapters take an interdisciplinary approach, combining psychoanalysis with aspects of queer theory and gender theory, while being mindful of the impact of the contemporary American political, social and cultural backdrop on the images emerging from Hollywood at the turn of the millennium.

In particular, more recent work on reproductive futurism by queer theorist Lee Edelman offers a valuable framework through which to consider cultural images of families, fatherhood and reproduction. Reproductive futurism describes the way in which the sociopolitical order is anchored to the symbolic figure of the Child, who represents the concept of survival. As such, reproduction becomes the acceptable face of narcissism, as society is structured in such a way as to drive towards a denial of individual pleasure (*jouissance*) in favour of perpetual investment in the next generation.[37] For Edelman, reproductive futurism – the 'genealogical fantasy that braces the social order' – is so pervasive as to be imperceptible, and to stand outside of this order is to adopt a queer position, denying the inherent superiority of a future anticipated but never seen.[38] This queer space is not intrinsically linked to sexuality but rather to resistance, to a refusal of this demand to continually move towards the 'perpetual horizon' of the child.[39] Queerness here signals negativity, a non-reproductive space that potentially threatens the myth of reproductive survival. Recalling Aronson and Kimmel's discussion of men being 'saved' through fatherhood, and informing my own suggestion of fatherhood as a 'saving mechanism', Edelman's designation of futurity as a 'saving fantasy' is important in crystallizing the power of futuristic myths not only to individuals but to society more broadly.[40]

At the heart of Edelman's claim lies an inherent contradiction, in that what the future promises is eventually death, yet this same future has the power to save. It is through reproduction that this future is realized, repressing today in favour of securing what is yet to come: 'our present … mortgaged to a *fantasmatic* future.'[41] Although reproduction and parenthood are often culturally constructed as selfless acts, a negation of the selfish impulses of youth and nonconformity (imagined by Edelman as queer *jouissance*), there is an equally self-serving impulse in the decision to reproduce. Freud identifies an enduring narcissism inherent in the desire to secure the future while being unable to experience it for oneself: 'At the most touchy point in the narcissistic system, the immortality of the ego, which is so hard pressed by reality, security is achieved by taking refuge in the child. Parental love … is nothing but the parents' narcissism born again.'[42] The child, in offering 'narcissistic solace', stands indefinitely as the symbol of the realization of this immortal survival.[43]

Fatherhood does not negate death. Indeed, in accepting a place within the linear temporality that underlies such generational relations, fatherhood only highlights the end to come, as the father sees the next generation emerge ahead of him. In Freudian psychoanalysis, there is an element of symbolic destruction inherent in this generational succession, as the son looks to eventually usurp the father, a tension explored further in Chapter 4. Rather, fatherhood qualifies death. It is an end that offers another kind of continuation, a variation on Elias Canetti's argument that man's desire is to 'exist when others are no longer there'.[44] The child carries the paternal legacy forward; they are 'the mortal vehicle of a (possibly) immortal substance', the 'temporary holder of an estate which survives him [sic]'.[45] Into this generational continuum the father sees his own child become the parent, and the cycle continues. Fatherhood therefore retains potent appeal, containing the promise of an indefinite future at a time in which contemporary masculinity was perceived to be under threat of obliteration.

The 'saving' of the man not simply by the child but by fatherhood highlights the cultural prevalence of reproductive futurism. Political rhetoric continually frames politics in terms of improving the world not simply for the current generation but for 'our children's children'[46] and even 'our grandchildren's grandchildren'.[47] Clinton's first inaugural address urged the nation to '[see] themselves in the light of posterity', just as the 'Founders' did: 'Anyone who has ever watched a child's eyes wander into sleep knows what posterity is. Posterity is the world to come: the world for whom we hold our ideals, from whom we have borrowed our planet, and to whom we bear sacred responsibility.'

This is what Edelman refers to as 'strategically misrecognised' narcissism, as the father's investment in his own survival is obscured by a rhetoric of responsibility to securing the future for these as-yet-unborn descendants.[48] Within this framework, the films discussed here can be seen as products of a particular political and social order that remains fixated on replication rather than change. Though the individual plays a central role in the American myth, the collective of the family is still the most politically desirable. Encouraging men to embrace their responsibilities as fathers is socially and politically expedient. Outside of a heteronormative familial structure, a man might find himself excluded from this promised future. In fatherhood, he is guaranteed survival even as, conversely, his place in the line of generational succession is a reminder of his eventual demise. Fatherhood bears the marker of immortality identified by Canetti: 'He wants to live longer than everyone else, and to *know* it; and when he is no longer there himself, then his name must continue.'[49] This is the ultimate triumph – to have survived – and at the turn of the millennium a reinvestment in fatherhood was the surest means by which to achieve this survival, and to know it.

Remakes, reissues and reinterpretation: Fatherhood reborn

As a film that laments a lack of paternal influence and drives towards the restoration of a suitable father figure, *Kindergarten Cop* is, however improbably, prescient of the representative shifts taking place in 1990s Hollywood. With Schwarzenegger at the helm, the film transplants 'one of the hardest hard bodies of the 1980s',[50] best known for action roles in *Conan the Barbarian* (John Milius, 1982), *The Terminator* (James Cameron, 1984), *Predator* (John McTiernan, 1987) and *Total Recall* (Paul Verhoeven, 1990), into a colourful, chaotic kindergarten classroom. Though the undercover aspect of Kimble's mission does permit some action heroics, largely his concerns are much more mundane: teaching a class of six-year-olds the Gettysburg Address, successfully evacuating in a fire drill and making sure kids get to the bathroom on time.

Hollywood was awash with remakes in the 1990s, but *Kindergarten Cop* represents a remake of a different kind. Here, it is the star who is made over for a new decade. Before his real-life transformation

Figure 1 Kimble wins the adoration of his young pupils in *Kindergarten Cop* (1990). Universal Pictures.

from movie star to politician, Schwarzenegger underwent an on-screen metamorphosis that exchanged muscles and machines for a more domesticated masculine image. Alongside *Kindergarten Cop*, his roles in *Junior* (Reitman, 1994) and *Jingle All the Way* (Brian Levant, 1996) point to a softer, more paternal imagining of heroism; in *Junior*, quite literally, as Schwarzenegger's hard body is softened and expanded in a male pregnancy plot. Even more traditional action roles in *Terminator 2: Judgment Day* (Cameron, 1991) and *True Lies* (Cameron, 1994) were infused with familial concerns. In the former, the Terminator is sent back in time to protect the young John Connor, becoming a pseudo-father figure in the process. In the latter, Harry Tasker must balance life as a spy with being a father and husband. If, as Susan Jeffords suggests, 1990s cinema was generally intent on 'redirecting masculine characterizations from spectacular achievement to domestic triumph', then Schwarzenegger's transformation from killing machine to kindergarten teacher is surely one of the decade's more impressive remakes.[51]

The film remake is an inevitable result of a Hollywood business model looking for a ready supply of viable stories and relatively low-risk projects. They form a significant subsection of films made in the 1990s, as major studios – now often subsidiaries of larger, risk-averse media conglomerates – pursued familiar stories that could be repackaged for a contemporary audience. These include cross-cultural remakes (*The Birdcage* [Mike Nichols, 1996]), remakes of cult movies (*Godzilla* [Roland Emmerich, 1998]), retellings of classic tales (*Robin Hood: Prince of Thieves* [Kevin Reynolds, 1991]) and updated literary adaptations (*Bram Stoker's Dracula* [Francis Ford Coppola, 1992]), frequently resulting in box office success.[52] Often, the changes made to the original are illuminating, imbuing an existing narrative with contemporary concerns, whether consciously or otherwise. The cult thriller *Cape Fear* is a notable example, one that further clarifies the paternal anxiety with which Hollywood was grappling, albeit with darker implications than a film such as *Kindergarten Cop*. Based on John D. MacDonald's 1957 novel *The Executioners*, the first adaptation was released in 1962, directed by J. Lee Thompson and starring Gregory Peck as Sam Bowden and Robert Mitchum as his nemesis Max Cady. In 1991, it was remade with Nick Nolte and Robert De Niro in the lead roles and directed by Martin Scorsese, who infuses the film with ambiguity.

Bowden is a man who, on the surface, possesses all the trappings of a successful life. He lives with his wife Leigh (Jessica Lange) and teenage daughter Danny (Juliette Lewis) in an attractive, affluent neighbourhood. His job as an attorney brings wealth, respect and a certain community standing. But *Cape Fear*'s preoccupation is with that just below the surface, much like the dark waters swirling beneath the family's houseboat, a safe haven that becomes the scene of a nightmare. And beneath the veneer of the good father, husband and citizen lies a less flattering image of Bowden, in which he is directly responsible for the threat posed to his family. The roaming, predatory presence of Cady, seeking revenge on Bowden for suppressing evidence that may have kept him out of prison, is the acknowledged embodiment of danger, but Bowden is far from being a convincingly moral hero. His ongoing flirtation with colleague Lori (Illeana Douglas) is a point of weakness, exploited by Cady when he targets Lori in a rape and beating designed to punish Bowden further. The film hints at Bowden's incestuous desire for his daughter, again projected onto Cady, whose interest awakens Danny's own sexual curiosity.[53] And everywhere, there are hints of Bowden's figurative impotence – the broken piano wire, the dead dog, the disrupted film screening – as he repeatedly fails to protect his family from Cady's invading presence.

Cape Fear takes the classic narrative of a father charged with protecting his home and family and imbues it with doubt. Like in *Home Alone* (Chris Columbus, 1990), another film that casts doubt on the parents' competence, the protection falls to a child.[54] On the boat, it is Danny who scalds Cady while her father is incapacitated. The film thrives on ambiguities, eroding Bowden's masculine authority and calling into question his status as the 'good' father while setting up Cady not simply as a monster but as a man who has been denied the signifiers of husband and father since being disowned by his family. Stripped of his fatherhood, Cady has nothing to anchor him to civilized life. Bowden, meanwhile, has failed to live up to the expectations of being a father and finds himself similarly adrift. The good/evil dichotomy established in the original fractures in the remake.[55] What remains is an uncertain, anxious portrayal of the American family that strays from idealized to troubled, with the father's failures at the centre. Cady's desire to reclaim his fatherhood is emphasized – 'I can have what you have,' he insists, referring to

Sam's wife and daughter – suggesting that it is capable of saving errant men such as him, if only they had the opportunity. Yet fatherhood is ultimately a site of near-failure, as Bowden struggles to contain his own destructive impulses. 'You're not allowed to stand up, Dad, remember?' Danny snaps at him as they hide from Cady. The image of the crouching, chastised Bowden is a reminder of this masculine deficit and the paternal failure it symbolizes.

In a telling piece of casting, Gregory Peck – the original Bowden and, as Atticus Finch, one of Hollywood's most beloved paternal heroes – returns in the remake as Lee Heller. A far cry from his performance of Bowden, Peck's Heller is a lawyer (recalling both Bowden and Finch) who defends Cady and attempts to disbar Nolte's Bowden in an act of 'dialogical subversion', whereby an actor recognized for his paternal appeal willingly calls into question the veracity of this image.[56] Certainly a duality runs through *Cape Fear*, of wanting to believe in the father and yet finding it increasingly difficult to do so. This same tension informs much of Hollywood's approach to its on-screen dads during this period. Writing about 1980s cinema, Robin Wood suggests that the 'Restoration of the Father' is Hollywood's 'ideological project', driving towards the ultimate reassurance: 'trust Father'.[57] In the 1990s, however, doubt began to creep in around the edges. For every triumphant paternal reclamation, there is a father struggling to change, a man on the brink of being de-fathered. And this duality is more than just the underlying premise of a swathe of Hollywood films; its roots go much deeper, tapping into the politics and culture of a nation. By the 1990s it was a cultural condition, nowhere more apparent than in the rhetoric that built up around Bill Clinton's presidential campaign and his ensuing years in office.

The American president is more than a political figurehead. For more than two hundred years, he has served as an ersatz 'national father'.[58] Susan Faludi, similarly, refers to the president as a 'public father'.[59] Much of the mythology surrounding the United States' construction is built upon the image of the all-knowing father, not only as 'one nation under God' (the ultimate Father) but in the imagining of numerous presidents as substitute fathers of the nation, from early leaders (George Washington, Thomas Jefferson) to wartime presidents (Abraham Lincoln, Franklin D. Roosevelt) perceived to have changed the fate of the Union. The continued dominance of the older, exclusively male presidential candidate into the twenty-first century reinforces this desired paternal authority, as Robin Lakoff suggests: 'Underneath, [Americans] want a daddy, a king, a god, a hero.'[60] But Clinton, the first baby boomer president and at 46 the third-youngest man to occupy the office, complicated this paternal image even as he entered the White House with his young daughter, Chelsea, by his side. In 1992, poet and men's movement activist Robert Bly made a case for revitalizing the role of the father in American life. 'There is not enough father,' he claimed, linking a lack of paternal influence to the uncertain masculinity afflicting adult men.[61] Clinton embodied this same concern: could he, a young, relatively inexperienced candidate with no war record, ever be 'enough father' for a nation built on a model of paternal politics as far back as the Founding Fathers?

Clinton's public persona was built in large part on elements of contradiction. Though Peberdy suggests that such contradictions were part of a voter-pleasing routine,[62] they also reflect competing notions of masculinity that contributed to the decade's perception of crisis and uncertainty. As a symbol of national manhood, Clinton embodied these uncertainties. Thus, he was part Arkansas 'redneck', part slick politician, a rural, working-class boy who was also a Rhodes Scholar and, according to opponent George H. W. Bush, a rich, privileged member of the 'tassel-loafered lawyer crowd'.[63] The image of a committed family man did battle with that of 'hypersexual womanizer'.[64] Brenton Malin explicitly links Clinton's presidency to the crisis of masculinity, observing that these myriad contradictions made him 'the model of a conflicted masculinity characteristic of the '90s'.⁶⁵ Faludi further emphasizes this perception of conflict and dysfunction, acknowledging public unease with Clinton's 'dysfunctional' masculine identity – 'Office lech or military virgin?' – as debate raged over his 'manly credentials ... as if his Y chromosome was the nation's greatest blight'.⁶⁶

Though such a pluralized construction of masculinity was characteristic of the 1990s, tension remained between Clinton's version of presidential masculinity and the more traditional, authoritative model that preceded him. If Ronald Reagan was 'the fantasy elder come to lead the sons in triumphal battle against the Evil Empire', then Clinton was the disappointing reality.⁶⁷ Reagan's Cold War rhetoric and invocation of mythical 1950s family values imprinted his presidency with a muscular masculinity that the electorate welcomed after the softer, more considered approach of Carter. That the 'triumphal battle' was more bluster than fact mattered little. Twenty-three years younger than Reagan was on entering office, to unforgiving commentators Clinton resembled a pretender to the throne who was unable to make the same promises to a generation of men struggling to come to terms with the changing landscape of their manhood.

Particularly damaging to Clinton were perceptions of juvenility. His own presidential campaign positively emphasized his youth, as he and running mate Al Gore (two years Clinton's junior) were heralded as a 'new generation of Democrats' in campaign paraphernalia. His opponents, however, pointed to his alleged draft-dodging and his admitted marijuana use (though Clinton maintained he 'didn't inhale'). The press dubbed him 'Slick Willie', a childish nickname that played on the conviction that he could not be trusted. His alleged infidelities and failure to control his philandering suggested a perennial adolescence unbecoming of the nation's leader.⁶⁸ This perceived irresponsibility cast aspersions on Clinton's ability to sacrifice, to not only know the difference between right and wrong but to adhere to it for the good of the family and the nation. In a period of struggle regarding a perceived loss of paternal reverence within American society, fatherhood at the highest level left much to be desired in the eyes of some sections of the media and the American public they served.

Mirroring Hollywood's project of paternal rehabilitation, Clinton's own restoration in the public imagination owes much to the conscious establishment of him as a father figure, particularly following the 1998 impeachment hearings regarding his relationship with White House intern Monica Lewinsky. A particular ambiguity surrounds Clinton's status as 'father' during his presidency, not least because despite his youth, his perceived inexperience and a public persona that, at its most unflattering, painted him as irresponsible and self-serving, he was the first president since Carter to have his child living in the White House. At the Democratic National Convention in 1992, Chelsea was pictured holding her father's hand, and she appeared beside him at his inauguration the following year. Clinton's reputation as a hands-on dad was emphasized by photo opportunities showing him playing minigolf and white-water rafting with his daughter. Perhaps inadvertently, it was further augmented by a popular news story regarding Chelsea's visit to the school nurse and her request that they 'call my dad; my mom's too busy'.[69] Though a misquotation often used to point to Hillary Rodham Clinton's dominant role within the White House, the story reinforced the president's involved relationship with his daughter. Clinton's lived fatherhood offered a valuable counterpoint to his symbolic fatherhood.

However, beyond this, Clinton's image as 'father' was crucial to gaining a second term and outlasting the threat of impeachment. He, like Schwarzenegger, would be remade. Dick Morris, advisor to the 1996 re-election campaign, traces Clinton's evolution from 'son' (of Arkansas, where he was governor) to 'buddy' (the down-to-earth 'regular guy' presented in the 1992 campaign) and finally to 'father' (post-1996): 'I told the president, "it's time to be almost the nation's father, to speak as the father of the country, not as a peer and certainly not as its child".[70] This strategy involved resisting the urge to show weakness or explain himself unduly, speaking directly to the electorate rather than engaging them in 'conversations'. As such, Morris engineered the shift from Clinton as father of Chelsea, to Clinton as symbolic father of the nation. In cultivating this image of 'national Dad' Clinton actually improved his approval ratings following the revelations of his relationship with Lewinsky.[71] Facing impeachment and widespread denigration, Clinton utilized fatherhood as a way of appealing to the nation and was able to cultivate a future in which his influence remained assured. Demonstrating this lasting legacy, in 2013, over a decade after Clinton left office, he was ranked third in Gallup's poll of outstanding modern presidents, behind Kennedy and Reagan.[72]

Clinton's presidency reflects wider ambiguities and complexities regarding masculinity and fatherhood. It also demonstrates the power of fatherhood as a tool for survival and redemption. The presidents who sit either side of Clinton, George H. W. Bush (1989–93) and George W. Bush (2001–9), reveal a further instance of paternal restoration. During his single term, Bush Sr oversaw a recession, the First Gulf War and the disastrous reversal of his 'no new taxes' pledge. As a somewhat unsatisfactory president, Bush Sr functions as the disappointing father, one who can nevertheless be redeemed through his son. Bush Jr's election, eight years after his father lost to Clinton, is an instance of real-life paternal rehabilitation, an attempt to impose a narrative of renewal and survival on a father who has previously failed to live up to expectations. If Clinton demonstrates the power of fatherhood to redeem the man, the Bushes demonstrate the potency of father–son succession and the saving potential (if not, in Bush Jr's case, the reality) of the child.

A crisis of fatherhood

As with men more generally, fears over the role and status of the father were not confined to the presidency during this period. Hollywood's compulsion to promote fatherhood is not simply the result of an existential masculine crisis but a product of more concrete changes taking place within many American homes. Burgeoning debates and discussions across the country, from newspapers and popular non-fiction to courtrooms, talk shows, churches, support groups and government offices, placed the father under increasing scrutiny. Of recurrent concern was absent fatherhood, an issue taken up by conservatives and liberals, feminists and fathers' rights campaigners alike, albeit from frequently different perspectives. In 1990, 24 per cent of American households with children were headed by a single parent, rising to 27 per cent by the decade's end.[73] Traditionally, single parent households were overwhelmingly headed by women; in 1996, the Census Bureau reported that 83 per cent of single parents were mothers.[74] One study revealed that almost a third of non-resident fathers visited their children less than once a year, or not at all.[75] There was, and remains, a demonstrable link between a father's absence and economic hardship, with 45 per cent of children who resided with only their mothers living near, or below, the poverty line.[76] What David Blankenhorn, founder of the conservative Institute for American Values, termed 'fatherlessness' became a symptom of fractured families and faulty masculinity, as men were accused of failing to take responsibility and commit to an acceptable version of adult manhood. Absent fathers were blamed for numerous social problems, including truancy, teenage pregnancy, drugs, suicide, educational failure and violent crime.[77]

The diminished presence of the father was frequently – and often hysterically – reported, with headlines decrying men's 'vanishing act' and proclaiming a 'father deficit'.[78] *Newsweek* ran a story titled 'A World without Fathers',[79] while the *Washington Post* simply asked, 'Where Are the Fathers?'[80] In his 1995 book *Fatherless America*, Blankenhorn declared absent fatherhood to be one of the nation's 'most urgent social problems', a sentiment echoed by the Clinton administration. As part of its determined policy of chasing so-called deadbeat dads, the government introduced the Deadbeat Parents Punishment Act in 1998, imposing a fine and/or a prison sentence of up to two years for parents – most often fathers – who avoided obligatory child support payments. It also developed various federal programmes to promote responsible fatherhood, including practical support for finding work and resources for more effective parenting, in a bid to tackle the problem.

Alongside Blankenhorn's bestselling book emerged similar titles reflecting on the damage done to families and children when the father was absent or devalued, including Norman Dennis and George Erdos's *Families without Fatherhood* (1992), David Popenoe's *Life without Father* (1996), Cynthia Daniels's anthology *Lost Fathers* (1998) and Ross D. Parke and Armin A. Brott's *Throwaway Dads* (1999). The emergence of extensive popular literature on fatherhood coincided with the establishment of fathers' rights organizations such as the American Coalition for Fathers and Children (ACFC), Fathers for Equal Rights (FER) and the National Fatherhood Initiative (NFI), as well as numerous local grassroots campaigns and support groups.[81] Many fathers' rights groups provide parenting advice and offer practical support, with a view to reinforcing the necessity of paternal engagement. In particular, the need for better legal representation and support in cases of custody, divorce and visitation is a common focus, with larger national organizations able to offer legal aid to some men. As discussed in Chapter 2, there is a persistent anti-feminist, anti-maternal slant to some fathers' rights' rhetoric, but these groups – like the surge of books lamenting the apparent dearth of fatherhood – also reflect a growing sense of loss and fear that the old paternal order was falling away.

Anxiety over the status of fathers and its increasing politicization coincided with growing debates over legal and biological definitions of paternity. High profile incidents such as the Baby Jessica (Michigan, 1993), Baby Richard (Illinois, 1995) and Baby Emily (Florida, 1995) cases, in which children were adopted without the consent of the biological father, contributed further to an atmosphere in which, for some, fatherhood was seen to be increasingly precarious.[82] Not coincidentally, the 1990s was also the decade of the talk show paternity test, as shows such as *Maury* (1991–present), *Jerry Springer* (1991–2018) and *The Jenny Jones Show* (1991–2003) thrived on the spectacle of revealing the identity of a child's father to a live studio audience. The reliance on DNA to prove the paternal relationship gives weight to the biological definition of fatherhood, a compelling and straightforward marker of proof in an era defined by multiplying characterizations of parenthood. The shifting definitions of who and what a father was, however, were further impacted by factors including the increased availability of alternative reproductive methods (such as artificial insemination, in vitro fertilization and gestational surrogacy), the growing numbers of stepfamilies and blended families, and the extension of parenting and adoption rights to same-sex couples and individuals. The insistence on biology enshrined in the televised paternity test reflects an anxious compulsion to return to an unequivocal definition of fatherhood at the exact point that the complexities of this definition were being debated.

Historian and family scholar Robert L. Griswold defines twentieth-century fatherhood in terms of uncertainty, 'its terms contested, its significance fragmented, its meaning unstable'.[83] As Griswold's history of fatherhood demonstrates, there is no previously uncontested definition of fatherhood, much like there is no mythical stable version of masculinity. Fatherhood is as much a sociocultural construction as it is a biological role. Though biology offers a singular point of clarity, it does not tell the whole story. Historically, paternity is linked primarily to marriage; legitimacy was bestowed via the presumption of marital fidelity.[84] Now, adoptive fathers may perform the legal, social and financial functions of being someone's dad regardless of biology. For children living with stepfathers, some or all of these aspects of fatherhood may similarly be fulfilled by a man who does not share their DNA. And, depending on how they become fathers, gay men may have similarly non-biological links with their children that do not preclude a paternal relationship. Historically, the role of a father has also been intertwined with financial provision, yet by the middle of the twentieth century this too was increasingly insufficient as a definition. In the 1960s and early 1970s, feminist campaigns made explicit the need for fathers to be more than material providers, suggesting that increased engagement with childcare and domestic labour would pave the way to gender equality. Though anxiety over fatherhood in the 1990s stems from some real demographic changes – chief among them the increase in divorce and the rising number of non-residential fathers – the reality is that it has always, to varying extent, been a role susceptible to redefinition. If the common factor of fathers' rights campaigners, politicians, talk show hosts, journalists, authors and judges' attempts to quantify fatherhood can be understood as a desire to put the genie back in the bottle, to establish a fixed and unequivocal definition along the lines of biology, legality, financial provision, social function or physical custody, the fact remains that the genie was never really there. Fatherhood, more so than motherhood, has always been troubled by questions of function. In the 1990s, the difference was simply one of visibility, as fathers found their role debated in numerous forums, both private and public.

As such, Hollywood undertakes a more complex task than simply flooding its screens with fathers during the 1990s. It must also navigate contemporary issues facing men and fathers, including divorce, custody issues, paternity disputes and the shifting legal definitions of fatherhood that sought to accommodate same-sex couples. Old models of fatherhood – the autocratic, unemotional patriarch, for example – are increasingly cast as undesirable and significant concessions are made to more emotionally available, involved iterations of fatherhood. The importance of being the breadwinner is questioned in a number of films that seek to demonstrate that good fatherhood is not intrinsically linked to earning power, while elsewhere on screen biology does not necessarily make a man a father. Even as Hollywood anxiously revamped its men into dedicated dads, the films here do not shy away from acknowledging the changing landscape of fatherhood in the 1990s. If anything, the concerns over what and who a father is fuelled many of these narratives, as men continued to negotiate the means of their symbolic survival.

Hollywood's new hero: The triumph of fatherhood

This symbolic survival is enacted on multiple fronts, and the following case studies are organized thematically in order to capture the extent of this project of masculine survival through fatherhood. Chapter 1, 'Fathers of the Future', focuses on disaster narratives, beginning with one of the decade's most successful and iconic films, *Jurassic Park*. Its themes of extinction and survival coalesce around Dr Alan Grant (Sam Neill), the lone adventurer who becomes a father figure to Lex (Ariana Richards) and Tim (Joseph Mazzello). This model of the single, self-sufficient man turning towards fatherhood in the face of disaster is a dominant trope in 1990s disaster films and the chapter continues with an examination of *Dante's Peak*, *Volcano* (Mick Jackson, 1997) and *Armageddon*, all of which prioritize the rehabilitation of the father – whether actual or surrogate – in the midst of an apocalyptic scenario. The revival of the disaster film produced spectacular cinematic manifestations of anxiety about the millennium and the future, threading together concerns about community, masculinity, technology and the environment and holding up a distorted mirror to the real-life tensions of late twentieth-century America. The Americanization of the disaster is notable, with big cities and idyllic small towns alike persistently cursed by lava, ash, meteors, tornadoes and alien invasion. Against this backdrop of imminent erasure, heroes are compelled to embrace a paternal role, perceiving the limits of their own survival should they fail to do so. In fatherhood and the realization of a reproductive future comes a second, more immortal form of survival, as heroism is reoriented towards an investment in the next generation.

In Chapter 2, 'Dad versus the State', disaster is relocated to the domestic realm. Here, dads are cast adrift, as divorce, restricted custody and legal bias temper their ability to father their children. *Mrs. Doubtfire*, *The Santa Clause* (John Pasquin, 1994), *Liar Liar* (Tom Shadyac, 1997) and *The Next Best Thing* (John Schlesinger, 2000) all engage with contemporary concerns over the family court and its reach into the hitherto private realm of the American family. The law threatens the integrity of a man's claim to fatherhood, and its influence must be curtailed if he is to maintain his link to his children and therefore his place in the generational continuum. Yet these fathers are often far from perfect. Transformation is crucial; men must change, as only through recommitting to their children, rediscovering responsibility and acknowledging the value of their fatherhood can they be restored. Those men who do not change – embodied by Bill 'D-Fens' Foster (Michael Douglas) in *Falling Down* – do not survive. However, the fantastical nature of some of these transformations, involving metamorphosis, magic wishes and cross-dressing alter egos, lends an ambiguous note to these tales of redeemed fatherhood, suggesting that same tension between belief and disillusion that characterizes so much paternal rhetoric, on and off-screen, during the decade.

Chapter 3, 'Boys, Interrupted', explores this ambiguity further, moving into more fatalistic territory by examining the death, or near-death, of a child. Dying children are not typical Hollywood fare and the prevalence of films in which a child – overwhelmingly a young boy – is erased from the screen is telling, as Hollywood demonstrates an unusual willingness to explore this taboo topic. Beginning with a discussion of *Lorenzo's Oil* (George Miller, 1992), the dramatized real-life story of a boy with an incurable disease, this chapter considers films produced on the margins of Hollywood, including Ang Lee's art-house crossover *The Ice Storm* and some lesser-known dramas (*Paradise, The Good Son* [Joseph Ruben, 1993]), as well as Steven Spielberg's big-budget production of the delayed Stanley Kubrick project *A.I. Artificial Intelligence*. Again, these films find fatherhood under threat, as men contemplate the contours of a future where they are stripped of their identity as 'father'. Vulnerable boys must take the lead in guiding these wayward men back to themselves. While maternal reactions to grief are commonly characterized as a prolonged state of melancholia, paternal grief is channelled towards the (re-)realization of a reproductive future, often symbolized through a surrogate relationship with another child. This chapter places such films in the context of masculine crisis, linking the deaths of young boys to a wider anxiety regarding the status of American manhood. Beyond this, it also considers these films as a response to the HIV/AIDS epidemic, considering the significance of a disrupted linearity in light of the tens of thousands of young men dying of the virus by the 1990s.

In Chapter 4, 'The Return of the (Lion) King', the discussion of death shifts to examine the premature death of the father. *The*

Lion King, *Twister* (Jan de Bont, 1996), *Contact* (Robert Zemeckis, 1997) and *Jack Frost* all feature children unexpectedly deprived of their dads. In *The Lion King* and *Jack Frost*, both of which focus on young sons, the father is compelled to return in supernatural form, having failed to adequately guide his son in life. That lack of paternal guidance that Bly laments and that Faludi locates at the heart of the masculine crisis, the disappointment in the father whose promises were not realized, manifests in these films in the form of rudderless sons needing a father's counsel. The temporary return of the father reorients the son towards a life of responsibility and success. The narcissistic impulse of reproduction must also be considered here, however, as the father's return serves not only his son but also himself, as his reaffirmed legacy ensures his continued influence on successive generations. Similarly, in those films concerning a bereaved daughter, the narrative drives towards a reproductive future in which the father may live beyond himself. Both Jo (Helen Hunt, *Twister*) and Ellie (Jodie Foster, *Contact*) must establish heterosexual romantic partnerships by the end of the film, ensuring that their veneration of their father is augmented by an investment in the next generation that will see them – and more importantly him – achieve a symbolic, generational immortality.

Elsewhere, Hollywood was somewhat more optimistic about its fathers, at least on the surface. Chapter 5, 'Guys That Say Goodnight', analyses three mainstream films released in the second half of the decade – *The Birdcage*, *The Object of My Affection* and *The Next Best Thing* – all of which portray gay men being, or becoming, parents. Issues around gay parenthood, adoption laws, surrogacy and reproductive technology entered the mainstream in the 1990s, as more and more same-sex couples became parents. Here, fatherhood comes to represent a tangible survival, the antithesis of HIV/AIDS and the devastation caused primarily (though by no means exclusively) among gay men. Such films represent ostensible progression; the caution, however, is in the details. The future offered to these fathers is heavily proscribed, reliant on an erasure of sexual and political autonomy and an expectation of conformity, through which fatherhood is bestowed as a reward rather than a choice. The conditional nature of the future offered to Hollywood's gay men, in which acquiescence to a heteronormative model of family is the only apparent source of fulfilment, ensures that fatherhood is always on someone else's terms. As the end of the decade approached, Hollywood continued to broaden the parameters of fatherhood, but progress remained circumspect.

Taken together, these chapters reveal Hollywood's abiding preoccupation with the father. Contrary to the past, the erstwhile hero is now the vulnerable party. Erasure, whether actual or symbolic, poses a threat to Hollywood's on-screen men. Deliverance comes in the form of fatherhood, capable of bestowing certainty and purpose in a period of intense speculation over the role and function of men. The child is often incidental in the films examined here, testament to the real focus on saving uncertain men and projecting them into a viable and meaningful future. When the child – most often a son or surrogate son – does play a more significant role, the ultimate goal is the same, to save the father and, in the son, the father of the future. The fear of being forgotten, of being left behind as that bridge extended into the millennium, drives this course of masculine rehabilitation, supplanting the muscular heroics of the past with a quieter, paternal triumph that would future-proof those men who chose to embrace fatherhood.

The enduring Hollywood image of the lone hero, the man necessarily estranged from family and home in order to prevail, is increasingly recast as lonely, selfish and misguided. In the opening scene of *Kindergarten Cop*, Kimble prowls the mall in pursuit of Crisp. The mall is traditionally a family space, symbolized here by the crowds of parents and children that form part of the milieu. Kimble is the visible antithesis of this, striding alone through the crowds in sunglasses and a scruffy beard, enveloped by a long trench coat. He pushes past a family on the escalator, his mind firmly elsewhere. By the end of the film, however, he is not only embracing Joyce but also doing so in a room full of children, all of whom have formed an attachment to their unusual kindergarten teacher, not least Joyce's son Dominic. For those men who have misunderstood the importance of family, Hollywood constructs for them one final chance to reclaim it. Similarly, in *Nine Months* (Chris Columbus, 1995) a stark comparison is made between Sam (Hugh Grant) and Sean (Jeff Goldblum), best friends who both enjoy a carefree, bachelor lifestyle. When his girlfriend Rebecca (Julianne Moore) reveals she is pregnant, Sam leaves, only to return when he discovers that Sean's example is ultimately unfulfilling. The film repeatedly uses Van Morrison's 'These Are the Days' to underline meaningful moments in Sam's life, first his anniversary with Rebecca and latterly as a lullaby to help their son sleep. The use of Morrison's song to bridge Sam's journey from carefree man with a sports car and a girlfriend to a father with an SUV – featuring the lyric, 'There is no past / There's only future' – suggests that Sam has made the right choice. His future is guaranteed while Sean is abandoned on the fringes, full of regret for making the 'wrong' choice when his own girlfriend proposed children. *Nine Months* highlights neatly the apparent dichotomy between the individualist natures of men like Sean, who desire freedom (and with it time, money and sex, although not the kind of sex that leads to children), and the willingness of other men, like Sam, to sacrifice some of this freedom for the good of the next generation. Hollywood's project is revealed in the othering of the non-father, while promoting the 'right' choice of self-sacrificing fatherhood. If 'the moment of *survival* is the moment of power', as Canetti suggests, then it is through this paternal claim that

Hollywood's men realize a latter-day heroism.[85] Self-sacrifice becomes its opposite: a self-saving bid for immortality. As Hollywood – and the United States – grappled with its own 'domestic apocalypse',[86] it placed its faith in fatherhood as a shield against fragmentation, anxiety and erasure, a means of harnessing the future visible just over that bridge to the millennium.

1

Fathers of the future: Extinction, survival and apocalyptic narratives

Steven Spielberg's blockbuster *Jurassic Park* is in many ways a quintessential product of 1990s Hollywood. Released in the summer of 1993, it grossed over $350m in the United States to become the top-grossing film of the year, more than $100m ahead of *Mrs. Doubtfire*. Based on the novel by Michael Crichton, it has spawned four sequels to date (*The Lost World* [Spielberg, 1997], *Jurassic Park III* [Joe Johnston, 2001], *Jurassic World* [Colin Trevorrow, 2015] and *Jurassic World: Fallen Kingdom* [J. A. Bayona, 2018]). The film utilizes recent advances in special effects and modelling technology to create a population of on-screen dinosaurs, embracing a commitment to spectacle ingrained in the decade's blockbuster films. These same dinosaurs could be bought as toys, experienced on theme park rides and seen emblazoned on T-shirts and lunchboxes the world over, reflecting the increasing value of auxiliary merchandise to the global film industry. That the *Jurassic Park* name and logo could be found on a dizzying array of said merchandise is wryly acknowledged in the film itself, as Dr Ian Malcolm (Jeff Goldblum) criticizes the park's financial motivations: 'You patented it, you packaged it and you slapped it on a plastic lunchbox.' In short, *Jurassic Park* epitomizes the Hollywood juggernaut of the late twentieth century. Beneath the looming Tyrannosaurus rex and swarming velociraptors, it also reflects Hollywood's preoccupation with the redemption of the father, albeit through a rather unlikely figure: the taciturn palaeontologist Dr Alan Grant.

After the reign of the hard-bodied heroes of the 1980s, of which Arnold Schwarzenegger, Bruce Willis and Sylvester Stallone are prime examples, Alan Grant is a somewhat unlikely blockbuster hero. The ascendancy of alternative heroes signals a loss of faith in those old, muscular heroics in favour of the ordinary man cast as Hollywood's saviour. The apocalyptic narratives of the 1990s, of which *Jurassic Park*, with its genetically modified dinosaurs accidentally let loose on a tiny island, is a microcosmic example, put their faith in comparatively ordinary guys to avert the crisis at hand. Rooting the survival of the family, the city or the world in a single man is not unusual in Hollywood, and while this model of masculine heroism continued, an important amendment must be acknowledged. The lone hero is now weakened by the very fact of him being alone. To succeed, collaboration is crucial. Most often, as this chapter explores, it is a familial relationship that provides the support and motivation to save the day and escape annihilation. What is significant about the films discussed here is the dual survival that is enacted within the narrative. Saving the world becomes secondary to saving the man himself, for he is also in danger. Time and again, his survival depends on his acceptance of a new narrative of heroism: that of the self-sacrificing father.

Alan Grant is a prime example of this paternal heroism in action. *Jurassic Park*'s narrative is built around themes of extinction and its reversal, of responsibility and of family. This is not to diminish its monster-blockbuster credentials but to reveal that just below the surface, it retains those same concerns over men and fatherhood that run like a thread through 1990s Hollywood. Central to this is Alan's transformation from an aloof, independent man to the protector of John Hammond's (Richard Attenborough) grandchildren, Lex and Tim, by the film's end. Above and beyond the spectacle of rampaging dinosaurs terrorizing the Pacific island of Isla Nublar, *Jurassic Park* is Alan Grant's redemption story.

Along with chaos theorist Dr Malcolm and palaeobotanist Dr Ellie Sattler (Laura Dern), Alan is invited to Isla Nublar by Hammond to certify the park's safety before it is opened to the public. This narrative conceit exposes one of the film's predominant concerns, namely nature versus man and the limits of human control over the natural world. Malcolm's repeated warnings that 'Life will not be contained. Life breaks free ... Life finds a way' go unheeded, resulting in a disaster scenario in which the island's dinosaurs literally break free, systematically circumventing the park's failing security and reverting to the hunting and herding traits determined by their DNA. Malcolm's statement, however, may also be applied to Alan, a man who is more concerned with fossils than with his own future.

Prior to arriving on Isla Nublar, Alan makes clear his views on children. Irritated by the presence of an obnoxious child who disputes his contention that dinosaurs descended from birds, he takes great delight in scaring the boy with an unnecessarily graphic description of a raptor attack. Taking a 6-inch raptor claw from his pocket, Alan asks him to imagine being surrounded by raptors, the claw slicing through his stomach. 'You are alive when they start to eat you,' he intones with barely hidden glee. 'So try and show a little respect.' Though Ellie chastises him, Alan remains incredulous that she would ever want a child, declaring them to be 'noisy, messy, expensive', and adding, 'They smell. Babies smell.' Though Ellie is open to the idea of children, for Alan fatherhood holds no appeal. He is committed to his scientific mission and has little time for emotional or familial distractions. It is this attitude that the film works tirelessly to change.

Predictably, Lex and Tim are fascinated by Alan, whose aversion to children is only heightened by their attentions. Yet when the park's security fails and he is reluctantly forced into the role of protector, Alan begins to forge a different relationship with the children. Battling for their collective survival, he, Lex and Tim must negotiate escaped dinosaurs, a car wreck and various accidents and obstacles in

Figure 2 *Jurassic Park*'s (1993) hastily created nuclear family in peril. Universal Pictures.

order to escape the carnage. This culminates in a scene in the Visitor Centre, in which Alan, Ellie and the children are pursued by the loose raptors. In these moments they physically resemble a nuclear family unit, with Lex and Tim as miniature versions of Alan and Ellie. As the T. rex crashes through the hall and devours the raptors, Grant is fully transformed from loner to father, shepherding his ad hoc family to safety.

As the surviving guests depart in a helicopter, leaving Isla Nublar to the dinosaurs below, Alan is framed in a shot with Lex and Tim, who have fallen asleep on either side of him. This mirrors a shot earlier in the film in which Alan watches over the exhausted children in his arms as the three of them shelter up a tree. The proximity craved by Lex and Tim in the early part of the film has been achieved. Yet it is now Alan who marvels at this opportunity. His expression is contented as he shares a smile with Ellie. As she watches him, he looks from Tim to Lex and back at her. His earlier reservations about children have disappeared, it seems, to be replaced with a silent acquiescence to her own desire for children.

Jurassic Park is, at its heart, a story of survival and evolution. The dinosaurs, in their natural state, did not survive the Mesozoic Age; it is only through genetic engineering that Hammond and his company InGen have brought these creatures back. Through the window of the helicopter, however, a flock of birds cuts through the sky. As Alan has endeavoured to prove, birds are the living descendants of dinosaurs, and in focusing on these birds as the film ends, *Jurassic Park* draws a parallel between them and Dr Grant. The old Alan is the dinosaur in this scenario, doomed to extinction if he fails to reproduce and embrace his potential as a father. The desire to triumph over nature has been proven folly; likewise, Alan must acknowledge his own natural instinct towards reproduction, whatever his practical objections to children may have been. In this new iteration he now has a future laid out before him. To embrace fatherhood is to embrace his own survival. Fleeing the unwelcome beasts of the past, Grant finds in fatherhood a tangible future, much like the birds that soar alongside the helicopter.

Symbolically, by the end of the film Alan has lost his hat, a minor but telling costume change that reflects the wider context of the domestication of the hero and the shedding of his lone-adventurer aspirations. Alan's hat, a beige straw fedora, serves a practical purpose, as his palaeontological work keeps him outside in the sun. However, it is also reminiscent of Indiana Jones's distinctive brown fedora and acts as a visual throwback to a previous Spielberg project. In *Indiana Jones and the Last Crusade* (1989), a flashback reveals a young Indy receiving the fedora from a treasure hunter, who sees the boy's potential as an adventurer. It remains a significant aspect of his costume throughout the franchise. Alan begins *Jurassic Park* in possession of a similar hat. On Isla Nublar, he first takes off his hat when he sees the herd of Brachiosaurus, a gesture of reverence as he gazes in wonder at the huge creatures before him. This wonder is reserved, in part, for the revelation that the dinosaurs are moving in herds – family groups – and it is interesting that it is here that he first removes his hat, in unconscious deference to this spectacle of family unity. He eventually loses it during the first T. rex attack, when he lures the dinosaur away from the children. Casting off this symbol of lone adventuring, Alan is plunged into the role of protector, whereby his heroism lies in his acceptance of the two children either side of him, not in the vanquishing of the monsters around them. Though Indiana Jones goes to great lengths to keep hold of his hat, performing the infamous hat grab in *Indiana Jones and the Temple of Doom* (Spielberg, 1984), Alan enacts no parallel millinery rescue. This is a key visual clue to his changing priorities. Conspicuously, the one man who does keep his hat is the park warden Robert Muldoon (Bob Peck), who continues to engage in macho heroics and is eventually outwitted and killed by a 'clever' velociraptor.

Spielberg is often discussed in relation to his representations of childhood.[1] However, the negotiation of masculinity in his films is equally significant, not least in the way that Spielberg's men are so often visible products of their time. Indiana Jones is the bold adventurer, the latter-day cowboy of Reagan's America: heroic, independent and (it transpires) looking for his daddy's approval. A decade earlier, Spielberg's trifecta of masculine almost-heroes – *Jaws*' (1975) Chief Brody (Roy Scheider), Hooper (Richard Dreyfuss) and Quint (Robert Shaw) – captured the uncertainty of 1970s America, a nation struggling with the aftermath of Vietnam and the destabilization of authority that followed Watergate. In the guise of the first modern blockbuster, *Jaws* – never just a movie about a shark – gave Hollywood audiences a vision of the nation's conflicted masculinity, fractured pieces of a troubled whole. Similarly, *Jurassic Park* taps into a particular narrative of contemporary masculinity that would play out across the decade and beyond. Ever preoccupied with narratives of paternal rescue, Spielberg himself would revisit similar themes of family and survival in *A.I. Artificial Intelligence* and paternity and redemption in *War of the Worlds* (2005).[2] Like *Jaws*, what lies beneath the monster is the true heart of the film.

This re-routing of heroism towards the paternal recalls *Kindergarten Cop* and its reimagining of Arnold Schwarzenegger as an emotionally engaged father figure. In *Kindergarten Cop*, the shift is still rather self-conscious, a plot device that plays on the ridiculous image of the physically imposing Schwarzenegger grappling with child-sized furniture and unruly kindergarteners. In *Jurassic Park*, the transformation is less obviously laboured, although the outcome is much the same. Alan must learn the same lessons in order to survive. The stakes are undeniably higher, as Alan, Lex and Tim evade being eaten, trampled or mauled, but for Alan, as for John Kimble, there are clear consequences related directly to his willingness to embrace a model of surrogate fatherhood. Professional success cannot compensate for personal fulfilment; true heroism comes with the final embrace of the child who has taught him such a lesson.

The defining feature of both men's newly discovered paternal role is a focus on physical protection. The role of the protector has been an integral legal and cultural aspect of American fatherhood throughout history. Though the expectations of fatherhood have continued to shift and change, the father's responsibility for the physical well-being of his children has been a constant presumption, while protection in other forms (financial, moral and sexual) has likewise largely been attributed to him.[3] The economic structure of the family mirrors this association with protection, maintaining the father's position as primary breadwinner far into the twentieth century, the person who stood between children and hardship.[4] Indeed threats to this position, in the form of increased numbers of women in the workforce and the growing necessity of dual-earner families to maintain a comfortable middle-class lifestyle, is one of the catalysts for the renewed cycle of masculine crisis in the 1990s. In the nineteenth century, the law enshrined the father as the absolute head of the family, responsible for property, money and children. Wives and children were legally obliged to obey the father, and in the case of parental separation, he would retain custody.[5] The father's role as the 'natural guardian' of the children in a legal sense shifted during the nineteenth century, yet culturally this interpretation of the role remained.[6] In lieu of a biological or legal relationship with the children they are compelled to protect, it is this commitment to their safety that marks out John Kimble and Alan Grant's success as stand-in paternal figures. In both cases, the man's willingness to take responsibility for the children in his care far outweighs any legal commitment or biological imperative.

To begin with, Alan must shield a panicked Lex from the prowling T. rex, coaching her to keep completely still and so remain undetected. He rescues Tim from the suspended wreckage of one of the tour cars and later catches him when he is thrown from a live electric fence. These acts bring Alan closer to both children. A distinction is carved between him and Hammond's lawyer, Donald Gennaro (Martin Ferrero), who abandons the children at the first sight of the T Rex and is punished for this desertion with a humiliating death, in which the T. rex devours Gennaro whole as he cowers in a portable toilet. Following the T. rex attack, a traumatized Lex continues to repeat, with some incredulity: 'He left us! He left us!' This may be understood as a reference to Gennaro. However, it is likely that on some level it also refers to Lex's own father. In a throwaway line at the beginning of the film an employee reveals that Hammond's daughter – Lex and Tim's mother – is going through a divorce. To Lex, Gennaro's swift abandonment mirrors the physical loss of her own father, and so Alan's protection is not only a practical necessity but also an emotional one, if Lex is to overcome the dual trauma of divorce and dinosaurs.

To this end, Alan makes Lex a solemn promise that unlike the others, he will not leave them. This vow and his commitment to fulfilling it are the basis of his paternal triumph. Later, when he and the children climb a tree to keep themselves safe from the escaped carnivores below them, he promises to stay awake 'all night' while Lex and Tim sleep. As they curl up beside him, Alan pauses to retrieve the raptor claw from his pocket – that same claw used to scare the young boy in the opening scenes – and tosses it to the ground, where the camera rests in a lingering close-up on the discarded artefact. Alan is no longer interested in scaring the children. His priorities are reoriented from gory stories to paternal reassurance, that same reassurance that is so notably lacking in the failed fatherhood of Sam Bowden in *Cape Fear*. Where Bowden repeatedly fails to protect his family, inviting trauma into the domestic realm, Alan – like Kimble – repels the trauma, reverses the pattern of paternal abandonment and shields the children from further physical and emotional harm.

Lost men and found fathers

Elsewhere in Hollywood, the same preoccupations recur with some regularity. Far from being isolated incidences of trauma over the lost father, the frequent return to this theme suggests a psychological attempt to work through this absence, reflecting an issue simultaneously afflicting a significant number of families in the audience. A similar narrative structure shapes *Dante's Peak*, starring Pierce Brosnan as Harry Dalton, a volcanologist with the US Geographical Survey who is sent to an idyllic Washington town to investigate potentially destructive seismic activity. In 'The Imagination of Disaster', Susan Sontag outlines a typical disaster narrative, beginning with the (inevitably male) hero – often a scientist – encountering a threat (the 'thing'). The scientist hero, in all Sontag's variations, is imagined as having either a wife or girlfriend, that is, someone to protect from the oncoming disaster.[7] Like Alan Grant, however, Harry is a loner, reluctant to form a meaningful relationship with anyone since the death of his partner Marianne in a previous volcanic eruption, seen in the film's opening sequence. And, like Alan, Harry is at risk precisely because of this reluctance. Early in the film, he declares that he has 'always been better at volcanoes than people or politics', preferring the scientific to the social. *Dante's Peak* is in no doubt that this is a flaw that needs correcting. Harry derives meaning in his life from the volcanoes he monitors yet, despite his best efforts, they evade understanding. He is fundamentally helpless, doomed to watch rather than participate. Redemption lies in a reversal of this state of affairs, in which Harry must learn that monitoring, measuring and predicting are fundamentally unfulfilling. If Alan is compelled to discover that fossils are no substitute for the future, Harry must come to understand that meaning lies beyond the readings on his seismometer.

In this case, Harry's chance for redemption comes in the shape of Mayor Rachel Wando (Linda Hamilton) and, more significantly, her children. Graham (Jeremy Foley) and Lauren (Jamie Renee Smith) have been fatherless for the past six years, since Rachel's ex-husband walked out. The first question that Lauren asks Harry is whether he has children; when he tells her no, she replies, 'You're lucky.' This is evidently based on Lauren's experience of her mother's loving but frazzled approach to parenting. Graham, meanwhile, shows all the signs of needing some paternal guidance. His attempts at independence – he and his friends have established a den in one of the town's mines – only incur his mother's disapproval. In contrast, Harry offers Graham a deep-sea fishing trip and recognizes the value of his knowledge of the mines, validating the rebellious, adventurous spirit that is traditionally coded as masculine. Graham appears to be a victim of that same lack of father posited by Robert Bly, a boy struggling to become a man without the guiding hand of his dad.

What is good for Graham, however, is equally beneficial to Harry. He rapidly becomes a part of the Wandos's domestic landscape, staying for dinner and fascinating the children with magic tricks; belatedly, Harry conforms to the expectations of Sontag's disaster hero. Much like Ellie in *Jurassic Park*, Rachel watches these scenes with an indulgent smile, enamoured of the familial image before her. When the volcano does erupt, proving Harry's calculations correct, his commitment is not to monitoring the eruption but to saving the children, who have taken Rachel's truck in an attempt to rescue their stubborn grandmother (Elizabeth Hoffman). Harry, too, has realized what is truly important to his long-term survival.

Dante's Peak enacts a relatively straightforward apocalyptic scenario and much of its second half is dominated by persistent images of destruction and chaos as the town collapses and the family attempts to stay alive. Through this landscape, Harry must not only navigate to safety but also ensure the survival of his ersatz family. At the beginning of the film Harry is framed alone, relentlessly doing push-ups in his cramped apartment. After arriving in Dante's Peak he remains a singular figure, the lone voice at the town meeting calling for safety measures to be implemented. Now, however, he emerges as the father figure, the central point towards which Rachel, the children and the townsfolk converge. He holds Lauren on the boat as they traverse an acidic lake, singing 'Row, Row, Row Your Boat' to calm her down. Later he manoeuvres his truck across a bed of lava and, despite the devastated landscape around them, the image places Harry firmly in the role of the patriarchal head of the nuclear family, with Rachel by his side and the children in the back of the car. He even stops, briefly, to rescue the family's dog. Around them the town is disappearing, but within the truck Harry has pieced together a family, with himself at the centre. His own survival is thus assured.

Dante's Peak ends with a strikingly similar shot to that of *Jurassic Park*, as the newly formed family are whisked away in a helicopter after being rescued from a collapsed mine. Inside the mine, Harry has been separated from the others and is rescued first. Though he and Rachel have formed a romantic (though so far chaste) attachment, it is not to her that he shouts when she and the children emerge but to her son. 'Graham! Graham!' he yells, as the four of them are reunited and embrace. Harry, it seems, has recognized the value of his newfound paternal role. On the helicopter, the children remain close to Harry, refusing to leave his side. 'Did you really mean what you said, about taking us fishing?' Graham asks hopefully. Harry assures him the fishing trip will go ahead and he and Rachel join hands, cementing Harry's new position within their family. Like Alan Grant, Harry has been given a second chance, surviving not only the volcano but his own fatal independence.

For the men discussed thus far, theirs is a symbolic, rather than reproductive, fatherhood, but the principles of reproductive futurism remain intact. Alan's commitment to Lex and Tim is embodied in the fact that it is he who takes charge of shepherding them back to civilization. For Harry, his dedication to his new paternal role is crystallized in his reiteration of an earlier promise to take the children fishing. It is not biology but commitment that shapes their chances of survival. In an era of apparently lacklustre paternal commitment, symbolized by the failed fathers of Lex and Tim, Graham and Lauren and most of the kids in Kimble's kindergarten class, the emergence of these formerly solitary men dedicating themselves to these children is particularly striking. It reinforces Hollywood's own commitment to engaged fatherhood as a means of masculine assurance, regardless of biological relation. Inevitably, however, hovering at the edges of these conclusions is the promise of a romantic relationship with the female protagonist and therefore the possibility of a reproductive future. Though Alan and Ellie are already a couple, this remains ambiguous for much of *Jurassic Park*, despite their discussions about having children. Ellie appears happy for Malcolm to flirt with her, while Alan glowers silently on the sidelines. Not until they are reunited in the Visitor Centre and rescued from the island does their romantic future seem secure, and this owes much to Alan's changed attitude towards the children. Their shared smile, and her indulgent gaze as their helicopter lifts away from Isla Nublar, is suggestive of a more assured future. Beyond the surrogate father role that Alan has accepted, this romantic reunion opens up a space in which a heterosexual reproductive future is also a distinct possibility. Likewise, it is only once they are rescued from the mine that Harry and Rachel finally kiss, but in this moment the suggestion is one of a shared future through their developing sexual relationship.

Balancing the aversion of disaster with a symbolic reproductive future is a common theme in Hollywood during this period. Yet for all their focus on establishing fatherhood, these films are often remarkably chaste. In part, of course, this is due to their status as family films. As Noel Brown notes, the family film offers a vision of cinema largely free of sex and violence, a reflection of the multi-demographic target audience, commercial imperatives and the family film's place within American culture as a comforting, conservative form of entertainment.[8] Therefore, despite the underlying drive towards heterosexual reproduction, these films tend to rely on the implication of sex rather than its realization within the frames of the film. In *Jurassic Park*, Ian Malcolm is the most overtly sexual character – he flirts suggestively with Ellie, and the most iconic image of him is one in which he reclines, shirt open, after being injured – and yet his status as father (he has three children) is precarious precisely because of his inability to commit to one woman. 'I'm always on the lookout for the next ex-Mrs Malcolm,' he tells Alan, wryly reflecting on his turbulent family life. In *Dante's Peak*, the first human casualties of the impending volcanic eruption are a young couple who have sneaked down to the hot springs to go skinny dipping. Their illicit encounter ends in them being burned alive by the rapidly heating water. Sex for pleasure is not the goal here. This goes some way to explaining the delayed consummation of Harry and Rachel's burgeoning relationship in the same film. Their first kiss is thwarted on no less than three separate occasions and it is only at the end of the film, when Harry has fully embraced his role as substitute father to Lauren and Graham, that he and Rachel finally take this next step, anchoring their sexual relationship to the pursuit of familial continuance.

Apocalypse averted

The commitment to a reproductive future is a common denouement to many of Hollywood's apocalyptic narratives. It is symbolized visually at the end of *Deep Impact* (Mimi Leder, 1998), as Oren Monash (Ron Eldard) glimpses the face of his newborn son for the first and last time, and in *Independence Day* (Roland Emmerich, 1996) as the president (Bill Pullman) is reunited with his daughter and Captain Hiller (Will Smith) with his son, a reminder of what was at stake had the alien invasion been successful. In its final scenes *Armageddon* shifts its focus from sex-for-pleasure to sex-for-reproduction when Rockhound (Steve Buscemi) declares to the woman he previously met in a strip club that he wants to 'make babies' with her. The end of the world crystallizes the desire of hitherto selfish or single men to 'make babies' and double down on their own survival. Having lived through the disaster, they turn now to the next generation and the prospect of living in perpetuity.

These are just some of the notable disaster movies in a decade that saw the genre flourish once more. Prompted in part by advances in special effects technology and in part by anxieties over the approaching millennium, some of Hollywood's biggest hits of the 1990s came from the action-disaster genre. *Independence Day* took the box office top spot the year of its release, and other significant successes include *Speed*

(Jan de Bont, 1994), *Twister, Volcano, Deep Impact* and *Armageddon*. *Titanic* (1997), James Cameron's epic romantic disaster film, was the runaway box office success of the decade and remains one of the most financially successful films on record. The 1990s invited these doom-laden scenarios, whether historical or contemporary, revealing a raft of underlying fears in the process. Disaster films, like the science fiction films discussed by Sontag, contain within them 'the deepest anxieties about contemporary existence'.[9] Though the anxieties may evolve, the methods of dealing with them within the realm of popular culture remain reliable: imagine the apocalypse, only to 'neutralize' it.[10]

A similar flurry of disaster films emerged in the early to mid-1970s, beginning with *Airport* (George Seaton, 1970) and including *The Poseidon Adventure* (Ronald Neame, 1972), *Skyjacked* (John Guillermin, 1972) *Earthquake* (Mark Robson, 1974), *The Towering Inferno* (Guillermin, 1974), *Airport '75* (Jack Smight, 1974) and *The Hindenburg* (Robert Wise, 1975). Writing about these films, J. Hoberman suggests that such disastrous scenarios on the big screen offer an audience the 'total breakdown of an institution hubristically imagined to be safe, and these ocean liners, airplanes, skyscrapers, theme parks, and cities, were, of course, microcosms of America'.[11] By 1974, the United States was struggling to extricate itself from the disastrous war in Vietnam. The same year, Richard Nixon resigned to avoid impeachment after the Watergate scandal destroyed his reputation and left the American public contemplating their trust in the office of the president and their own 'national father'.[12] Just five years later Carter would seal the fate of his own presidency when he questioned the nation's confidence and its citizens' commitment to it and to each other. Reagan was on the horizon, waiting to promise the American public 'hope', 'confidence', 'strength' and 'inspired leadership'.[13] But Carter tapped into a truth about the malaise dogging the United States during this decade, and Hollywood reflected this back at its audiences. It takes three men to tackle the shark in *Jaws*, and it is Brody – a man who is afraid of the water, a man whose wife propositions *him*, a man who cannot shoot straight – who emerges as the ultimate hero. The disaster scenarios that populated the box office during this same period are similar indications of a nation grappling with itself, its future and its chances of survival.

Of course, in playing out these disasters on the big screen, Hollywood provides an expectation of resolution: the monster will be vanquished, the disaster will be averted, and so to envisage the disaster is to engage in a game of cinematic *fort-da*.[14] Hoberman quotes Theodor Adorno's maxim: 'Psychology knows that he who imagines disasters in some way desires them.' Adorno goes on: 'But why do they come so eagerly to meet him? Something in reality strikes a chord in paranoid fantasy and is warped by it.'[15] The persistence of disastrous narratives in 1970s Hollywood is suggestive of this perverse desire for destruction, that same desire that underpins Freud's theory of the death drive, whereby the desire to '*restore an earlier state of things*' (i.e. to return to a state of inertia) resides in the unconscious even as one remains conscious of their 'self-preservative instincts'.[16] On screen, this drive is kept in check by the safety valve of the Hollywood narrative, which dictates that disaster ultimately be averted and order be restored.

In the 1990s a similar impulse is revealed in the succession of films noted above. These disaster scenarios often extend beyond single institutions to encompass not only the country but the world itself. Christopher Sharrett perceives a thread of 'American apocalypticism' running through the cinema of this period, the result of a postmodern crisis of meaning disrupting notions of truth.[17] Certainly, there is a wider apocalyptic narrative running through Hollywood in the build-up to the millennium. Crisis, it seems, reigns: a crisis of masculinity, a crisis of fatherhood, a crisis of confidence as the nation faced the end of the 'American century'. Hollywood responds with a plethora of natural disasters, alien invasions and races against time. Crucially, these disasters are no longer the institutional 'microcosms'

Hoberman identifies, but the real thing. *Independence Day* and *Deep Impact* both '[revel] in the destruction of vast metropolitan centers', not least *Independence Day*, which takes great cinematic delight in destroying the White House with a beam of energy direct from an alien spaceship.[18] In *Volcano*, the city of Los Angeles is the target, with locations continually flashed up on the screen: Wilshire and Western, the Beverly Center, La Cienega, the Hard Rock Café, Cedars-Sinai Hospital. The localization of this disaster is an opportunity for geologist Amy Barnes (Anne Heche) to reflect on the arrogance of man, those who would have the audacity to build a subway in an area of seismic activity. Beyond that, it is an opportunity for the film to underline that most persistent of fears, that the impending disaster was a distinctly American one. If the whole world was under threat, the epicentre of the disaster was resolutely located on US soil. Similarly, in *Dante's Peak*, the fictional town is depicted as a vivid, colourful idyll. The film opens on a volcano erupting fire and ash over a Colombian city. People stagger through the grime with their possessions. A bike is wheeled through the grey ash as others shield themselves with umbrellas. This monochrome landscape is a contrast to the first glimpses of Dante's Peak, where a yellow balloon floats against a brilliant blue sky, the backdrop to a cascade of white-tipped mountains and lush green forests. The camera tracks in on Main Street, a cacophony of colour and noise. A carousel whirls in the distance, while a marching band advances in the foreground. This is the Pioneer Days Festival, a colour-saturated celebration in the heart of America's 'Second Best Place to Live'. The festivities, the awards and the cheerful population are all testament to its small-town charm, revealing exactly what is under threat. And at the heart of these disasters, battling for his own survival as much as that of the planet, stands the American man, who will finally be anchored by a turn towards the paternal.

While for men like Alan Grant and Harry Dalton this process begins with the care of someone else's children, for other male protagonists the battle is one of recognition and a reharnessing of their existing fatherhood. In *Volcano* and *Armageddon*, Mike Roark (Tommy Lee Jones) and Harry Stamper (Bruce Willis) are already fathers, but this in itself is not enough. If they are to survive, they must ensure their link to the next generation is secure. The precarity of post-divorce fatherhood is well established in Hollywood during the 1990s and is discussed in more detail in Chapter 2. Accordingly, *Volcano* takes one of Hollywood's most persistent figures, the divorced father, and places him at the centre of the disaster narrative. Mike is head of the Office of Emergency Management, a task force responsible for overseeing disaster response in Los Angeles. Though he is ostensibly on vacation while his teenage daughter Kelly (Gaby Hoffman) visits him, when an earthquake hits the city he returns to work. Kelly, frustrated by this response, complains that he is breaking his promise that he would honour their vacation time. Kelly and Mike's fractious relationship is established in typical Hollywood shorthand: he insists on leaving her with a babysitter, and in retaliation she threatens to pierce her nose. His offer of a trip to Disneyland is met with derision, as Kelly declares she would rather go shopping at the Beverly Center.

It is, predictably, the disaster that brings them together. When a second earthquake hits in the middle of the night, Mike is forced to take a frightened Kelly to work with him, only to find chaos engulfing the city as fire, ash and balls of lava begin to rain down. Here the film emphasizes Mike's competing commitments. He must remain on the ground and begin to coordinate the response efforts, but he must also care for his daughter. The two of them engage in the following loaded exchange:

Kelly: You can't just leave me.
Mike: I have to stay.
Kelly: Why?
Mike: Because it's my responsibility.
Kelly: So am I.

Mike's survival quest, therefore, is twofold. He must attempt to rescue the wounded, discover the source of the lava and prevent it from erupting on the site of the Cedars-Sinai Hospital, thereby saving the city. He cannot, however, neglect his own personal quest to forge a better relationship with Kelly and so solidify his paternal role. Having dispatched his daughter to apparent safety at Cedars-Sinai, Mike is horrified to discover that he has in fact sent Kelly to the very place the volcano is likely to erupt. It is only as he authorizes the detonation that will create a route for the lava to flow into the ocean that Mike spots Kelly in the shadow of the Beverly Center. The camera zooms in twice on Mike's face in this moment, as realization dawns. If the first can be read as the surface horror of this moment – his only daughter is in imminent danger – the second zoom might be read as a deeper sense of realization. Mike's own future is suddenly in danger of being wiped out. In slow motion, Mike runs towards Kelly, pulling her out of the way as the building collapses. The final moments of the film cement Mike's new-found commitment to his own fatherhood. 'I'm on vacation,' he informs his colleague, refusing to involve himself in the immediate strategy for dealing with the aftermath of the disaster. 'I'm going home with my daughter.' Mike puts his arm around Kelly as the camera tracks out, leaving them to navigate through the ash and rubble of what remains of LA. The city may be in partial ruin, but Mike's own survival is assured now he and his daughter are reunited.

In effect, Mike experiences a rebirth in the face of extinction. His own immediate survival means little if Kelly does not also survive. In *Crowds and Power*, Elias Canetti suggests that '[man] wants to live longer than anyone, and to *know* it'.[19] The child's survival is the 'knowing' in this scenario. If Kelly lives, then Mike's own future is secured. Yet this is also dependent on him rebuilding a successful relationship with Kelly, ensuring that he remains a substantial part of her life. Significantly, for much of the film Kelly becomes responsible for two young children. It is the disappearance of the young boy in her care that leads her to the Beverly Center and puts her in danger. There are hints here of Kelly's own (reproductive) future, as she assumes temporary maternal responsibility for the boy. Mike's double-zoomed look of horror occurs as he sees not only Kelly but the young boy too. It is a distorted vision of the future, a vision in which he glimpses the generations that may follow him. This is what Mike, above all, is running to save.

These themes of survival beyond the self are integral to Hollywood's construction of fatherhood as a saving mechanism in the 1990s, nowhere more so than in films where the father dies, discussed in more detail in Chapter 4. *Armageddon* plays with similar ideas of extinction and reproduction, demonstrating that even when the father does not survive the disaster, what remains crucial is the consolidation of his legacy. Another blockbuster hit, grossing over $200m despite a lukewarm critical response, *Armageddon* concerns a mission to destroy an oncoming asteroid before it wipes out the planet. At its heart it is built around the strained relationship between Harry Stamper and his daughter Grace (Liv Tyler). As the film drives towards a conclusion where the earth is saved from destruction, it pushes also for Harry's rehabilitation and the securing of his own reproductive future even as he sacrifices himself for the greater good. The immortality promised through fatherhood is not a physical defiance of death but a spiritual and psychological one. By mending his relationship with Grace, Harry's survival beyond himself is restored.

Harry leads the team of oil rig drillers enlisted by NASA to deal with the asteroid. Included in his team is Grace's boyfriend A.J. (Ben Affleck), of whom Harry is openly disapproving. 'She's better than that,' he declares to the rest of the team. 'She's better than all of us.' Here Harry adheres to the narcissistic parental belief that his child's life should be and will be an improvement on his own, echoing the Freudian assumption that the child 'shall not be subject to the necessities which [the parents] have recognized as paramount in life. Illness, death, renunciation of enjoyment, restrictions on his own will, shall not touch him [sic].'[20] Yet Harry and Grace, much like Mike and Kelly in *Volcano*, have a fractious relationship, as indicated when Grace refuses to call him 'Dad'. Even in the shadow of an approaching asteroid, this is a threat to Harry's survival. If he is not remembered and rehabilitated as Grace's father, his own legacy ends with him.

Accordingly, *Armageddon* becomes a narrative of individual, rather than collective, survival. To complete their mission, one of the crew must leave the spaceship, manually trigger the malfunctioning equipment and blow up the asteroid, guaranteeing the safety of the planet below. It is A.J. who draws the short straw among the crew, but at the last moment Harry forces A.J. back into the airlock and embarks on the mission alone. With A.J.'s safety assured, Harry tells him, 'You gotta take care of my little girl now. That's your job.' His next lines demonstrate his own commitment to a paternal legacy, as Harry rewrites the past on the spot: 'I've always thought of you as a son,' he claims of the man he formerly disparaged. 'Always. I'd be damn proud to have you marry Grace.' Harry's final words, as he is left alone and exposed in space, are simply, 'My son.'

Figure 3 Harry protects A.J. and sacrifices himself in *Armageddon* (1998). Buena Vista Pictures.

In terms of action, this is the precursor to the film's big moment. Yet for Harry, this *is* his big moment, even before he triggers the bomb that will destroy the asteroid. His demise is what Elena Woolley terms an 'intimate death'.[21] Woolley suggests that in many Hollywood apocalyptic-disaster films, the protagonists are 'gifted' with a death imbued with meaning as opposed to another instance of faceless annihilation, as is the fate of the masses. In Harry's death, we see nothing less than his survival. He has successfully rehabilitated himself, inserting himself into the presumed reproductive future of Grace and A.J. and claiming them both as his children. His reference to their marriage underlines this presumption, and indeed *Armageddon* ends on this official union. At Grace and A.J.'s wedding, the aisles of the church are flanked by large pictures of the astronauts who died on the mission. Most prominent among these images is one of Harry, whose greatest triumph in death has surely been to establish himself not only as Grace's father but A.J.'s surrogate father too, the preserver of their union and the benevolent figure, smiling from his photograph, who has ensured both their and his own survival. No longer the estranged father, Harry can now be assured of a continued generational legacy. This is neatly mirrored in an extra-textual moment of father–child bonding, as Liv Tyler's own biological father Steven Tyler provides the film's signature song (Aerosmith's 'I Don't Want to Miss a Thing').[22]

The harnessing of paternity as the key to masculine survival extends beyond Harry to other surviving members of the mission's crew. Chick (Will Patton) has previously been denied visitation with his son by his ex-wife. However, on landing back on earth, Chick and his son are reunited. Meanwhile, Rockhound, firmly established as a womanizing, sex-obsessed gambler before the mission, returns an apparently changed man. His aforementioned declaration that he wants to 'make babies' reiterates the film's central theme: in itself, survival is worth little unless it can be extended beyond the self into the next generation. Released shortly before *Armageddon* in the summer of 1998, *Deep Impact* concerns a similar narrative of potential extinction, as a meteor hurtles towards the earth. Once again, the meteor's greatest impact is reserved for the North American continent, a literal manifestation of the United States' fears for the upcoming millennium and beyond, reiterating that same 'American apocalypticism' discussed above. Beyond these narrative similarities, *Deep Impact* also shares a preoccupation with establishing the father's legacy before death. Astronaut Oren Monash is essentially on a suicide mission, committed to driving his ship into the advancing meteor in order to divert it and so prevent its impact with the earth. He is, however, permitted to say goodbye to his wife via video link, during which he sees his newborn son for the first and only time. Even as Oren faces his own death, it is his fatherhood that promises another form of survival beyond the self. Like Harry, he can die knowing a part of him continues to live on.

Mastering the apocalypse

Discussing the proliferation of apocalyptic narratives in American cinema, Wheeler Winston Dixon theorizes that the end of the twentieth century marks a point at which cinema itself was facing up to its own end. 'As we enter the 21st century,' he writes, 'there are signs of exhaustion everywhere. The narrative structures of feature films ... are being shamelessly recycled from one film to the next, and sequels now predominate the box-office.'[23] Dixon's assessment of twenty-first-century Hollywood reveals an industry crippled by a commitment to the safe bet, shunning risk in favour of guaranteed reward, in a climate where recognizable narratives, characters and pre-sold properties are used to capture the attention – and the money – of the audience. The films discussed here largely fit within this Hollywood model. They represent a fleet of high-concept, easily exportable products whose star names and universal narrative motifs of destruction, danger and survival attracted large audiences in both national and global markets, promising a safe return on their large budgets.

The recycling and repetition that these films engage in, however, can also be read as an extension of the anxiety encased within them. Repetition brings mastery, as Freud's work in 'Beyond the Pleasure Principle' observes. It is passivity reconstituted as action, with the fearful event a 'necessary preliminary' to its vanquishment.[24] To persistently enact apocalyptic visions on screen only to neutralize them by the time the credits roll suggests that the threat has been mastered, at least temporarily, through a 'compulsion to repeat' that offers the illusion of command.[25] Despite the fact that these films 'exhibit a phenomenally unlikely degree of survivalism in the face of the planet's hypothetically destructive forces', they ultimately come to symbolize 'a kind of hopefulness and defiance of death'.[26] With the exception of those men who do willingly sacrifice themselves for the rest of the population (Harry Stamper, Oren Morash and Russ Casse in *Independence Day*, another disappointing father redeemed through heroic death), there is a persistent theme of survival against unbelievable odds in these films. That this survival is attached to the spectre of fatherhood and an embrace of paternal responsibility underlines the decade's parallel preoccupation with rescuing men from a scenario of crisis, whereby precarious men are reborn as future-proofed father figures.

For those astronauts, drillers and volcanologists who feature heavily in these scenarios, danger is already a facet of their work. These apocalyptic events are merely an opportunity for mastery of the ultimate danger: extinction. To come back from the brink and live to tell the story: there is a potent power in this triumph, not unlike that power discussed by Canetti regarding survival and death. This same desire to master erasure is embedded in Alan Grant's work in *Jurassic Park*, albeit with one crucial difference. Before the events on Isla

Nublar, Alan is a man largely protected from death and destruction, despite his profession. The dinosaurs he has made his career from have been dead for millions of years. Alan is engaged in his own process of mastery: digging, studying and categorizing, all in the name of demystification. Extinction is an abstract concept for him, something to investigate rather than contemplate, and so the precarity of his own future has not yet been revealed to him. Hammond and InGen's revival of the dinosaurs disrupts this place of safety, however. The power of nature quickly supersedes Alan's own power. In one scene, as he and the children navigate through the park, they stumble across some hatched dinosaur eggs. 'The dinosaurs are breeding,' Alan says, observing the broken shells. 'Malcolm was right. Life found a way.' That which man believed he had mastered has evaded control; it is here that chaos resides.

This scene is a reminder of *Jurassic Park*'s preoccupation with reproduction and replication, and the narrative drive towards Alan realizing his place in this reproductive order, order being the operative word, which suggests that this is the true means to mastering his own fate. At Isla Nublar's science facility, Hammond introduces a video explaining the process by which his scientists have managed to clone dinosaur DNA, a literal repetition of genetic sequencing that reverses extinction. The real-life Hammond is joined by a video version of himself; this image continues to multiply, until numerous Hammonds are all talking to each other. This replication of the self is a more literal rendition of the drive behind human reproduction. Here, Hammond is only giving birth to more versions of himself, but the implication is the same. While ever these replications exist, Hammond lives, just as the millions of years old dinosaurs now live on.

Alan's own mortality is only thrown into relief by the appearance of these living dinosaurs. To gain mastery over his own ultimate demise, Alan turns to the spectre of procreation, as symbolized by Lex and Tim, and embraces it (and them). In essence, reproduction is another form of repetition, one that ensures Alan will continue to exist beyond himself. It is this form of repetition that promises true mastery over his own future. There are symbols of reproduction scattered throughout *Jurassic Park*, from the hatching dinosaur egg and Hammond's delight that the baby dinosaurs will imprint on him to the way Alan lays his head rapturously on the Triceratops' stomach, an image reminiscent of a father listening to the heartbeat of his unborn child and emphasized by a soundtrack dominated by the sound of steady breathing. These moments signal the film's ultimate intention to subvert the threat of extinction, establish Alan's own reproductive future and ensure life 'finds a way' for him, above all.

Conclusion: Transcending disaster

End-of-the-world scenarios are Hollywood's bread and butter in the 1990s, driven on an industrial level by almost certain box office return and on a thematic level by the fears generated by the millennial moment. The repetition of apocalyptic spectacle reveals the anxiety of possible destruction. Ostensibly this destruction threatens the nation, but symbolically it taps into those fears at the heart of the crisis of masculinity, that men were in danger of being cast adrift. Battling against this threat, whether natural, man-made or extraterrestrial, the ordinary heroes that populate these films are offered the opportunity to regain control and master the threat, both physical and existential.

This control is perpetually linked to fatherhood. The uncertainty of the future and the United States' place within it can be mitigated, it is suggested, through a commitment to the next generation (and those subsequent generations that logically follow). The end is not the end so long as man can lay claim to the immortality promised to him through reproduction. Crucially, it is a form of heroism that does not rely on spectacular physical stunts or improbable feats of strength but one that is available to all these on-screen men, providing they recognize the potency of their own paternal potential. The disasters may be spectacular, but the heroics are reassuringly mundane. Alan Grant may be dodging dinosaurs, while Harry Dalton and Mike Roark may be racing against a volcano spewing lava, but none of these men require immense physical strength, gadgets or superpowers to survive. As Hollywood faced the end of the world, it repeatedly promised that the planet could be saved by its fathers and that its men could be saved by fatherhood. The birds flying by the InGen helicopter at the end of *Jurassic Park* are a striking visual testament to this survival narrative, in which the future comes to be represented by a long line of descendants that have transcended extinction to live forever.

2

Dad versus the state: Hollywood's courtroom battles

Hollywood's blockbuster disasters were a reliable source of box office income throughout the 1990s, as anxiety over the approaching millennium merged with advances in technology and special effects. Anchoring survival to paternity in these multi-million-dollar pictures reinforces a central message of masculine hope: threatened with annihilation, men could rescue themselves through a renewed commitment to the next generation. Closer to home, however, on-screen fathers were facing erasure of a different kind. Beyond aliens, dinosaurs and natural disasters was something far more mundane, yet it retained the potential to cast men out beyond the sanctuary of the family. In short, Hollywood's dads were getting divorced.

As discussed in the previous chapter, the turn towards fatherhood is paramount to the survival of American men in the 1990s. The survival of these men through fatherhood marks an attempt to circumvent the pitfalls of traditional masculinity, assumed to be in crisis, and presumes instead a future based on the apparently unassailable structures of a paternal identity. Yet if fatherhood holds the promise of a tangible future, the realization of this future is not without its obstacles. Across a multitude of genres, Hollywood put a domestic spin on the precarity of masculinity, casting its men out of the family home and into considerable uncertainty, reflecting what Faludi calls a 'domestic apocalypse'.[1] It may be a more prosaic form of apocalypse, but it is still anchored to the same fear of erasure.

Without his children, these films wondered, just how secure is the father's future?

Shifting patterns of marriage and divorce in the United States in the late twentieth century ensure that such questions are more than hypothetical. The divorce rate increased during the 1980s, with one in every two marriages projected to end in legal separation.[2] This rate remained steady, only falling slightly in the late 1990s; the 1980s and 1990s have the highest divorce rates in US history.[3] As the 1990s dawned, the familial landscape of the United States was one that included significant incidences of separation, divorce, one-parent families, stepfamilies and non-residential parenting. The nuclear family so beloved in popular culture and political rhetoric was changing irrevocably.

Much of this change fuses around the figure of the father or, in many cases, around the spectre of his absence. As discussed in the Introduction, paternal absence or lack of engagement was of primary social concern during the 1990s, a decade in which half of American children would be subject to legal custody arrangements.[4] Of those children, a significant majority would reside apart from their fathers. In the 1980s, Hollywood protested a little too much over this state of affairs, constructing a raft of 'fathered-only child[ren]' as mothers were marginalized and men took over the domestic and parenting duties.[5] Men left holding the baby, such as the trifecta of bachelors Tom Selleck, Steve Guttenberg and Ted Danson in *Three Men and a Baby* (Leonard Nimoy, 1987), grappled with diapers and dinner until, inevitably, they realized that self-fulfilment lay not in work or women but much closer to home. Valorizing the newly domesticated father, such films reinserted dads into the family at a point when, in reality, increasing numbers of children were growing up in fatherless homes. By the 1990s, however, a notable shift occurs. Though Hollywood remains intent on rehabilitating its fathers, these men are now often outside the family home and find themselves susceptible to marginalization. Furthermore, this marginalization is not simply spatial but legal, as divorce and separation invite the law into the sanctity of Hollywood's family home.

As seen in Chapter 1, divorce is a common narrative element in the 1990s. Both children and parents are seen dealing with the effects of separation, with many films drawing on contemporary fears that divorce was irreparably distancing fathers from their children. In some cases, such as *Dante's Peak*, the potential damage caused by such distance is projected onto the children. However, more commonly, Hollywood advances the notion that the estrangement of fathers and children – whether voluntary or otherwise – is primarily bad for the father. This chapter examines the tension between fatherhood as a means of masculine survival and as a site of continued power conflict in Hollywood's depictions of the family court. Films including *Mrs. Doubtfire*, *Falling Down*, *The Santa Clause* and *Liar Liar* take concerns over divorce, custody and the role of the non-resident father and address them within a domestic context. The role and rights of the father take centre stage in these films; it is remarkable that three of the decade's most successful family films (*Mrs. Doubtfire*, *The Santa Clause* and *Liar Liar*) are essentially about the impact of divorce of men. What they document is a battle for paternal authority and a continuation of the link between father and child, all of which is threatened by the legal institutions governing the American family, the resounding villains of the decade.

Family courts were established in the United States during the 1940s to legislate on various issues relating to divorce, separation, alimony and custody. Their aim was to 'offset the harsh effects of adversary divorce' (no-fault divorce was not legalized until the 1970s).[6] Despite its on-screen ubiquity, by the 1990s the family court was a last resort. Most cases of divorce and custody were mediated privately, without the need of a judge. However, these films all engage with a more adversarial model of legal intervention, raising the stakes of the father's removal from the family. Central to this discussion is the extent to which the law is able to inhibit the paternal future on offer.

Research into fathers post-divorce reveals a variety of issues associated with the non-custodial father role, including emotional stress, humiliation, despair, emptiness and feelings of disempowerment.[7] This perceived 'powerlessness' stems from various key factors, chief among them issues of child support and access, the role of the child's mother and the intervention of family courts, lawyers and other associated professionals such as child therapists.[8] Hollywood's representations of divorced fathers take power as their central concern, constructing the family courts, the legal system, the mother and the stepfather as obstacles to the father's own survival through a continued relationship with his child. Shades of common fathers' rights narratives concerning access and maternal bias, which became increasingly prevalent in the 1990s, can also be discerned.

These films owe a considerable debt to *Kramer vs. Kramer* (Robert Benton, 1979), in which Ted and Joanna Kramer (Dustin Hoffman and Meryl Streep) engage in a lengthy custody battle over their 5-year-old son Billy (Justin Henry). *Kramer* is an early example of Hollywood representations of divorce and parenting, not as a backdrop to a broader drama but as a theme unto itself. Its iconic scenes within the courtroom elevate a dispute between parents to a hostile face-off, a visual tactic replicated in later films to heighten the dramatic tension. When the court awards primary custody to Joanna, invoking an approximation of the outdated 'tender years' doctrine, the film interprets this as a grossly unfair maligning of Ted's fatherhood.[9] The law fails to recognize Ted's contribution to Billy's upbringing, a contribution romanticized in some of the film's most iconic scenes, including one in which Ted teaches Billy to ride a bike. 'Don't go too far!' Ted yells as Billy pedals into the distance. But in *Kramer*, as in the case studies below, it is the law that ultimately threatens to carry his child away. The film also invests heavily in Ted's transformation into an emotionally engaged primary caregiver, and narratives of transformation remain common as fathers face off against their legal adversaries.

The on-screen visibility of the family court lends an element of heightened drama to a rather banal aspect of civil law.[10] The imposing setting of the courtroom, more commonly the preserve of crime dramas and legal thrillers, imbues proceedings with an antagonistic quality. It is also a location that is resolutely not-home. In *Mrs. Doubtfire*, an abrupt cut shifts the action from the warm, bright family home to the darkness of the courtroom and the stern figure of the judge (Scott Beach), delivering his judgements from an elevated position. The emotional nature of custody cases provides a further reliable source of narrative tension. This tension underlines the building anxiety over the courts' role in contemporary family life and the law's power to define fatherhood. If fatherhood provides the answer to the question of how to deal with the crisis of masculinity and the precarity of the future, the law is capable of unravelling fatherhood with a second familiar question: what makes a man a father? If, as Richard Collier suggests, family law is concerned primarily with 'ascribing status', the legal definition of 'father' is often represented as being narrow enough to exclude otherwise good fathers.[11] It is this legal erasure that fathers must battle to overcome. At the end of *Mrs. Doubtfire* and *The Next Best Thing*, similar scenes usher in the credits, with the restored father driving away with his children in the car. In both cases, he has been the victim of a restrictive custody arrangement based on a judgement about his status as a father. For Daniel (Robin Williams) in *Mrs. Doubtfire*, it is his unconventional approach to parenting that leaves him vulnerable. For Robert (Rupert Everett) in *The Next Best Thing*, his sexuality and lack of biological relation to the son he has raised place his own fatherhood in jeopardy. In these final scenes, placing the father – literally – back in the driving seat ensures the influence of the law is finally, symbolically subdued.

This paternal triumph is crucial to the father's continued survival. Hollywood's stance remains unequivocal in its belief in the father, maligning the external powers that limit his autonomy, even as it is careful not to dismantle the patriarchal framework of the law itself.

'Just us': The law as intruder in *Mrs. Doubtfire*

Mrs. Doubtfire was one of Hollywood's most successful films of the 1990s, and Williams's portrayal of divorced dad Daniel Hillard remains one of his most iconic roles. After his wife Miranda (Sally Field) files for divorce, Daniel invents a female alter ego, Euphegenia Doubtfire, in order to see his children Lydia (Lisa Jakub), Chris (Matthew Lawrence) and Nattie (Mara Wilson). The film grapples with themes of fatherhood, paternal love and responsibility, which form around the contemporary cultural anxiety of the law's influence on the family and especially on the father.

Daniel's custody is restricted due to his precarious employment and unsatisfactory living situation. In the opening scenes, he is at work voicing a cartoon bird, a role he promptly quits after a disagreement over the bird smoking a cigarette. Although audiences are invited to understand Daniel's decision as a moral one, it is reinterpreted by Miranda and the judge as irresponsible. For Miranda, this irresponsibility, compounded by the wild impromptu birthday party he throws for Chris, is the final straw. 'I want a divorce,' she declares, as Daniel visibly crumbles. And no wonder; suddenly, his fatherhood becomes visible to the law. As breadwinner and homeowner – traditionally masculine roles – Miranda's position is secure. Daniel, meanwhile, is at the mercy of the judge. His sporadic employment patterns and his poky apartment are subject to a scrutiny they would not otherwise be afforded. The judge gives Daniel three months to 'get a job, keep it and create a suitable home' and thus adhere to the court's accepted image of fatherhood.

Daniel's moral values and his desire to make his children happy are swiftly reimagined and rejected. The court is interested in measurable outcomes, not professions of fatherly love. Daniel dutifully adheres to the conditions, submitting to his court liaison Mrs Sellner (Anne Haney), accepting an unglamorous job and learning to keep house. However, unsatisfied by the custody arrangement, he resorts to masquerading as Mrs Doubtfire and is soon declared indispensable by Miranda, unaware that her ex-husband has infiltrated his former home. Eventually and inevitably unmasked during a disastrous family meal, Daniel is reprimanded by the judge and punished with extremely limited, supervised visitation in a second custody hearing. Daniel's commitment to his children is of little consequence. The moment that the law becomes involved in the Hillards' post-divorce parenting arrangements is the moment that his fatherhood, and so his future, is put at risk.

In effect, *Mrs. Doubtfire* enacts a double home invasion narrative. As a director, Columbus has form here: *Home Alone* also centres on the middle-class, suburban family home under siege. In this instance, 10-year-old Kevin's (Macaulay Culkin) sole defence of his home suggests a fundamental failure of parental authority.[12] In *Mrs. Doubtfire*, this loss of authority is attributed to the invading force of the law, whereby a symbolic violence is perpetrated on the relationship between father and child. The watchful eyes of Max Cady in *Cape Fear*, trained on the windows of the Bowdens' home, are transplanted by the law's intrusive monitoring. Yet a second invasion must be noted too, in which Daniel uses Mrs Doubtfire as a way back into the home. While the law's influence is deemed insidious, this incursion is framed as a reasonable – if comedic – solution to his limited visitation. At one point in *Cape Fear*, Cady dresses in the murdered maid's dress to escape detection. *Mrs. Doubtfire* reimagines this scenario – an unwelcome man masquerading as a woman to gain access to the home – as a necessary means of seeing his children and celebrates it accordingly.

In framing the law as the real intruder, *Mrs. Doubtfire* reflects contemporary concerns over the role and reach of the family court. Feminist legal scholar Martha Fineman suggests that the law 'has begun to reflect an assumption that the family may be harmful to an individual's (economic, emotional, and physical) health', disrupting the dominant construction of the family as a benign entity.[13] This assumption is criticized by numerous conservative commentators, whose approach to family law reflects a neoliberal distaste for outside regulation. Stephen Baskerville, president of the American Coalition for Fathers and Children (ACFC), describes the 'discovery of fatherhood' by government agencies (including those that police child support and legislate on custody) as 'disturbing', criticizing the government's ability to intrude on the private lives of families.[14] Likewise, Dana Mack argues that the United States was becoming an increasingly 'family-hostile culture' by the 1990s, removing the rights of parents to raise their own children in favour of external institutions.[15]

These criticisms reflect an uneasy negotiation of the family along a public/private axis. Though the family is a legally defined institution,[16] society is often keen to imagine the family as a private concern, off-limits to the very legal structures that determine its existence.[17] The preference for viewing the family as a private entity conveniently ignores socio-political issues ranging from a lack of economic and residential security to domestic violence and abuse, all issues that may necessitate the intervention or support of government and legal agencies. Yet the multifarious reality of American family life is often ignored in favour of an image of white, heterosexual, middle-class families whose default position is one of affluence, property ownership, good (physical and mental) health and availability of opportunity. Hollywood, too, prioritizes this model of the apparent 'dream family'.[18] This is a family who has no need of legal intervention; only the (relatively amicable) dissolution of the parents' marriage invites legal scrutiny. Single-parenthood and absent fatherhood consistently correlate with poverty in the United States and disproportionately impact on non-white families.[19] But in keeping the focus on the white, middle-class, self-sufficient family that has hitherto existed largely unmonitored by the state, the law represents an intrusion rather than a necessary aide. Just as the United States adheres to an economic model of global, free-trade neoliberalism in the 1990s, Hollywood's families are also shown to benefit from diminished regulation and increased autonomy. In *The Santa Clause*, when Scott (Tim Allen) takes his son Charlie (Eric Lloyd) to the North Pole, his ex-wife Laura (Wendy Crewson) reports it as a kidnapping. Non-custodial parents taking their children when under explicit instruction not to would usually constitute a serious police incident, yet here it is reconstructed as a misunderstanding, in which Scott's desire to see Charlie is excuse enough. The police response is presented as unfair and heavy-handed,

Figure 4 Daniel is reunited with his children at the end of *Mrs. Doubtfire* (1993). 20th Century Fox.

testament again to the neoliberal assumption that the affluent, white family – and in this case the father – knows best. Similarly, within this paradigm Daniel's fatherhood is suddenly, and unnecessarily, under threat from a hostile, proscriptive exterior force, regardless of the unconventional means he uses to see his children.

This, then, is the real triumph of *Mrs. Doubtfire*'s final scenes. As Lydia, Chris and Nattie watch television, Mrs Doubtfire appears on screen, dispensing sage advice to her young viewers. Once again, Daniel has breached the boundaries of the family home in the guise of his alter ego. Miranda interrupts to introduce the children to their new nanny, at which point it is revealed that Daniel's reinsertion into the home is twofold. Not only is his voice coming from the living room, but he is standing, in person, outside the house. A contrite Miranda confirms there will be 'no more supervised visits, no more court liaisons', as Daniel is now free to take the children after school. Nattie, seeking clarification, asks her father: 'Just us?' 'Just us,' Daniel promises, as he prepares to drive away with the children. With this conclusion, *Mrs. Doubtfire* affirms the mistake of letting the law interfere with the family unit. It is Daniel, waiting on the doorstep, who truly knows what is best for his family. This recognition is critical to the realization of his future through fatherhood, which the law has attempted to usurp. Left to their own devices, families are shown to best be able to mediate among themselves, more capable of healing their own wounds than having someone else prescribe a cure.

The 'access bitch': Mothers and the law

Throughout the 1990s, the government developed various programmes to promote responsible fatherhood. It also reinforced a commitment to punishing those fathers who did not meet the requirements of this responsibility. The Deadbeat Parents Punishment

Act (1998) suggested a fine and/or a prison sentence of up to two years for parents who avoided child support payments, the centrepiece of a determined policy of chasing and shaming so-called deadbeat dads. David Blankenhorn suggests that the deadbeat dad was the 'reigning villain of our contemporary fatherhood script', a man reduced to his inability to pay for his children.[20] The term became a headline staple. In May 1992, *Newsweek* featured a mocked-up Wanted poster of a man accused of owing over $22,000 in child support, under the headline 'Deadbeat Dads', while *People Weekly* dedicated a September 1995 front page to 'America's Worst Deadbeat Dad'. Clinton returned to the subject frequently. 'We cannot renew our country when children are having children and the fathers walk away as if the kids don't amount to anything,' he declared in his 1994 State of the Union address,[21] echoing the promise made at the Democratic National Convention in 1992: 'Take responsibility for your children or we will force you to do so.'[22]

The political imperative to punish deadbeat dads stems from the lingering influence of the New Right's 'family values' platform, enacted under Reagan, and from the economic realities of absent fatherhood. Non-payment of child support often led to greater dependence on welfare and government assistance, tellingly revealed in the language used by Clinton when he called for fathers to 'reinvest' in their children.[23] Once again, the government's commitment to enforcing responsible fatherhood largely applied to men who were, through divorce, separation or estrangement, outside the family home and therefore visible to the authorities.

The 'deadbeat dad' narrative casts the father in the role of uninterested and potentially criminal party, a man who must be forced to take financial responsibility for his children.[24] *Falling Down* engages explicitly with the deadbeat dad, the problems of a father expelled from the family home and the fear of a mother who is aligned with the law. Bill 'D-Fens' Foster embarks on an epic odyssey across Los Angeles in order to 'get home' to his young daughter Adele (Joey Hope Singer), who lives with Bill's ex-wife Beth (Barbara Hershey). Released the same year as *Mrs. Doubtfire*, the broad strokes of the narrative are similar – a divorced father who wishes to see his child is deemed 'not good enough' by the law – but the execution is not. *Falling Down* offers a bleak depiction of divorced fatherhood that owes much to the narrative of disenfranchisement advanced by fathers' rights groups and reflected in research on divorced fathers.[25] What emerges as Bill traverses the city, committing a variety of increasingly violent acts, is that he is estranged from his daughter, unemployed and losing his grip on reality.

It is the twin blows to Bill's masculinity – the loss of his job in the defence industry and the breakdown of his marriage – that send him spiralling into despair. This despair manifests in anger and violence towards a Korean shopkeeper, a gang of young Latino men and a construction crew, among others. Bill is the quintessential disenfranchised white man of 1990s America.[26] Michael Douglas's casting is interesting here, as in the space of a decade Douglas epitomized the changing parameters of American masculinity. In *Romancing the Stone* (Robert Zemeckis, 1984) he plays the rugged, romantic hero opposite Kathleen Turner; three years later, as Dan Gallagher, he is a somewhat contented family man who finds himself out of his depth after an affair in *Fatal Attraction* (Adrian Lyne, 1987). By 1989, he was getting ostentatiously divorced from Turner in *The War of the Roses* (Danny DeVito, 1989). *Falling Down* continues this progression from masculine power to powerlessness and includes a visual throwback to *Fatal Attraction* in the family photo Bill finds in a drawer. The photograph is strikingly similar to the one over which the end credits of *Fatal Attraction* play. In the earlier film, this photograph symbolizes that which has been saved. In *Falling Down*, it represents everything that Bill has subsequently lost.

Like numerous other on-screen men who find themselves adrift, Bill knows enough to yoke his quest for survival to his fatherhood.

Unfortunately, the law has other ideas. A restraining order prevents Bill from seeing Adele. The film thus engages with another common image of post-divorce parenting, the mother as 'access bitch', a woman who 'fabricate[s] allegations of violence and abuse in order to gain tactical advantage in family law disputes' and 'derive[s] spiteful satisfaction from denying men contact with children'.[27] In *Mrs. Doubtfire*, a brief shot of Miranda and her female attorney quietly celebrating while Daniel despairs hints at a similar conceit about the privileged position of mothers in relation to family law. *The Next Best Thing* projects the same advantage onto Abbie (Madonna), who deprives Robert of his paternal rights by revealing that their son is not biologically his. The 'access bitch' is a touchstone in many fathers' rights narratives, a response to this presumed legal bias and perception of paternal oppression.[28] Though fathers' rights groups have multifarious aims and purposes, as a whole they have often been criticized for their attitudes towards women and their propensity to cast fathers as uncomplicated victims.[29] In *Falling Down*, positioning Beth in the quintessential malicious 'access bitch' role merely accentuates the fact that Bill sees himself firmly as a victim: 'I'm the bad guy?' he whines incredulously, as he is confronted by Detective Prendergast (Robert Duvall). For Bill, a violent killing spree is excusable as long as Beth has failed to invite him to Adele's birthday party.

Beth's role in Bill's downfall is made clear when she calls the police after Bill repeatedly threatens to come to the house. In her panic, Beth is unable to remember the exact terms of the restraining order. 'He can't come within one hundred feet of us,' she tells the officer (Benjamin Mouton) and his partner (Dean Hallo). 'Or is it yards?' Her uncertainty is brief but damning. Surely, the audience is forced to ask, if Bill was a real danger she would remember the exact distance. This scepticism is filtered through the police officers, who remain unmoved by Beth's concerns about Bill's 'horrendous temper'. When she suggests that Bill 'could, I think' be a threat, one officer offers a cynical response: 'You *think*?' Though the audience has witnessed Bill's violent rampage through the city, there is still a sense of antipathy towards Beth. Her confession that the judge 'said we should make an example of him' reinforces the perception of an unfair collusion between the mother and the law. Jude Davies and Carol Smith suggest that the audience is 'encouraged to resent' Beth and invited to presume her 'ridiculous' even though Bill clearly poses a legitimate threat, not only in Beth's telling but in the unfolding of the film itself.[30] Bill is maintained as the true victim, regardless of the violence he perpetrates and the fear he instils.

The language surrounding custody and access is by nature combative.[31] Parents 'fight' for access in custody 'battles'; it is possible to both 'win' and 'lose' custody. As a result, children become 'part of a nexus of power within family relations',[32] no longer simply objects of love but objects of power, or 'assets'.[33] When Samantha Cole (Jennifer Tilly) is unfairly awarded custody in *Liar Liar*, she snatches her children away from her ex-husband, snapping, 'They're mine. Don't you have some cheques to write? You haven't paid for them yet.' Mrs Cole is in many ways a caricature of a vindictive ex-wife, her behaviour reducing the children to tokens of financial gain. This possessive language, however, is common. In *Mrs. Doubtfire*, when Miranda arrives at Daniel's new apartment to pick up the children, she asks, 'are my children ready yet?' Daniel is quick to correct her – 'no, *our* children are not ready yet' – but the sense of ownership is indicative of the power relations that the law's involvement has laid bare. Likewise, Bill's repeated mantra of 'I'm going home to *my* daughter' reveals an assumption of possession and a desire to reclaim something that is in danger of being lost to someone else.

This conflict mentality suggests that to retain custody is to retain control, whether that control be emotional, financial or physical. Repeatedly, Hollywood configures its custody battles as arenas of masculine failure. But to construct a loser, a winner must also be crowned. Legal victory is routinely conferred on the mother, resulting in a loss of paternal identity, what Blankenhorn describes as the process of being 'de-fathered'.[34] The men in these films are at risk as long as their fatherhood can be reduced to visitation schedules, child support requirements and court-mandated expectations. Crucially, what the law's intervention presages is a narrowing of the role of father to a traditional paternal model centred primarily on financial and material provision, a model that by the 1990s was increasingly outdated and untenable. The conflict, therefore, extends to the expectations of a father versus the individual reality, with little regard for the emotional attachment between father and child. This, Hollywood suggests, is where the danger lies. The father must overturn the legal obstacles in his way if he is to resist the process of 'de-fathering' inflicted on him by the law.

The overturning of legal intervention is most often twinned with the capitulation of the mother, allowing for the father's symbolic return to power on two fronts. In both *Mrs. Doubtfire* and *The Santa Clause*, this is achieved in a scene in which the mother burns the custody papers. Miranda rejects the custody arrangement, relinquishing the privilege conferred on her by the family court in favour of transferring this authority back to Daniel. She visits him on the set of Mrs Doubtfire's television show and throws the custody papers into the fireplace of the fictional living room. With this gesture, Daniel's family life is no longer confined to a stage set that replicates a warm family home. Similarly, in *The Santa Clause* Laura signals her own mistake in having a judge revoke Scott's visitation by burning the custody papers in front of him: 'It's my Christmas present to you.' The displacement of the law comes in the form of maternal apology, a realization that the legal power granted to them was misplaced. There are, inevitably, shades of a familiar anti-feminist narrative here, as women find their new power unwieldy. Miranda goes so far as to tell Daniel, 'I don't want to hurt our kids anymore', reorienting the blame firmly towards herself. Laura and Miranda's ability to reverse the court's decision when Scott and Daniel cannot is suggestive of a lingering paternal weakness, but it also suggests a belated recognition that father still knows best. Trust has temporarily been placed in the wrong 'father', in this case the law. In correcting this decision, credence is once again given to the neoliberal desire to retain authority over one's own family, allowing the father to regain – and even strengthen – his own power.

'My dad's a liar': The other side of the courtroom

If Hollywood's divorced fathers were generally at the mercy of the law, *Liar Liar* presents audiences with a twist on this particular tale: a divorced dad whose job is to disenfranchise other fathers. The film opens with 5-year-old Max (Justin Cooper) declaring to the rest of his class that his dad is a 'liar'. His teacher corrects him – 'you mean a lawyer,' she says reassuringly – but Max's apparent slip of the tongue reveals the film's disdain for the legal profession, an arena in which lying, evasion and greed are not only commonplace but encouraged. This is one thing when it involves defending ATM robbers and gang members, it seems, but when the issue at hand is one of paternal custody, the film is unequivocal in its condemnation.

Liar Liar is a typical mid-budget Hollywood comedy that combines various familiar narrative threads – the workaholic father, the perpetually disappointed child and a custody dispute that favours the mother, however unsuitable – and packages them up as an opportunity for Jim Carrey to bounce, undulate and gurn his way through a performance as Fletcher Reede, an unscrupulous attorney who is oblivious to the numerous ways in which he lets down his son on a weekly basis. Fletcher is both the father on the brink of becoming powerless and the lawyer responsible for a parallel act of paternal disenfranchisement. The central conceit of the film – that for one day

Fletcher is rendered incapable of lying after Max's birthday wish is granted – begins the unravelling of Fletcher's professional life and throws into relief his own precarious fatherhood.

Michael Asimow observes the widespread negative portrayal of lawyers in 1990s cinema and highlights a number of common traits often attributed to these characters, including their 'mostly unhappy personal lives and dysfunctional families'.[35] *Regarding Henry* (Mike Nichols, 1991), for example, features Harrison Ford as yuppie lawyer Henry Turner, a self-obsessed workaholic oblivious to the impact of his thoughtless behaviour on his young daughter. Gennaro, who abandons the children in *Jurassic Park*, is also a lawyer. Such characterization is particularly pertinent when considering those lawyers who are involved in custody decisions. In *I Am Sam* (Jessie Nelson, 2001), Sam's (Sean Penn) custody of his daughter Lucy (Dakota Fanning) rests with Rita (Michelle Pfeiffer), a successful lawyer whose family life is disintegrating. Rita's lack of control over her own family life contrasts with the high level of control she has over Sam's. In the same way, Fletcher's own shambolic approach to parenting and his frequent infidelity while married to Audrey (Maura Tierney) are no barrier to his role in depriving more committed fathers of their children, as in the case of Richard (Eric Pierpoint) and Samantha Cole, with Fletcher cynically representing Mrs Cole against the evident best interests of the Cole children.

A lack of emotional involvement from judges and lawyers is in keeping with the expectation of professional impartiality, yet such distance is recast in these films as a deficiency. By failing to recognize declarations of paternal love, the family court is established as a peculiarly anti-family institution, even though the lawmakers are often parents themselves. In *The Santa Clause*, the judge who revokes Scott's visitation delivers his verdict from behind a desk on which sits a framed photograph of his own son. In *Liar Liar*, Fletcher's colleague reduces children to pawns in a power game, announcing cheerfully,

'I love children. They give you so much leverage in a case like this.' The exploitation of children and parents for financial gain places the legal professionals – and, by association, the law itself – in the role of villain. Their lack of empathy advances the belief that families are not well-served by the court that claims to represent them. Instead, children become objects of 'allocation', as the law lays bare that which is generally hidden in a narrative of middle-class American family life: that children are not simply subjects of love but often objects of power, generating that very 'leverage' that Fletcher's colleague identifies.[36] Fletcher's ambition for promotion leads him to engineer a custody win and larger financial settlement for Mrs Cole, despite her own maternal apathy and her confession that her ex-husband is a 'wonderful father'. As his boss Miranda (Amanda Donohoe) reminds him, 'You get paid to win,' recalling frequent accusations that the family courts are motivated by money rather than justice.[37] Whether or not Fletcher's actions are morally sound is beside the point; another colleague is fired from the case for questioning its ethics. Again, the law is characterized as broadly unsympathetic, uninterested in the consequences of its rulings and fighting for the wrong reasons. In short, Fletcher and his ilk are 'a greedy pack of liars and thieves', rather than the upholders of justice.[38]

As a lawyer, Fletcher is stereotypically amoral and self-serving. As a father, he is not much better. He begins the film as a casually dishonest, workaholic dad, a staple of 1990s Hollywood.[39] He is frequently late to see Max, offering flimsy excuses or else forgetting entirely, prompting Audrey to accept her boyfriend Jerry's (Cary Elwes) proposal to move the family to Boston. Oblivious to the parallels, Fletcher continues to take his own fatherhood for granted while pursuing the curtailment of Richard Cole's paternal role. It is not his involvement with the Cole case that makes Fletcher re-evaluate his approach to fatherhood but rather Max's ill-timed birthday wish: 'I wish, for only one day, that Dad couldn't tell a lie.'

As a comedy vehicle for Carrey, Fletcher's inability to lie informs much of the film's humour. He is forced to submit to his new-found compulsion to tell the truth, his face and body contorting with the effort. But in his relationship with Max the truth becomes a revelation. When his secretary Greta (Anne Haney, appearing again as a woman tasked with watching over an errant father) reminds him that he promised to collect Max from school, Fletcher retorts, 'Oh, I'm such a shit!' Later, he is stunned by his own blunt realization: 'I'm a bad father,' he declares morosely, as Audrey catalogues his disappointing behaviour. These epiphanies are the crux of Fletcher's own survival. Faced with being usurped by Jerry and consumed by his soulless job, it is his son who engineers Fletcher's moral and paternal rescue, making Max the quintessential saviour of Aronson and Kimmel's reckoning. By the end of the film, now fully cognizant of the importance of his own fatherhood, Fletcher quits his job for alternative legal work that is both ethical and less demanding on his schedule. The reward for such a transformation is Fletcher's re-entry into the family. On Max's next birthday, Fletcher and Audrey share a kiss while Max looks on, beaming. Fletcher has been rehabilitated, the label of 'lawyer' (or, indeed, 'liar') subjugated by the renewed role of 'father'.

Much like *Mrs. Doubtfire* and *The Next Best Thing*, *Liar Liar* must negotiate the tricky line between repudiating the law without dismantling it entirely. In a discussion of *To Kill A Mockingbird* (Robert Mulligan, 1962), Amy Lawrence argues that a subtle undermining of the law is necessary to shore up the father's authority. Atticus Finch, the quintessential cinematic lawyer–father, turns a blind eye to Boo Radley's killing of Bob Ewell. Following this decision, his daughter Scout (Mary Badham) is shown curled up in his lap, which Lawrence reads as a symbolic shift that maintains the primacy of Atticus's paternal authority, suggesting that he 'can now be restored because the law has been subtly but firmly displaced'.[40] A similar scenario shapes the conclusion of *Regarding Henry*, in which Henry quits his prestigious New York law firm, declaring, 'I can't be a lawyer anymore.' Telling his wife 'I want us to be a family,' suggesting that the two things – law and family – are fundamentally incompatible, he removes their daughter from her boarding school so Henry can make up for missing out on so much of her early life. Likewise, though Fletcher is far from being the benevolent father–lawyer figure of Atticus Finch, the same displacement must be enacted at the end of *Liar Liar*. Fletcher's own fatherhood, like Henry's, is restored, the fallibility of the law is acknowledged, and only then can the film fade out on the Reedes' re-established familial harmony.

Transforming the 'bad guy'

One crucial element linking these films is the necessity of the father's transformation. The catalysts are various, ranging from the voluntary adoption of an alter ego (*Mrs. Doubtfire*), to a medical condition (*Regarding Henry*), to those transformations that require a more supernatural explanation (the force that grants Max's birthday wish in *Liar Liar* is never elucidated). Retaining this supernatural element, *The Santa Clause* also concerns the adoption of an alter ego, in this case an involuntary undertaking accompanied by a permanent physical transformation that sees Scott Calvin become Father Christmas.

These transformations are integral, because they imbue a relatively banal narrative concerning a divorced or disinterested father with comedy, drama or tension. However, such a focus on transformation also calls into question Hollywood's faith in its own fathers. That Fletcher must be afflicted by an inability to lie, or Scott struck by the inescapable duty of being Santa, or Henry literally shot in the head, suggests that something more than the threat of separation is required to shock these men into re-evaluating their fatherhood. While these men are worth saving, there remains room for improvement. Even

Daniel, whose commitment to his children is unusually unwavering, is positively impacted by Mrs Doubtfire and her more responsible, capable approach to parenting. From the late 1960s onwards, the women's movement called for men to embrace equal parenting and become more domestically and emotionally engaged with their children. A similar transformation takes place in these films, as men re-evaluate their priorities, develop their domestic skills and, most crucially, learn how to bond with their child. A sleight of hand ensures that feminism is not credited for this shift, however. Circumstances out of the father's control drive him towards the initial change; finally, in the closing moments of the film, his own autonomous decision to choose a more engaged, responsible model of fatherhood determines his rehabilitation.

Nevertheless change, these films suggest, is not only preferable but necessary. The perils of refusing or being unable to change are revealed all too bluntly in *Falling Down*, in which Bill's inability to adapt seals his fate. Bill's rage at the shifting world around him, a world in which he has become, without realizing, 'the bad guy', achieves nothing. It is merely a sign of stasis, a commitment to a model of masculinity and fatherhood that is no longer viable. Doggedly pursuing this outdated model, Bill finds himself ill-equipped to survive. The final scenes are set on a pier, itself a symbolic end point. Bill faces off against Detective Prendergast and his police-issue gun with a plastic water pistol, like Bill a poor facsimile of the real thing. Only in death can Bill still envisage his own worth as a father, safe in the knowledge that his life insurance will help provide for his daughter. It is here, as Davies points out, that Bill is finally transformed 'from maniac to hero', but the transformation comes too late to save him.[41] Adele is destined to know her father only from home videos and old photographs. It is against this fate that men such as Daniel, Scott and Fletcher battle, with transformation the key to success.

A focus on transformation further recalls Rowena Chapman's theory regarding the 'new man' and his proliferation as a cultural model of masculinity. Chapman suggests that although the new man proposes a break with traditional masculinity, in reality he represents a continued bid for power.[42] By adapting just enough, male power can be retained under the guise of real change. Likewise, the extreme transformations seen in these films ultimately ensure that the father retains his paternal privilege. In *Mrs. Doubtfire*, Daniel essentially proves himself as both a father and a surrogate mother figure, doubling his influence in the same home for which he was previously incapable of taking responsibility. Fletcher and Scott, meanwhile, are made heroic through their fierce attempts to remain in contact with their sons (Fletcher going so far as to hijack a set of airport stairs to apprehend a moving plane). The fact that both men must be forced, by powers beyond their control or comprehension, to recognize their deficient parenting is not interrogated. It is the transformation that matters most. After years of benign indifference, these signs of change are enough to restore the father.

Crucially, these transformations serve another final purpose. In constructing a 'before' and 'after' version of fatherhood, they allow for a further indictment of the law. Through his incarnation as Father Christmas, Scott is evidently a man changed for the better. Yet so often these positive transformations are rendered negative by a legal system struggling to quantify good fatherhood. When *The Santa Clause* begins on Christmas Eve, Scott is a company man more concerned with the self-congratulatory staff party at which he is honoured than being on time to visit his son. Though Scott pays lip service to 'families' in his speech, his own family life is almost non-existent. The Christmas Eve he and Charlie spend together is an awkward affair, beginning with Charlie begging Laura to pick him up as early as possible the next day and going downhill from there. Scott sets the kitchen on fire, blasts the turkey with a fire extinguisher and drags Charlie to a Denny's for a cheerless dinner. Before bed, he half-heartedly reads 'The Nightmare Before Christmas', skipping out half

Figure 5 Scott and Charlie bond after Scott's transformation in *The Santa Clause* (1994). Buena Vista Pictures.

the pages and failing to disguise his impatience at Charlie's incessant questions. The culmination of this evening is the accidental death of Santa as he falls from Scott's roof. As the first man on the scene, Scott inherits the title of Father Christmas and all that it entails. This is Scott's transformative moment, but it is also the moment at which his fatherhood comes under threat, not from his own neglectful behaviour but from the assessment of the law.

As Scott accepts his new role, his priorities begin to change along with his physical appearance. He and Charlie bond as he embraces his unlikely new responsibilities, the two of them now enthusiastic about spending time together. Rather than oversee the manufacture of lucrative, poor-quality toys, Scott becomes passionate about developing creative, durable toys, much to his colleagues' dismay. Essentially, Scott becomes a committed, ethical, interested father only to see his visitation revoked and fatherhood severely curtailed. *The Santa Clause* borrows the Santa-on-trial motif from *Miracle on 34th Street* (George Seaton, 1947; Les Mayfield, 1994) but updates it to reflect concerns over divorce and custody. The catalyst for the legal intervention is the concern raised by Laura and her husband Neal (Judge Reinhold) that Scott has filled Charlie's head with delusional fantasies about the North Pole, elves and reindeer. The very thing that has united father and son becomes a source of danger. Not only must Scott contend with Laura and Neal but with Charlie's head teacher and the family court judge. Scott, as a father, becomes answerable to various professionals, echoing those concerns of divorced fathers who perceive an institutional bias against them. Even his boss suggests that he see 'a doctor, a shrink, a dietician', while the judge is unrepentant in his decision to prevent Scott from seeing Charlie.

Like *Mrs. Doubtfire*, the issue becomes one of misinterpretation. In one scene, Scott sits on a park bench while children queue up to tell him what they would like for Christmas. To Laura, this is alarming. Her ex-husband, whose appearance now resembles a much older man, is encouraging unfamiliar children to sit on his lap in the park. Even Scott is willing to acknowledge that 'this probably looks pretty odd'. Yet what the children – and, importantly, the audience – can see is what Laura, Neal and the judge cannot: that this version of Scott is a distinct improvement on his old self. To the courts, however, this is unquantifiable. On paper, the disinterested but solvent, unremarkable father from the beginning of the film is preferable. Once again, the law struggles to legislate when faced with a father who does not fit the narrow mould of court-mandated parenting. This is the same issue that afflicts Daniel, whereby his evident love for his children, of which the audience is in no doubt, bears little legal weight. That Tim Allen and Robin Williams both shaped their star personas around the image of the loving if buffoonish father in the 1990s – Allen in *Home Improvement* (1991–9), Williams in a raft of films throughout the decade[43] – only emphasizes what is at stake. As fathers embrace a more nurturing, involved brand of fatherhood, the courts are seen to be playing catch up, refusing to acknowledge the shifting parameters of fatherhood and so jeopardizing the very men who have realized the value of their paternity and are working to redeem themselves.

Phased out: The threat of the stepfather

It is telling that the fathers in these films do not forge successful relationships post-divorce. Beyond a token gesture of heterosexuality – Daniel, in disguise, attempting to buy a young woman a drink, or Fletcher leering at a female colleague in the elevator – there is no hint of a romantic future with another woman, or any second chance at parenthood. Hollywood is firm in its conviction that these men are in danger of losing their one and only chance at fatherhood if they do not maintain a relationship with their existing children. Robert, too, frames his opportunity to parent with Abbie as a once in a lifetime chance, a view his own mother reiterates. He too is denied a romantic future, as discussed further in Chapter 5. It is imperative, therefore, that these men subdue the influence of the law and reclaim their paternal recognition.

This struggle manifests in a tangible threat that exists beyond lawyers, judges and ex-wives: the stepfather. Blankenhorn likens stepfathers to 'replacement fathers, perhaps able to offer the functional equivalent of fatherhood to children whose fathers have departed'.[44] Here is the threat of a man who can easily supplant the father and take on a paternal identity through his attachment to both mother and child.[45] Blankenhorn suggests that, given the stepfather's primary attachment to the mother, the child remains an object of secondary importance to him. It is an unsurprising generalization, given Blankenhorn's conservative commitment to traditional family structures. However, Hollywood's imagined stepfather is far from disinterested. Rather, he is eager to replace the father and in this benign eagerness the real threat emerges. In 'Totem and Taboo',

Freud suggests that the child mediates an ambivalent relationship with its father 'by displacing his [*sic*] hostile and fearful feelings on to a *substitute* for his father'.[46] Here this manifests with the stepfather as substitute for the law. He is an individual on whom the father – rendered as a symbolic child through his loss of power – can take out his frustrations and fears. The stepfather exists not just as the literal (threatened) father substitute, but as a substitute for the hostile presence of the law, that which may strip the father of his paternal status.

In *Mrs. Doubtfire*, it is Stu (Pierce Brosnan) who threatens to usurp Daniel. Much like Brosnan's character in *Dante's Peak*, Stu is a man formerly uninterested in children who, on meeting Miranda's kids, abruptly warms to the idea of fatherhood. Stu's interest stems not only from his romantic pursuit of Miranda but also from a personal realization that fatherhood may offer lasting fulfilment. 'I'm pushing forty,' he tells a sceptical friend. 'I don't want to spend the rest of my life by myself.' For Stu, children have gone from being a hindrance to a lifeline, a way of harnessing meaning beyond the sports clubs, nice cars and successful career that have so far characterized his adult life. In *The War of the Roses* Danny DeVito's lawyer Gavin D'Amato confides, 'My father used to say there are four things that tell the world who a man is: his house, his car, his wife and his shoes.' Adrift of the yuppie aspirations of the Reagan years, Stu might add to this, his children. Daniel's eviction from the family home has presented Stu with an undeniable opportunity to acquire this fifth pillar of manhood.

The problem is that Stu's quest for paternal fulfilment risks Daniel's own future. As Mrs Doubtfire, Daniel overhears Stu claim he is 'crazy' about the children, 'especially that little Natalie', with whom Daniel shares a particularly close bond. Stu finishes with a clear advance into Daniel's territory: 'God knows they need some kind of stable father figure in their life right now.' Stu's presence challenges both

Daniel's masculinity and his fatherhood. While Stu is charming and attractive, Daniel spends all of his time in Stu's company dressed as a large middle-aged woman. Even as himself, he is financially insecure and, according to Miranda, his chief appeal to women is that he makes them laugh. Daniel's own insecurities emerge from behind the façade of Mrs Doubtfire, who implies benignly on numerous occasions that Stu has a small penis, but these are the limits of his challenge. Daniel must watch as Stu steps on his paternal territory. These threats are not dissimilar to those posed by the law. Yet while he is unable to eliminate the law, Daniel can eliminate Stu's presence by the end of the film. After the disastrous meal in which Daniel is unmasked, there is no further mention of Stu. Whether or not he and Miranda continue their relationship, his absence from the screen suggests his diminishment in favour of Daniel's renewed paternal authority.

A similar process governs *The Santa Clause* and *Liar Liar*, which feature strikingly similar stepfather figures. If Stu is the suave interloper, Neal and Jerry are almost cartoon-like in their eagerness and dorky enthusiasm. Neal is fond of childish, patterned wool jumpers and functions almost entirely in wide-eyed inanity, dispensing nuggets of pop-psychiatric wisdom. Jerry, meanwhile, is unrelentingly corny and try-hard, to the point that even Audrey is unable to take him seriously, rebuffing his 'I love you' with a startled 'thank you'. Both men are set up as faintly ridiculous figures, belying their secondary status, yet despite this they remain a real threat to the fatherhood of both Scott and Fletcher. When Fletcher, faced with a buoyant Jerry, quips that 'my plan to phase myself out is almost complete', he reveals what is actually at stake: his own future.

In the United States, the majority of stepfamilies are composed of a mother, her children and a stepfather. However, Gold and Adeyemi suggest that while stepfathers often have physical proximity, fathers are often emotionally closer to their children.[47] In these films, this emotional bond must be maintained if the father is to resist being 'phased out' by his successor. Commonly, this manifests in an in-joke between father and child, acting as shorthand for a special connection between the two of them. It recalls Bly's suggestion of a 'healing' bond established between father and son when they spend significant time in each other's company.[48] This is evident in Greta's assessment of Fletcher and Max's relationship. When Fletcher suggests 'my son hates me', Greta is quick to reassure him. 'Max loves you,' she says. 'I've seen you together.' What Greta has seen is unquantifiable. Yet it speaks to something that transcends description, a connection that binds father and son together to benefit them both.

Fletcher's performance of 'The Claw', which involves tickling Max with a comically clawed hand until he shrieks with delight, underlines their bond. When Jerry tries to replicate 'The Claw', Max is perplexed and underwhelmed by the attempt and Audrey asks Jerry to stop. 'It's like they have their own little world together,' she shrugs, when pressed to explain. To Jerry – who has experienced first-hand Fletcher's tardiness, lies and forgetfulness – it seems unfair that he will never be granted the same privileges, but this is the narrative of fatherhood to which Hollywood cleaves. Fletcher's bond with Max may be difficult to explain, but their connection – underpinned, though not defined, by biology – must endure.

Similar connections are foregrounded in *Mrs. Doubtfire* and *The Next Best Thing*. It is Daniel's ability to 'do the voices' while reading *Charlotte's Web* to Nattie and make his children laugh that give him an advantage. In *The Next Best Thing*, Sam's inability to pronounce 'roast beef' leads to an ongoing joke between him and Robert. This joke re-emerges in the final scene, when Abbie tells Sam he is spending the afternoon with his father. When Robert asks what they should eat for dinner, Sam triumphantly yells, 'roast beast!' It is this, more than biology or physical custody, that cements their bond, that same 'little world' shared by Fletcher and Max. It becomes a link, and this link must remain in order to effect the passing on of the father's legacy. If the father is to survive through the child, another man – just like the law – must not be permitted to disrupt the paternal connection.

This shared world between father and child, and the maintenance of a generational legacy, is most explicit in *The Santa Clause*. Scott is in the most overt danger of being usurped by a stepfather figure. Neal is married to Laura and shares a family home with her and Charlie. He has started to have a noticeable influence on Charlie, who routinely spouts snippets of psychological jargon he has absorbed, telling his dad that he 'learn[s] a lot' from Neal. Scott, meanwhile, can only teach Charlie 'the importance of having a high-quality fire extinguisher in the kitchen' as he narrowly avoids setting the house on fire, a lesson that Charlie absorbs with disdain. The restored connection between Scott and Charlie relies, once again, on the establishment of a shared world and a repudiation of the stepfather's efforts to replicate this bond. When Scott becomes Santa, it is Charlie who understands best what is happening. Without question, he believes in the North Pole, the elves, the workshop and the enormity of Scott's new role. This world becomes one that Scott and Charlie can experience together, not only as a shared space but a shared belief. At the end of the film, Charlie diagnoses Neal as 'denying [his] inner child', leading Neal to observe that Charlie will be a 'great psychiatrist someday'. Charlie, however, is firm. 'No, I think I'm going to go into the *family* business,' he asserts, looking up at Scott. The linear generational progression has thus been restored. Charlie will follow in his father's footsteps, while Neal's influence is confined to the margins. Once again, the film ends with a father driving away with his child. This time, it is Scott manoeuvring reindeer and sleigh through the air, his son by his side, but the implication remains the same. The father is once again in his rightful place; the threat has been neutralized.

Conclusion: The best interests of the father

In a period of masculine uncertainty, the fear of erasure is heightened. Hollywood's divorced dads reflect this particular fear. Here are men who recognize the value of their fatherhood – often belatedly – only to have it taken away. On screen, a three-pronged conspiracy of paternal erasure is constructed, as the mother, the stepfather and the law itself, all conspire to divorce the father from his future. These fathers must transform just enough to secure their own survival. Taken together, these films demonstrate a persistent narrative of maintaining faith in the father, however fallible he may appear. Above all, the link between father and child must be upheld. When Daniel tells the judge that he and his children 'have a history', he is bidding for a future in which this history can be continued. The law, capable of severing this generational connection, can only ever be cast as an unwelcome force, an unnecessary invasion into the American family home.

The common standard of custody cases, the 'best interests of the child', is repeatedly evoked in these films. It explicitly underpins the judge's rationale to award full custody to Laura and Neal. While the judge in *Mrs. Doubtfire* acknowledges that 'it is not in a child's best interests to deprive him or her of a loving father', this does not alter his decision to grant Miranda custody. Elsewhere, these 'best interests' are obscured by biology (*The Next Best Thing*) and financial gain (*Liar Liar*). Yet the children at the ostensible centre of these films are, in fact, a secondary concern in Hollywood's quest to rehabilitate the father. What is paramount is whether the father's best interests have been served. A restoration of paternal authority must therefore be accompanied by a curtailment of legal power. The law is not dismantled but removed at its most intrusive from the individual family so that the father may once again exercise his paternal privilege in private, his judgement rendered superior. It falls to Scott, not the judge, to define Charlie's family at the end of *The Santa Clause*. 'I can't be with you all the time,' he tells his son. 'We're a family. You, me, your mom ...' After a pause, he adds, '... and Neal.' Scott's apparently magnanimous statement is in fact a reclamation, as what the law previously had the power to determine now falls once again to Scott. This brief moment captures Hollywood's wider project of shoring up the father's authority, subduing the influence of external agencies and restoring paternal order. In a period of masculine anxiety, this restoration of his fatherhood is crucial to ensuring the man's continued survival. Ultimately, in the final frames, power is handed back to the father who still knows best.

3

Boys, interrupted: Fathers, sons and loss

'Kill the child and you kill the future.' Vicky Lebeau's stark statement regarding the death of the child on screen neatly encapsulates what is at stake when a child fails to reach adulthood.[1] Quite simply, the erasure of the child is the erasure of the future. If, as Edelman suggests, 'we are no more able to conceive of a politics without a fantasy of the future than we are able to conceive of a future without the figure of the Child', then killing the child is a symbolic interruption of salvation.[2] It fractures the expectation of future survival, both on- and off-screen. While Hollywood tethered masculine survival so vehemently to fatherhood, the frequent death of the on-screen child – overwhelmingly the son – ruptures this saving narrative. It is the flip side of the fatherlessness debate, with fathers now floundering without the child that cements this identity. The fragility of paternal salvation is revealed. To kill the child raises questions about the precarity of the future for two generations of American men, both fathers and sons. The loss of the son places the father in jeopardy, as he negotiates the brutal reality of being – perhaps permanently – de-fathered.

In a discussion of fatherhood and survival, it may seem counterintuitive to focus on films in which a father loses his paternal status. However, these films illuminate some of Hollywood's own paradoxical anxieties around the father, already glimpsed in those narratives of involuntary transformation discussed in Chapter 2, as he becomes characterized by precarity. How fathers deal with the death of their child in the end shores up the very narrative that, on the surface, such films seem to contradict. Threatened with losing their link to the future, men are notable in their drive towards being re-fathered, whether anchoring themselves to another child or recommitting to family and the potential of a reproductive future. Investment in the next generation remains paramount, regardless of the temporary challenge posed by the child's death. This chapter examines the negotiation of the relationship between father and non-father, future and no-future (which, in Edelman's framework, remains a queered position) that structures a range of films including *Paradise*, *Lorenzo's Oil*, *The Good Son* and *The Ice Storm*. Frequently here the son – or surrogate son – takes centre stage, a reminder of what is at stake should this quest for the future fail.

These examples represent a darker, more final form of domesticated apocalypse. Mick Broderick suggests that apocalyptic mythology 'seeped into the very *zeitgeist* of contemporary cinema' during the 1990s, the more bombastic ramifications of which were explored in Chapter 1, as scenarios of extinction, annihilation and erasure played and replayed on the big screen.[3] In action–disaster films, an emphasis on preserving the child prevails. It is the root of both Mike and Kelly's desire to save the unknown young boy in *Volcano*, despite considerable risk to their own safety. In *Deep Impact*, journalist Jenny (Téa Leoni), who has no children, relinquishes her space in a safe bunker to her friend and her friend's young daughter, sacrificing herself for the next generation. In the same film, teenager Sarah (Leelee Sobieski) and her new husband Leo (Elijah Wood) are entrusted with her baby brother, pushed into their arms as her parents resign themselves to their own deaths. While films such as *Paradise* and *Lorenzo's Oil* do not feature the kinds of 'extinction level events' that structure many of these blockbusters, they retain the same apocalyptic undertones, simply relocated to the ordinary American family. To not only allow the threat of death to invade the realm of the child but to also allow the child to perish is fundamentally unsettling to an audience used to seeing children shielded or snatched from the jaws of danger. The 'extinction' in these cases may be singular, but its impact is just as devastating.

Research on bereaved parents suggests that they not only lose a child but also 'the future that the child and they would otherwise have created together. They lose the immortality of being survived by the child and the child's descendants.'[4] Just as the aliens must be defeated and the meteor diverted, the child's death must be overcome to maintain the promise of paternal survival. Some sense must be made of the loss, lest that queer notion of anti-futurity prevails. These films see father and son entangled in this project of masculine continuance, the screen populated both by men seeking paternal purpose and emotionally vulnerable young boys craving the guidance of a father figure whom they have, for various reasons, been denied. The dead or dying child is largely peripheral. Instead, the focus is on the boys left in their place and the bereaved fathers who must negotiate their own grief, reflecting how Hollywood largely sidesteps the event of the child's death in favour of its anxious aftermath. If this aftermath might be read as a queer space and temporality that invites the shattering of the future, then the child – they whom Edelman designates 'the obligatory token of futurity' – must somehow be restored, rescuing the father from an existence devoid of apparent meaning.[5]

Hope for the future: Children on screen

On screen, children are frequently figured as universal symbols of hope, innocence and renewal. There are exceptions: most notably, horror films have persistently subverted this expectation to create unsettling or horrific images of children, figures of evil rather than symbols of purity.[6] However, it is far more common that children signify 'the future and the hope of forthcoming generations'.[7] Young children, particularly boys, often experience a great deal of independence and adventure on screen, emphasizing the link between childhood and a sense of freedom and exploration.[8] While a loss of innocence often characterizes films about childhood this only serves to underline the fact that young children are generally associated with innocence until some significant event determines otherwise.[9] Elsewhere on film, a child's birth is routinely used to signify the continuous, forward movement of life, often in the face of death. *Autumn in New York* (Joan Chen, 2000) juxtaposes the death of Will's (Richard Gere) girlfriend Charlotte (Winona Ryder) in one hospital room with the birth of his first grandchild in another, while *In America* (Jim Sheridan, 2002) ends with the death of HIV-positive Mateo (Djimon Hounsou) and the birth (and successful blood transfusion) of a baby to Johnny (Paddy Considine) and Sarah (Samantha Morton), whose son Frankie died before the start of the film. The famous baptism scene in *The Godfather* (Francis Ford Coppola, 1972) is an ironic take on the same principle, intercutting the baptism of Michael Corleone's nephew with the mafia killings of the family's rivals.

In cultural, political and religious rhetoric alike, birth is symbolic of redemption and renewed possibility. 'With each newborn child,' suggests Ellen Handler Spitz, 'comes the possibility of future salvation and a better world.'[10] Here again is the assumption that the child's life, and the world it inhabits, will be an improvement on the present. This belief resides at the heart of reproductive futurism, justifying reproduction through the apparent promise of new hope and opportunity. For the parents, their desire to nurture this hope coincides with the potent appeal of seeing themselves live on through the child in question. The death of a child irrevocably ruptures this promise. In a decade characterized culturally as one in which men needed salvation, their survival is thrown into sharp relief by the child's demise.

Hollywood has always maintained an intimate relationship with death. It imbues the disaster movie, the melodrama, the superhero film, the Western, the war film, the horror movie and more besides. Indeed, cinema as a whole has a complex and close association with death, what George Toles characterizes as an 'immense preoccupation'.[11] Cinema not only has the power to depict death but also to bring the dead back to life as no other medium can do with quite the same veracity. On screen, the audience sees 'time fossilized'.[12] Geoffrey Gorer argues that in the twentieth century, the visual spectacle of death in media became pornographic in its violence and intensity,[13] and a preoccupation with visual depictions of the dead body, for so long a cultural taboo, continues into the twenty-first century.[14]

Despite its ubiquity, there remains a demand for meaning when presenting death on screen. Toles frames this in terms of 'proportion', where any death must be weighed against a character's 'value' to ensure it is not trivialized, unduly rushed or forgotten too soon.[15] Death may be visceral in a broad sense (faceless victims of disaster, enemies killed en masse, peripheral characters as collateral damage), but for those deaths that carry more emotional weight their inclusion must be justified. This is particularly the case with children, as 'to be a child on screen is to be not anonymous enough to die just for the sake of the explosion'.[16] François Truffaut suggests that depicting a child's death is tantamount to an 'abuse of cinematic power'.[17] The reluctance to kill the child is reflective of the death of the future it signifies. It is also, particularly for western audiences, a profoundly unnatural and disconcerting concept. Whether a child's death is anticipated or not, it is always 'untimely'.[18] In the West, a child's death is increasingly unusual, with improvements in healthcare and science contributing to relatively low child mortality rates.[19] Such rarity conveys a sense of unnaturalness as the expectation of surviving into adulthood is shattered. This, combined with the cultural place of children as symbolic indices of futurity, ensures that in cinema the death of a child cannot be inconsequential.

That is not to say that it cannot be depicted, but that its realization on screen must be understood as weighted with particular meaning. European cinema has been less reluctant to portray child death and parental grief, as evidenced in films including *Olivier! Olivier!* (Agnieszka Holland, 1992), *Trois couleurs: Bleu* (Krzysztof Kieslowski, 1993) and *La stanza del figlio* (Nanni Moretti, 2001), contemporaries of those discussed in this chapter.[20] Though Hollywood has not traditionally tended towards the same explorations of parental bereavement, it is remarkable that in the 1990s it repeatedly returns to the theme. If a child threatened with death seems unthinkable, the fact that the world's primary purveyor of family-friendly entertainment elects to represent this scenario so persistently during the decade invites investigation. Serge Leclaire maintains that the child's death is incomprehensible, as it resists meaning. 'We rediscover the sacred horror,' he states. 'It just can't be.'[21] And yet an ambivalence is revealed, as Leclaire observes: 'A child's death is unbearable: it fulfills our most secret and profound wishes.'[22] Though horrific to comprehend, it also reveals an impulse towards death that both exists and must be denied in all humans, the crux of the death drive.[23] The denial of this negativity is crucial. The child's death reveals an anti-reproductive, anti-futuristic space – that which Edelman claims as queer – and it is this negative space that must be rejected. Hence the films discussed in this chapter all drive towards the re-establishment of reproduction and the desire to make meaning from that which, on the surface, appears to collapse all comprehension.

There are shades of the same quest for mastery observed in Hollywood's many disaster films. When Lebeau asks 'Who, after all, would want to kill a child?', the answer, it seems, is a Hollywood intent on mastering the fear of erasure.[24] The films examined here are not isolated examples but sit within a wider body of mainstream films of the period that engage with the prospect of a dead or dying child, including *Stand by Me* (Rob Reiner, 1986), *My Girl* (Howard

Zieff, 1991), *Boyz N the Hood* (John Singleton, 1991), *Juice* (Ernest R. Dickerson, 1992), *Above the Rim* (Jeff Pollack, 1994), *The Cure* (Peter Horton, 1995), *The Mighty* (Peter Chelsom, 1998), *The Virgin Suicides* (Sofia Coppola, 1999), *A Map of the World* (Scott Elliott, 1999), *Pay It Forward* (Mimi Leder, 2000), *George Washington* (David Gordon Green, 2000) and *Mystic River* (Clint Eastwood, 2003), as well as those that acknowledge a dead child in the immediate past, such as *The Accidental Tourist* (Lawrence Kasdan, 1988), *Dead Calm* (Philip Noyce, 1989) and *Jacob's Ladder* (Adrian Lyne, 1990). As the millennium approached, Hollywood's repeated killing of the child reflects a fear that the future was somehow out of reach and must be restored as swiftly as possible. In the end, the future is revealed to be only as secure as the children who fulfil its promise. Their death is the ultimate destruction of fatherhood, and these films repeat this trauma only to negate it through the assuaging of grief and the rehabilitation of a paternal identity by the closing credits.

The life of one boy: Fathering a dying child in *Lorenzo's Oil*

Films about a dead or dying child are often paradoxically reimagined as stories of survival and *Lorenzo's Oil* is a prime example of this reconfiguration. Based on the true story of Lorenzo Odone, it documents his parents' battle to keep him alive after he is diagnosed with the degenerative neurological condition adrenoleukodystrophy (ALD). Faced with the loss of their formerly bright, capable child, Augusto (Nick Nolte) and Michaela Odone (Susan Sarandon) are compelled to find a cure. ALD primarily affects boys, the majority of whom die of the incurable condition within two years of diagnosis, and against this reality the Odones endeavour to prove medical science wrong. Writing in the *New England Journal of Medicine*, William

B. Rizzo accurately refers to *Lorenzo's Oil* as 'a Hollywood tale of promise', focusing as it does on a possible cure.[25] This optimistic note, though criticized by medical professionals, ensures the possibility of survival is foregrounded even against considerable odds. However, it is not only the survival of Lorenzo – and numerous other boys with ALD – that is at stake. Underlying this is the parallel narrative of Augusto's own survival, as he emerges as the driving force behind the quest for a cure.

Like the films discussed in Chapter 2, *Lorenzo's Oil* adheres to a neoliberal ideology that pits Augusto and Michaela against the behemoth of the medical institutions that control Lorenzo's fate. Though they are reliant on doctors and scientists for diagnosis and treatment, their aims are often incongruous with the medical professionals whose own concerns understandably extend far beyond an individual case. While they consider the evidence and risk associated with any potential treatment, Michaela is withering in her condemnation, observing, 'The life of one boy is not enough reward for you to risk the reputation of the institution and the esteem of your peers.' For the doctors, Lorenzo is a point of data. For the Odones, he is the joint vessel of their love, hope and future.

These disparate aims are emphasized during a conference debate over the value of anecdotal evidence and lived experience of ALD parents, during which Michaela challenges the doctors present: 'So what you're saying is that our children are in the service of medical science. How very foolish of me. I always assumed that medical science was in the service of the sufferers.' Like the legal bodies in Chapter 2, medical institutions work on one hand to protect the family and yet on the other hand undermine the family's autonomy by suppressing the personal fight for Lorenzo's (unlikely) survival in favour of a broader quest to understand ALD. The link between parent and child is interrupted as a result. When doctors dismiss Augusto's attempts to source an effective treatment, he declares vehemently, 'I am not a scientist. I am a father.' And as a father, Augusto is fighting not for all the boys but for one: his own son. 'I claim the right to fight for my kid's life,' he yells at members of the ALD Foundation. 'And no doctor, no researcher, no bloody foundation, has the right to stop me from asking questions which might help me save him!' Unspoken but undeniable is the extension of this logic: in saving Lorenzo, Augusto retains the possibility of also saving himself. When Michaela's sister Deirdre (Kathleen Wilhoite) suggests sympathetically that 'there has to be a life beyond Lorenzo', she misunderstands Augusto's drive: without Lorenzo, what lies 'beyond' offers him no enduring link to this ostensible future.

These outbursts need no justification, reflecting the desperation of a father who is doomed to watch his son die. There is, however, an added dimension to this desperation. For Augusto, Lorenzo represents perhaps his final chance at fatherhood. His two adult children from a previous marriage live in Rome and are peripheral figures in his life. ALD is a genetic disorder, passed down from mother to son, and Michaela is a carrier. The fathers' reaction to this maternal pathology is documented at an event where Michaela is surrounded by women discussing the husbands and partners that left them following the ALD diagnosis, with one confessing that her husband divorced her specifically because he wanted more sons. Though Augusto does not ever suggest leaving Michaela, he does erupt at her in a vicious outburst, accusing her of being 'tainted' and castigating her 'poisoned blood', an accusation weighted with allusion to the AIDS crisis, as discussed further below. Despite its maternal origins, ALD is rendered as a disease that primarily disrupts the link between father and son, adding this secondary dimension to Augusto's quest for a cure. It also returns, uncomfortably, to that notion of mothers being at least partially responsible for the curtailing of the father's role.

Though films such as *Lorenzo's Oil* broadly deal with the issue of parental grief, there is a notable difference in how Augusto and

Michaela deal with Lorenzo's diagnosis, mirrored in the films below. Its depiction of maternal and paternal grief reflects the common notion that both are distinctly separate experiences.[26] Maternal grief is described as 'timeless',[27] a lifelong 'shadow grief'[28] stemming from the loss of what Celia Hindmarch characterizes as a 'vital sense of self' for the mother.[29] Talbot similarly suggests that underpinning maternal grief is a fundamental loss of identity.[30] In comparison, paternal grief – comparatively under-researched – is characterized as less enduring and more tangible.[31] It is the loss of the provider/protector role that is often felt most keenly,[32] with many bereaved fathers using increased workloads as a coping mechanism.[33] In *Lorenzo's Oil*, Michaela prioritizes spending time with their son before he dies and expresses concern that their amateur medical research will make them miss what remains of Lorenzo's life. Augusto, meanwhile, channels his efforts towards action, putting in hours at the library and painstakingly compiling his research.

Just as the doctors' priorities deviate from the parents', Augusto's primary concerns do not always align with his wife's. After one particularly distressing attack, Lorenzo shakes and moans uncontrollably while Michaela tries to soothe him, whispering, 'if this is too much for you, my sweetheart, you fly as fast as you can to baby Jesus.' Unseen by Michaela, Augusto looks on in considerable distress at this suggestion. It is a cure, not comfort, that he seeks. He proposes instead that they 'take responsibility' for Lorenzo's condition, advocating for a knowledge-based approach that treats ALD 'like another country' that can be understood and mastered through education. His hope is focused on reversing the death sentence they have been given, protecting Lorenzo not through palliation but through action.

This distinction in parental approaches to grief and death recalls Freud's 'Mourning and Melancholia', in which he suggests that mourning is a process that can be completed, while melancholia has no discernible end point. Freud determines that the difference between the two states lies in that which is diminished: 'In mourning it is the world which has become poor and empty; in melancholia it is the ego itself.'[34] In the films discussed here, including *Lorenzo's Oil*, the mother's grief is closely aligned with this melancholic state, as she accepts the permanence of being de-mothered. Her own ego, her identity as a mother, is shattered. The shattered self features prominently in Leo Bersani's work on queerness and negativity; like many prominent queer theorists, including Edelman, Bersani links queer subjectivity with a negative space of incoherence, ambivalence and melancholia.[35] The mother's embrace of melancholia repositions her in a queer temporality (the anti-future), in which the future is diminished in favour of an endless present, in which the inclination – if any – is towards the past. The fathers, however, appear to drive towards an eventual cessation of mourning. In this renewed future, they may reclaim their fatherhood not only symbolically but also tangibly.

For Augusto, this potential future is symbolized by his breakthrough discovery, leading to the development of the eponymous Lorenzo's oil. The efficacy of Lorenzo's oil remained unproven until 2005; while able to prevent the development of symptoms in susceptible boys, it has little effect on those who already have ALD.[36] The end of *Lorenzo's Oil*, however, chooses a redemptive path, with the closing scenes forming a tribute not to those boys lost to the disease but to those who live on. A caption informs the audience that Lorenzo has recovered his sight and some head movement, finishing with a look towards the future: 'And so he waits for what will come next.' A collection of short home video clips of real-life boys with ALD follows, with the boys – healthy, playing, smiling and laughing in front of the camera – recounting how long they have been taking Lorenzo's oil. Lorenzo Odone eventually died in 2008 at the age of 30, but as far as the film is concerned, he – and his father[37] – have won a second chance at survival as the credits roll.

Restoring hope: The surviving child as future salvation

In her research on trauma, Cathy Caruth suggests that a child's death raises an 'urgent and unsettling question: *What does it mean to survive?*'[38] Persistently, Hollywood's answer lies in the figure of another child. Despite the death of one child, another holds the promise of salvation. Much like the fathers in Chapter 2, cast out of the family home only to be reinstated, the child's death both acknowledges the fragility of the father and, in revealing a second child in need of guidance, offers a redemptive solution.

This conceit structures both *Paradise* and *The Good Son*, where the death of one boy is twinned with the survival of another. In both cases, the second boy is portrayed by Elijah Wood, at that point an emerging child star frequently enlisted to play wide-eyed, innocent young boys. Will, in *Paradise*, has recently (and unknowingly) been abandoned by his father and sent to live with family friends. In *The Good Son* Mark moves in with his aunt and uncle after the death of his mother. In both films, the boy's trauma mirrors that of the central couple, who are grieving the loss of their own son. As with *Lorenzo's Oil*, the father's response to this death is markedly different to the mother's. However, while Lorenzo's debilitating illness determines that Augusto must drive the action, elsewhere primacy is given to a young boy whose need for a stable father figure drives the restoration of paternal authority. Propelled by an emerging relationship between the grieving father and the boy, the focus is on moving forwards and investing the father's paternal energies into the future, while simultaneously saving the vulnerable boy at the film's centre. Recalling Aronson and Kimmel's discussion of the child as the saviour of the father, these films both adopt and extend this notion. The boys' own desire for a father figure and their emotional demands on him force the bereaved

Figure 6 Macaulay Culkin as the epitome of innocent childhood in *My Girl* (1991). Columbia Pictures.

fathers to modulate their grief and recognize the potency of their joint survival. In essence, father and (surrogate) son save each other.

As an unexpected vehicle for Macaulay Culkin, *The Good Son* exists as the darker cousin of the more successful *My Girl*, the latter featuring Culkin as doomed boy Thomas J. Sennett, whose fatal bee allergy sees him confined to a tiny white coffin in the third act of the film. *The Good Son* is similarly resolute in killing off the biggest child star of the 1990s. If children on screen have traditionally signified innocence, then Culkin is surely the epitome of this childish purity in the early 1990s. Characterized as 'impish and heartwarming',[39] a cheeky yet endearing 'munchkin',[40] Culkin is imbued with a 'natural goodness' that makes his death in both films ultimately alarming and unsettling to an audience.[41] (His younger brother Kieran would similarly meet his end in *The Mighty*, discussed briefly below.) Culkin's portrayal of the disturbed, sinister Henry in *The Good Son* further undermines this wholesome image. Against this, Wood's Mark emerges as a more solid prospect for his Uncle Wallace's (Daniel Hugh Kelly) rehabilitation as the Good Father.

At the beginning of the film, Wallace and Susan Evans (Wendy Crewson) are grieving for their younger son Richard after he drowns in the bath. The couple has two other children, Henry and Connie (Quinn Culkin), the former displaying persistently sadistic behaviour. Henry causes a traffic accident by throwing a lifelike dummy from a bridge, shoots a cat, kills a dog and pushes Connie through the ice while skating. Unsurprisingly, he is eventually revealed as Richard's killer. In a chilling final scene, Henry attempts to push his mother off a cliff, while Mark attempts to save her. Both boys fall. Faced with an impossible choice, Susan lets go of Henry and saves her nephew.

The central figures of *The Good Son* are, clearly, Henry and Mark; Wallace and Susan's roles are comparatively minor. Nevertheless, the representation of their grief chimes with wider cinematic images of bereaved parenthood during the decade. While Susan's grief over Richard conforms to the 'shadow' model described above by Peppers and Knapp, Wallace is sombre yet pragmatic. Susan makes a daily pilgrimage to the cliff-top near their home in an act of private remembrance. She keeps Richard's bedroom intact and in one scene sits among her son's old toys, crying. A child's preserved bedroom is common to films dealing with parental bereavement, including *Ordinary People* (Robert Redford, 1980), *Paradise* and *Rabbit Hole* (John Cameron Mitchell, 2010). The image of the mother returning to this space and going through their child's belongings is similarly prevalent. Wallace, however, sees little use in this activity. Again, the distinction between mourning and melancholia is recalled, with Susan's commitment to the past overriding any consideration of the future. This is captured in an exchange between the couple, in which Wallace suggests that Mark could sleep in Richard's bedroom, rather than share with Henry. For Wallace, the logic is simple. One boy needs a room and they have a room to spare. Susan, however, is adamant that the room should remain as it is. 'We have to face it,' Wallace argues, perceiving her reluctance as denial. 'I face it every day,' she counters, yet it is clear that father and mother have distinct ideas about what 'facing it' constitutes, and which direction they are facing.

Wallace clearly opposes Susan's potentially endless mourning and her determined grip on the past. He is keen to help Mark through his grief for his mother, a process that in turn enables Wallace to heal himself. For Wallace, Mark represents another chance to get fatherhood right, something made doubly necessary by Henry's pathological tendencies, which threaten Wallace's survival just as surely as Richard's death did. Henry speaks frequently of death – 'you're gonna die anyways,' he declares to Mark in one of his many fatalistic moments – and throwing the dummy from the bridge symbolizes a surrogate suicide on Henry's part. Neither of Wallace's sons are a secure bet for the future, but in his nephew he finds another valuable opportunity that he instinctively knows to take.

The centrality of Mark and Henry to *The Good Son* reveals the importance of the son to these narratives of survival. It is not Wallace's needs that are foregrounded but Mark's. Mark is a vulnerable, bereaved child. His own dad has left on an extended business trip, in a somewhat insensitive move recalling the unthinking father so beloved of 1990s Hollywood; in a short space of time, Mark has essentially been abandoned by both parents. He and Henry are constructed as two sides of one coin, one boy beyond the reach of compassion and reason, one who can still benefit from them.

This is a shift in focus from those films discussed in previous chapters, which centre the flawed-but-redeemable father. Here instead is a glimpse of the consequences of failed redemption: the floundering, unsure sons of the future or, in Henry's case, the nihilistic spectre of no future at all. With Henry as the antagonist, *The Good Son* stresses the dangers of a son who has rejected the guidance of his parents – particularly his father, as a model of functional masculinity – and refuses to countenance his place in the generational continuum. The film works hard to convincingly construct Henry's inherent evilness, lest Wallace be found responsible. Accordingly, Henry's destructive and nihilistic behaviour apparently arises from within, much like his counterpart Rhoda Penmark (Patty McCormack) in *The Bad Seed* (Mervyn LeRoy, 1956), on which *The Good Son* is loosely based. Though he is in therapy, no explanation for his conduct is forthcoming. As such, Wallace is vindicated. No doubt is cast on his fatherhood and, by extension, Mark is safe to put his faith in him.

Faludi identifies a 'layer of paternal betrayal' in American masculinity of the 1990s. 'The fathers had made [the sons] a promise, and then had not made good on it,' she suggests, and this landscape of broken paternal promises is visible in these films.[42] Henry perceives this promise as one of singularity. He will be his father's only son, he will be enough. Killing Richard (and attempting to kill Connie) is a manifestation of this feeling of betrayal. Mark, meanwhile, must come to terms with his abandonment, whereby his parents – though not maliciously – have not made good on the implicit promise of parenthood, that they will be there to protect him. This betrayal can only be reversed by another father figure, in this case Wallace, but Mark must be the catalyst. Faludi observes that 'what undid [the sons] was their fathers' silence.'[43] Mark, who has suffered the silence of two grown men wrapped up in their own grief, forces Wallace to find his paternal voice again by reminding him of his responsibility to a living boy who can still be saved. Here, fatherhood is only of value if it has a purpose. It is Mark, rather than Henry, who represents an enduring belief in both mother and father, encapsulated in his race to save Susan and thus preserve the family that will be the source of both his and Wallace's redemption. As discussed further below, the importance of the son in these narratives is telling in what it reveals about the multi-generational layers of masculine anxiety such films are navigating.

The care of another child as the solution to paternal fears of erasure is explored at greater length in *Paradise*, which again features Wood as the young protagonist desperately seeking male guidance. Ben (Don Johnson) and Lily Reed (Melanie Griffith) are mourning their son James when Will, the son of Lily's old school friend, moves in with the couple during his mother's pregnancy. His father has recently abandoned the family, although Will stubbornly insists that he is simply on navy duty. In Ben and Will, *Paradise* sets up a man and a boy who are similarly adrift, though while Ben is painfully aware of his position, Will maintains a degree of naivete. Initially, Ben does not welcome Will's intrusion on the couple's grief, viewing their young visitor not as a fellow sufferer but as an annoyance. Their first encounter sets this prickly tone. Will, entering an unfamiliar diner, asks for directions to the Reeds' home. One customer grunts that, if he's lucky, 'your visit will be a short one. They've changed,' he adds. Only later does Will realize this customer was Ben, offering not gossip but painful self-reflection.

In these early moments it is Ben who appears to have fallen into a melancholic state, his devastation manifesting outwardly as brooding, prickly behaviour that reveals no impulse towards overcoming his grief. Yet a reversal soon occurs. Lily's instinct to lavish unspent maternal attention on Will is abruptly tempered when Will unintentionally begins to encroach on James's memory. As Lily withdraws, Ben's attitude also shifts, as he awakens to the potential to recapture his own dormant fatherhood. This shift colours a scene in which Will discovers a model plane hidden in a cupboard. Lily, uneasy, refuses to let him play with it, but Ben lets Will take the plane and patiently teaches him how to fly it. Observing the boy's delight as the plane soars around the garden, Ben suggests that he keep it. Thus begins Ben's thawing towards Will, revealing the differing approaches to James's death taken by him and his wife. Lily, like Susan in *The Good Son*, is a preserver. James's bedroom remains untouched, and Lily is seen in one scene sitting among his possessions, contemplating a pair of small wellingtons. She appears unprepared for Will to occupy the same space as James, whether physically or figuratively. For her, Will is a reminder of what was; for Ben, he becomes a suggestion of what could be again. The plane is symbolic of this new attitude. Ben argues that he made the plane to be played with and would rather another boy get some pleasure from it than it be shut away and unused. Much the same can be said of Ben's own fatherhood. Made useless through James's death, it can be reanimated by Will's presence.

Ben's escape from his melancholic state, however, leaves him at odds with Lily. This burgeoning conflict is encapsulated in a scene in their small community church. The camera isolates the three characters from the rest of the congregation and neither Ben nor Lily acquiesce when instructed to join hands with their neighbours. The scene highlights the disconnection not only between the couple and the rest of the community, none of whom (they assume) can comprehend Ben and Lily's loss, but between each other. Ben attends church under duress, while Lily sees an opportunity for solace. The following exchange underlines Ben's shifting priorities, as he asks Lily where her 'spirit' went:

Ben: Why are you buying all this sanctimonious crap?
Lily: It comforts me.
Ben: Well, there's more to life than being comforted.
Lily: Like what?
Ben: Like living.

This inducement to 'living' is not simply a quest to stay alive. That Will's presence has inspired this shift in Ben recalls Canetti's suggestion that the act of living contains within it the 'satisfaction' and 'continually repeated pleasure' of survival.[44] Lily's dedication to her grief, meanwhile, leaves her stranded in a melancholic state, one condition of which is 'an overcoming of the instinct which compels every living thing to cling to life'.[45] Ben's fear that Lily's 'spirit' is gone suggests the ultimately destructive power of melancholia, as Lily's desire to live is erased not through a compulsion to end her own life but in a refusal to see beyond her current grief. She exists in a queer, anti-futuristic space, one that in these films is only ever configured as negative, stagnant and to be transcended. Her stalled state is ultimately unproductive. If the future is entwined with the concept of survival-as-forward-motion, it is this very instinct towards survival that Lily appears to lack, and towards which Ben is now driving with considerable intent.

Paradise does not attempt to deny Ben's own grief but rather channels it towards something more productive, in this case ensuring Will's own successful navigation of boyhood trauma (his absent father, his new sibling, his fear of the unfamiliar). Faludi, discussing contemporary masculinity, observes men 'clinging to a phantom status' as they struggle to articulate meaningful manhood.[46] This same concept of a 'phantom status' is pertinent to Ben, whose fatherhood, already threatened by James's death, is worth little if it cannot respond to Will's needs. Phantom fatherhood is useless, but Will's demands on Ben's time, patience and emotional maturity can bring it back to life. Once again, as in *The Good Son*, the presence of a proxy son for whom a paternal intervention would be of evident untold benefit drives the redemption of the father. Accordingly, Will's own struggles provide Ben with a sense of paternal purpose, a chance to reclaim the identity of 'father' that he unwillingly gave up when his own son died. Ben's recovery becomes Will's, and vice versa, mirroring the relationship between Wallace and Mark. Ben fills the space left by Will's absent father, taking him fishing and teaching him to fly the plane. These traditionally masculine, outdoor activities, with which Will is unfamiliar, reflect the received wisdom that young boys need their fathers if they are to develop a coherent masculine identity. In this way, Ben 'rescues' Will from the potential damage of a fatherless childhood, echoing those contemporary cultural concerns of absent fatherhood and its impact on a generation of children.

Will, for his part, gives Ben a renewed sense of purpose, offering him an outlet for all the things he might expect to have taught James. The film's climactic scenes cement this mutually beneficial relationship. Will runs away after his friend Billie (Thora Birch) suggests that his dad has met someone else, speculation that upsets Will's fragile belief in his missing father. A desperate Ben finally finds Will atop an old water tower, tentatively completing a circuit around its perimeter, an act that symbolizes Will facing his fears as he conquers both the water tower and his dread over his father's disappearance. Ben's watchful yet hands-off approach suggests that he recognizes the importance of Will achieving this by himself. When Will stumbles, however, Ben intervenes and hauls him out of danger. In letting go of one father – back on the ground, he calls his mother and demands the truth – Will is caught by another.

Re-establishing reproduction: The should-be father

The water tower incident charts a successful move towards adolescence for Will, reinforcing the value of an interested father figure to a young boy. Through its young protagonists, *Paradise* continually revisits the distinction between 'good' and 'bad' fathers, establishing Ben as the 'good' father against a collection of other, far less edifying examples. Aside from Will's absent father, the film constructs three other 'bad' fathers, namely Billie's biological father (Rick Andosca), her older sister Darlene's (Sarah Trigger) unseen father and their stepfather-to-be Earl (Greg Travis). Paternal disillusionment is a tool the children use to wound each other in moments of vulnerability – Billie is sceptical of Will's father's 'sea duty', for instance – and both are keenly aware of the longing for a stable father figure that constructs the absence at the heart of their childhood. It is this absence that good men such as Ben can fill, while the bad fathers that surround Billie only make the lack sting more. *Paradise* also hints that Darlene's promiscuity results from growing up without a father, recalling those suggestions of the damage wreaked by paternal absence. Having seen the difficulties faced by her mother Sally (Sheila McCarthy), caused in great part by these disappointing fathers, Billie laments the fact that she must grow up as a woman ('It makes me sick,' she declares). Yet she harbours a secret fantasy of visiting her dad at his ice rink and impressing him with her skating skills, a dream that inevitably ends in disappointment. Perceiving a family resemblance as she contemplates a poster outside the rink, her fantasy is quickly shattered when she approaches her father only for him to tell her to get off the ice. When Billie declares that she is his daughter, he simply walks away. Billie is crushed, not least because at home she faces a more chilling prospect in the shape of her mother's boyfriend. Sally openly admits that she finds Earl odious and cannot bring herself to kiss him even as they announce their engagement, yet she craves the stability and financial security he offers. He, meanwhile, covertly threatens Billie with violence ('Once I'm your father …') if she misbehaves.

Against these absent, uninterested and violent father figures, Ben is a welcome if anomalous alternative. Faced with a frightened young boy, Ben chooses empathy. When Will claims that 'it doesn't matter' if his father is coming home, Ben is adamant that this is not the case. 'It does matter. Don't run away from things just because they scare you. If you do, you'll always be afraid,' he counters. This message has resonance for Ben too, a reminder that he must embrace that very thing – fatherhood – that has frightened him since James's death. It is also a reminder to refrain from his own act of running away, in this case by leaving Lily when their relationship breaks down. As the 'good' father, Ben must realize his mistake before it is too late, not least because in Lily a more concrete image of the future lies. Ben's reconstruction as the good father serves a dual purpose. It allows him to save Will, but it also cements the idea that Ben is the father who *should be*. His relationship with Will is only the first step. If Ben has so much to offer as a paternal figure, the film must also work to give Ben renewed access to his own reproductive future. The inclusion of a number of 'bad' fathers in *Paradise* – a theme also apparent in *The Mighty*, where Kevin's father is absent and Max's is a murderer, and in *The Cure*, where both Dexter and Erik's father are absent – only heightens the need for Ben (and Lily) to emerge from mourning and prepare to reinvest in the next generation.

For this to occur, a reconciliation must take place. For much of the film Ben and Lily are distant, both physically and emotionally. When they are together, they fight and snap at each other. More often they are framed apart, as in one scene where they passive-aggressively use noise (Lily's sewing machine, Ben's television) to aggravate one another. In this instance, Will's presence brings the destructive nature of their relationship to Ben's attention. Seeing Will sitting alone, wearing headphones to block out the noise, he recognizes the boy as a possible way out; soon after, Ben hands over the toy plane. Later Will chastises Ben for neglecting his duties around the house, such as fixing the garage, reminding him of the familial obligations expected of a father and husband. There is a flicker of hope here for Ben, a realization that investment in the child might yet bring salvation as he rediscovers a sense of purpose. The challenge then becomes convincing Lily to adopt the same salvific outlook. Here, *Paradise* temporarily enters uncomfortable territory. Tentative scenes of familial harmony are soon shattered by Ben's attempt to kiss Lily as they sit on the porch. 'I can't!' she sobs repeatedly as she retreats. Later that night a drunk Ben tries to force himself on Lily. This is the culmination of Ben's reawakened fatherhood and his desire to 'live', manifesting as a sexual impulse and the implication of reproduction.

The breakdown of intimacy, both emotional and sexual, is an enduring trope of films dealing with parental bereavement. As in *Paradise*, frustration over this loss of intimacy often resides with the father, consistent with the findings of actual grief research.[47] Given that Ben's pursuit of sexual reconciliation only emerges following the rediscovery of his paternal role, it must be understood as symbolic not simply of a desire for sex but a desire for reproduction. 'Are you sick of me?' he demands of Lily, as she backs away from him. 'Or are you just dead inside?' This reference to being 'dead inside' implies sterility and the threat of an unrealized reproductive future, once again positioning the mother as anti-future, the barrier to Ben's compulsion to survive. Faced with this prospect, Ben's rage erupts in an outburst that recalls John Baxter (Donald Sutherland) in *Don't Look Now* (Nicolas Roeg, 1973) shouting at his wife Laura (Julie Christie) that their daughter Christine is 'dead dead dead dead dead!' 'Jimmy's dead, goddamn it!' he yells. 'And you can't bring him back by turning this house into a graveyard ... But I'm alive. And I'm not going to pretend to be dead any more, just to keep you company.' Although Lily asks Ben to let her go, he continues to shake her and tear at her nightshirt, telling her, 'I'm just playing by your rules, Lily. My heart's not in this any more than yours is.' This air of obligation, in a moment fuelled more by desperation than ardour, suggests that Ben is being propelled by something other than straightforward desire, whether consciously or not. Instead, a demand to 'play by the rules' suggests a recognition that the continued adherence to reproduction and the heteronormative family is crucial to Ben's survival.

Lily's self-confessed numbness, her aversion to being touched and her vigilant commitment to James's memory are not unusual responses to maternal bereavement, but nevertheless they have troubling implications for Ben's own future. For the father, death becomes a form of impotence. They cannot prevent the child's death, rendering one of the fundamental expectations of good fatherhood – protection – unsuccessful. They must also overcome the loss of sexual intimacy so that their own eventual death might be tempered by the knowledge of a generational legacy, that 'immortality' that Talbot identifies. *Paradise* eventually ends with a romantic reunion, as Ben and Lily are reconciled at another point of loss, this time Will's return to his mother. In a torrential rainstorm – a symbolic cleansing after the stifling southern summer of the film's setting – Ben comes to Lily's aid, and the two kiss passionately on the porch. Like the weather, Lily's resistance is broken, and in this moment a future becomes possible for the Reeds. Notably, their reunion occurs outside, a space which, in *Paradise*, is perpetually associated with the children and is in itself symbolic of renewal. In this moment, Ben and Lily's emotional embrace signifies the reproductive possibilities now once again on the horizon.

Returning to the void: Vulnerable boys and narratives of crisis

As in *The Good Son* and *Paradise*, the survival of a second child is central to *The Cure* and *The Mighty*, both of which pair a sick boy with a troubled counterpart whose survival is assured by their association with the former. In *The Cure*, Dexter (Joseph Mazzello) contracts HIV/AIDS from a blood transfusion and eventually dies but not before his friendship has imbued the troubled Erik (Brad Renfro) with a renewed sense of purpose. In *The Mighty*, Kevin (Kieran Culkin) dies of complications associated with Morquio's disease, but his life has not been in vain. The confidence he has inspired in his awkward, bullied friend Max (Elden Henson) sees Max thriving in the film's closing scenes. The legacy of both dead boys lives on in another, physically stronger boy. Likewise, in *My Girl* Thomas's death is eventually transcended by the survival of Vada (Anna Chlumsky), who learns to overcome her crippling phobias and become a well-adjusted young girl by the closing credits, albeit with some misplaced optimism about Richard Nixon's re-election in her final voiceover. The thriving, surviving child marks a point of relief, ensuring the death of the first child fulfils the demand for meaning.[48]

The question remains, however: what does it mean that so many young boys, specifically, are dying on screen? As stated at the beginning of this chapter, the death of the child raises the prospect of these films as apocalyptic narratives, reflecting a wider sense of crisis. The demise of a raft of young, white boys on screen reflects a very particular anxiety, what Marita Sturken calls a kind of 'paranoia' regarding the place of the white male in contemporary American culture.[49] It recalls Faludi's suggestion that American boys can no longer expect to inherit that to which they might once have felt entitled. Their future as men has been curtailed and this is rendered on screen as a literal death of the boys who are no longer assured of their future power and status. Faludi's study of American masculinity in the 1990s found that many adult men were battling feelings of disappointment and abandonment, aimed at the fathers they felt had failed to deliver this vision of the future.[50] It is therefore telling that Hollywood often roots the child's death in the past. In *Paradise*, James's grave reveals a 1980s setting, the same decade *Lorenzo's Oil* takes place. *My Girl* and *The Ice Storm*, discussed below, are set in the 1970s. Even those films with contemporary settings frequently construct a rural milieu that suggests some disconnection with modern life. There remains an anxious denial, a nervous claim to 'not-now' even as these stories repeatedly manifest on the screens of 1990s cinemas across the country. These dead and dying boys should be understood as the adult men of the millennium – the boys of the 1970s and 1980s – where contemporary crisis is reimagined as an earlier obliteration. Unfulfilled by their fathers, promised an undelivered vision of their future as men, sons fail to thrive. In these multi-generational narratives of masculine anxiety, the death of the son on-screen is a symbolic, if extreme, manifestation of this paternal disappointment and the father's failure to guide his son effectively.

Beyond these narratives of masculine crisis, there is another element to consider. The 1990s played host to a much more tangible crisis: the AIDS epidemic. The United States' first case of HIV/AIDS was recorded in 1981. By 1992, over 250,000 people had been diagnosed with AIDS; of them, almost 230,000 had died.[51] The same year, the Center for Disease Control recorded HIV/AIDS as the leading cause of death among American men aged 25–44.[52] By 1994, it was the leading cause of death for all Americans in the same age bracket.[53] Though AIDS was, and remains, a global pandemic, within the United States there was a sense that it was a peculiarly national phenomenon, in which the country itself had been infected with the virus.[54] Like the death of a child, AIDS disrupts the expected timeline of death, impacting most visibly on the bodies of young, virile men whose own futures were cut short by the ravages of the virus. Hollywood ventured to make a film about AIDS in 1993 with Jonathan Demme's *Philadelphia*. Yet it is around, rather than within, such films that cultural anxieties about AIDS are better glimpsed. Monica Pearl's work on 'reincarnation films', for example, explores the attempt to 'give meaning' to the 'unbearable meaninglessness' of AIDS,[55] while monsters in horror films, the quintessential Other, have also been read as allegories for fears about AIDS.[56] Just as the virus refuses definite boundaries, AIDS films cannot be easily categorized, leading Alan Nadel to identify thematic branches of 1980s and 1990s cinema that can be understood in the context of AIDS, including pastoral 'death-as-a-loss-of-innocence' films such as *My Girl* and *Paradise*.[57] In such films, a child's death symbolizes a breakdown of meaning and order, replicating the virus itself.

In the 1980s, AIDS was commonly constructed in opposition to the heterosexual family, but by the 1990s the reach of the virus was such that it could no longer be plausibly contained in the same way.[58] *The Cure* comes closest to an explicit AIDS narrative, albeit one that recalls the troubling distinction between 'innocent' victims (commonly, those who contracted the virus through blood transfusions, as in Dexter's case) and those less worthy of sympathy, chief among them men who had sex with other men. *Lorenzo's Oil*, too, sees parents briefly discussing AIDS activism as a model for increased medical funding. However, more broadly films in which a child dies are a displacement for concerns over AIDS and, specifically, its potential to intrude on the sacred domain of the American family. In its disruptive, meaningless nature, AIDS operates in a queer space. It is capable of destroying or denying the future; it obeys no logic regarding age, health or strength when it comes to infection, which before treatment breakthroughs in the mid-1990s often meant death. That it primarily – though far from exclusively – impacted on men having non-reproductive sex is further testament to this anti-futurity. The death of the child represents a similar loss of a future and a failure of survival that must be overcome by re-closing the circle of the family and ensuring that a future is re-established. As such, these films exist both as reflections of the AIDS crisis and its denial, a refutation of the queer, future-shattering narrative it imposed on the United States during the 1990s.

This duality is reflected in *The Ice Storm*, which both kills a boy on screen (unusually, the death is depicted within the frame) and yet seeks to re-establish the family on stronger ground after the tragedy, disavowing the very disorder it careens towards. Released by Fox Searchlight, a subsidiary of 20th Century Fox, *The Ice Storm* exists on the boundaries of Hollywood and independent cinema, pairing star names (Sigourney Weaver, Kevin Kline and Christina Ricci) with an art-house aesthetic. It provides an interesting case study not least because the dead child, Mikey, is portrayed by Elijah Wood, an inversion of Wood's role as the surviving boy in two of the films discussed above. Rather than the aftermath of parental bereavement, the film is an examination of families in crisis that culminates in a child's death. Though this crisis is once again displaced to the 1970s, the film reflects many of the same issues facing a contemporary audience: the splintering of the American family, the wavering trust in a presidential figure and the marginalization of the father. In the two central families, the Hoods and the Carvers, the fathers are both present and not, another duality that hints at fractured foundations.

The Ice Storm is an apocalyptic film in two senses. First, it relies on the meteorological phenomenon of a vast, unrelenting storm to signify the human crisis within. It is this storm that finally kills Mikey Carver, as he is electrocuted by a fallen power line. Secondly, the narrative is structured in such a way that it drives towards tragedy from the outset, gathering speed as it examines the breakdown and collision of the two families. The family is a site of disappointment and disillusion, from the affair that Ben Hood (Kline) is having with Mikey's mother Janey (Weaver), to the shoplifting habit of Ben's wife Elena (Joan Allen) and the bored sexual experimentation that occurs between Wendy Hood (Ricci) and the Carver brothers, Mikey and Sandy (Adam Hann-Byrd). The film presents the family as a destructive force, whereby the apocalypse it faces is of its own making. Visual hints of the devastation to come are resolutely domestic, from close-ups of ice cracking in liquor glasses to the hanged figure of Sandy's GI Joe, rooting destruction as much in the mundane as in the spectacular.

The film is bleak in tone, both narratively and visually. If the child's death disrupts the 'space of safety' that childhood and the family symbolizes on-screen, then *The Ice Storm* subverts this safe space from the outset, with the families plagued by amorality and a general sense of malaise.[59] In the affluent suburb of New Canaan, a landscape of privilege and security, the next generation trade only in cynicism and muted despair. Children and parents remain detached;

the strongest bond unknowingly exists between Elena and Wendy, the latter inheriting her mother's propensity for shoplifting at the local pharmacy. Wendy is transfixed by the Watergate scandal unfolding on television, seduced by this vision of national destabilization. Meanwhile, Mikey craves clarity, clinging to the 'perfect spaces' of geometry and the 'clean' molecules of ice he studies, even as everything around him is revealed as murky and unsatisfying.

The disillusioned son is at the centre of *The Ice Storm*. Like his sister Wendy, Paul Hood (Tobey Maguire) lacks respect for Ben, who is riled by Wendy's interest in Watergate and out of touch with Paul, whom he awkwardly (and very belatedly) attempts to advise on masturbation. Paul is disappointed when his romantic interest in classmate Libbets (Katie Holmes) is foiled by her interest in their more self-assured friend Francis (David Krumholtz). Likewise, Mikey's desire for clarity and order goes unfulfilled. It is his fascination with the ice and its molecular perfection that drives him outside in the storm, seeking the same certainty that is lacking in his own life, a lack rooted in his own paternal disappointment.

Paul and Mikey are those betrayed sons of Faludi's imagining, promised everything and granted little. In New Canaan, the epitome of white, Anglo-Saxon, Protestant (WASP) America, their lives may be materially comfortable, but spiritually they remain unfulfilled and disappointed by a visible lack of paternal vitality. The two fathers, Jim Carver (Jamey Sheridan) and Ben, remain at the margins, distant and lacklustre figures throughout. Ben's affair with Janey only serves to highlight his inadequacies, as she labels him 'boring' and rejects his attempts at non-sexual intimacy ('I have a husband, I have no need for another'). Jim, meanwhile, is largely invisible. In one scene, returning home from work, he remains only partially visible in the door frame. He announces his return to his sons, only for them to respond, 'You were gone?' The non-father status that jeopardizes men such as Augusto Odone, Wallace Evans and Ben Reed is already on its way to being established here. Against the backdrop of Watergate and the failure of Richard Nixon to live up to the expectations of a 'national father', the fathers in *The Ice Storm* are largely useless figures, reflecting a wider disillusionment with paternal authority, both from the children who reject it and the men unable to wield it.

Mikey's death is the film's climax. Much like the storm itself, his death represents a release, the culmination of the characters' desperate quest for meaning amidst the unfulfilling fragments of their lives. However bleak and nihilistic the film up to this point is, the death of Mikey plays by the rules. He does not simply die, in this case, for the sake of the storm. Instead, his death marks a reversal, a restoration of the family and, crucially, of the father. The Carvers and the Hoods, whose individual members have been drifting further away from each other for much of the film, are thrown back together by the force of the tragedy. As Janey wakes up to a sobbing Jim, the icicles outside their window begin to melt, a thawing that implies reconciliation. An emotional Ben likewise breaks down as he drives Elena and Wendy to the train station, a moment that may ordinary be read as weakness but here suggests the same kind of splintering, not as destruction but as the first step to coming back together.

This final drive to the station reveals that the opening scene, in which Paul is travelling home by train, is in fact the final scene. Mikey is already dead and the Hoods, so fractured up until this point, have reunited to meet Paul. As *The Ice Storm* begins, this scene is overlaid with Paul's narration, as he considers his comic book: 'That was the meaning of the Fantastic Four, that a family is like your own personal anti-matter, your family is the void you emerge from, and the place you return to when you die. And that's the paradox. The closer you're drawn back in, the deeper into the void you go.' At the beginning of the film, these words appear to sum up Paul's feelings towards going home for Thanksgiving. Being 'drawn back in … deeper into the void' has negative connotations, reinforced by both

Figure 7 The Hoods reunite the morning after Mikey's death in *The Ice Storm* (1997). Fox Searchlight.

Paul's awkward relationship with his father and the family members' inability to connect. Yet at the end of the film, this statement takes on a different meaning, highlighting the form of survival that the child and the family as an entity offer to the father. For Ben, Mikey's death is the catalyst for realizing the significance of his relationship with his own son. If the family is 'the place you return to when you die', this ties Ben's mortality as a father to his children. In this opening/final scene, it is not only Paul returning to his family but Ben returning to his, a closing of the family circle that re-secures Ben's future survival. The family finally becomes a 'space of safety' in which death is both possible and yet postponed, a reassurance (and realization) that overrides the tragedy of Mikey's own death.

Conclusion: Survival and the limits of futurity

As the 1990s ended, one film began production after many years in limbo. In another act of cinematic inheritance, *A.I. Artificial Intelligence*, originally conceived by Stanley Kubrick, was eventually realized by Steven Spielberg and released in 2001. The film grapples with some of the anxieties of a dying child in a futuristic milieu. It presents mecha David (Haley Joel Osment) as the solution to Henry and Monica Swinton's (Sam Robards and Frances O'Connor) impending loss of their biological son, Martin (Jake Thomas). Mechas are artificial beings, valuable though somewhat maligned in a post-climate change world that 'strictly licenses pregnancies' to preserve resources. David is unique as a child mecha programmed to love and Henry and Monica are deemed ideal test subjects.

Like those films above, *A.I.* is primarily concerned with a vulnerable boy who functions as a substitute for the son and, in this case, his relationship with a mother who embraces and, latterly, rejects him. Unusually, the film is structured around a mother quest, as David's desire for his mother's love survives intact two thousand years into the future, when humans are extinct. Once again, the mother–child bond is rendered timeless, outside of the demands of linear generational progression. David's final vision, in which Monica assures him that she has 'always loved' him, exists in memory, beyond time and reality.

David and Henry do not enact a parallel narrative of father–son redemption. However, Henry's reaction to David is worth reflecting upon, not least because it crystallizes that broader link between fathers, sons and the future. Initially, adhering to the familiar pattern, Henry is keen to bring David into their home, while Monica remains unconvinced. 'There is no substitute for your own child!' she yells furiously. Nevertheless, David's potential as a substitute is clear, not least in a striking visual moment in which his reflection overlays a framed photograph of Martin. However, a reversal soon occurs. Monica 'imprints' David, binding them together, while Henry becomes increasingly wary and advocates for his destruction. He begins to see David as a threat, particularly once Martin recovers and returns home. Arguably, Henry has no need for David once Martin is restored, but the threat of David goes beyond this: David cannot age. He therefore represents both an endless future and no future at all.

Should Henry accept David as his son, he would do so in the knowledge that this son would live – or rather, exist – forever. Yet David cannot promise the immortality of a multi-generational legacy, because he himself cannot reproduce. There is only David, an artificial boy frozen in time, and this stasis has more in common with death than life. *A.I.* takes the scenario of the second, redemptive child and complicates it with an ironic twist. A son who can live forever is no more use that a son who dies too soon, if neither can promise the father's extension into future generations. Thus it is revealed what is truly at stake in these films. The father must be saved, so he in turn might save the father of the future.

Hollywood remains both uneasy over, and inextricably drawn to, the dying child throughout the decade. If fatherhood might deliver men from the uncertainties of millennial masculinity, such rescue is inevitably dealt a blow when the child on which their fatherhood is predicated is revealed as vulnerable and mortal. The continued reiteration of these scenarios again recalls Freud's work on mastery and repetition. In a culture where child death is uncommon, the impulse is often to deny the possibility. Films in which a child dies or is threatened by death, however, present another option. They repeatedly imagine the child's demise (that which 'just can't be') in a quest to conquer the fear it conjures. It is, perversely, a form of taking control, that same cinematic game of *fort-da* observed in the replaying of Hollywood's disaster scenarios, offering both the traumatic incident (*fort*) and the triumphant reversal (*da*). This reversal is not necessarily the child's resurrection (though *Lorenzo's Oil* and *A.I.* do both save their dying boys) but the father's, and herein lies the real triumph: confronted with the unthinkable, the father is eventually reborn.

Edelman sums up the attitude towards parenthood and reproduction as being one of a refusal to imagine any viable alternative: 'And the trump card of affirmation? Always the question: If not this, what?'[60] The same attitude applies here as, though the death of the child has the power to turn fathers into non-fathers, this position of non-father must be rendered temporary. This is the rhetorical 'what?' of Edelman's question, and by insisting that these men return to the safe parameters of fatherhood these films disavow the potential queering of the family that the death of the child threatens. The family may temporarily shatter, but it does not break, and as such it continues to hold the most concrete promise of a securely masculine future for America's anxious men.

4

Return of the (lion) king: Fatherhood beyond death

If the child's death is unnatural and traumatic, then the death of the father on screen is characterized as no less devastating. Though the trauma remains, however, the violation of expectation is erased. Simonds and Rothman suggest that successful parenting can ultimately be reduced to 'dying before they do', a bald yet irrefutable statement that reinforces the idea of a child as the living embodiment of the future.[1] To die before they do keeps the illusion of survival intact. Oren's introduction to his son via video screen moments before his death in *Deep Impact* is a classic example. His wife reveals that she has named their son after him, and Oren dies secure in the continuation of his paternal legacy, offered a glimpse of immortality even as death looms. If the father's death is inevitable, his erasure is not. Against a backdrop of crisis and doubt, Hollywood works to make meaning from his death, emphasizing the importance of his legacy both for the child's survival and his own. If the death of the father reflects a paranoia over the threat of erasure, then the restoration of his influence and the spectre of his returning self marks the mitigation of this fear. Whatever his failings, the father will not be forgotten.

Wheeler Winston Dixon suggests that 'when we cease to exist, the world ceases to exist because we can no longer apprehend it. And it is this moment that we fear and anticipate above all others because it represents the complete disintegration of the self.'[2] Narratives of paternal death and resurrection work against this disintegration, installing the child as the bearer of the generational legacy. The concept of the father living on through the child is the heart of reproductive futurism, that very promise of the future to which society and the individuals within it subjugate their own desire. It is narcissism turned outward, an apparently selfless investment in the next generation that, in fact, benefits the ego through the promise of living forever. This chapter examines four films – *The Lion King*, *Twister*, *Contact* and *Jack Frost* – all of which target a mainstream family-oriented market and all of which concern the father's own immortal survival, the puzzle that must be solved before the final credits. In this, these films owe much to *Field of Dreams* (Phil Alden Robinson, 1989), in which a father returns from the dead to reconcile with his son and reaffirm the primacy of the patriarchal family. *The Lion King*, *Jack Frost* and *Contact* all similarly rely on the spectral manifestation of the father. This visual reminder of the father's presence reinforces his place in the 'generational continuum'[3] as the child's survival once again becomes his own. As in the previous chapter, the child is crucial in driving the father's redemption and rescuing him from the obscurity of death.

The Lion King is another of the 1990s' biggest box office hits. It was Disney's most successful film of the decade, a period that marked the studio's commercial resurrection and the so-called Disney Renaissance. Much like Disney's *Bambi* (David Hand, 1942), it hinges on a moment of traumatic parental loss, in this case the death of lion Mufasa (James Earl Jones) as he is thrown from a cliff by his vengeful brother Scar (Jeremy Irons) after rescuing his son Simba (Jonathan Taylor Thomas) from a wildebeest stampede. Simba's discovery of his father's body is a shocking, visceral moment.[4] His cries for help echo around the deserted gorge as he realizes, with creeping horror, that he is alone. Tugging at Mufasa's lifeless paw, his distress is compounded by Scar's calculated observation, 'If it wasn't for you, he'd still be alive.' Shattered, Simba promptly runs away, no longer interested in reigning over the very kingdom he once coveted. It is at this point that

Simba's survival is jeopardized as, exiled from his pride, he must fend for himself. Mufasa's own future is similarly threatened by this chain of events. The danger lies not in his own death so much as Simba's rejection of his familial duty, and this must be restored if both father and son are to be rehabilitated.

The Lion King acknowledges the unique trauma that comes with the death of the father and reinforces the son's responsibility in maintaining the generational continuum. For a time, Simba is permitted to reject the pain associated with Mufasa's memory and deny the knowledge that he must succeed his father. Yet this can only be temporary. He must eventually face the reality of Mufasa's death in order to realize his own future, and within this future immortalize his own father. When the baboon shaman Rafiki (Robert Guillaume) announces triumphantly that 'the king has returned', he is referring to both the return of Simba and the return of Mufasa through him. Here is a reassurance that the father's death is not the end. It does not mark the end of his patriarchal reign but merely its continuation. Any threat to this continuation necessitates an intervention, and it is this intervention that structures the films discussed here.

Like father, like son: The myth of the 'new régime'

In 'Beyond the Pleasure Principle', Freud outlines the concept of traumatic neurosis, of which the first element is 'fright' (*Schreck*), as distinct from 'fear' (*Furcht*) or 'dread' (*Angst*), the defining quality of 'fright' being surprise.[5] This distinction informs Boaz Hagin's contention that 'death must have its sting', recalling the demand for meaning that death impels in Hollywood.[6] This 'sting' also refers to the sharp psychic pain that accompanies the death of a loved one, a trauma-through-fright that occurs as 'a consequence of an extensive breach being made in the protective shield against stimuli'.[7] Though this 'sting' might be assumed to be more prevalent in films depicting the child's death, the frequent absence of this death within the frame often denies such an impact. However, in films depicting the father's death the impact is more immediate, bringing with it the sting of 'fright' inherent in Freud's rendering of trauma. The sense of loss and abandonment is brought into sharp relief. It is this same trauma that informs Faludi's reflections on an anxious millennial masculinity, in which the father's perceived abandonment looms large. Like the death of the child, the death of the father in mainstream 1990s family films reflects the cultural anxiety of destabilization, as a figure of male authority is erased before the son, made vulnerable by his premature loss, is fully grown.

Fright imbues the scene in which Simba sits by Mufasa's body. The feeling of being alone and overwhelmed overrides all other emotion, including the ability to fathom Scar's devious plan to take control of the pride. Teresa de Lauretis observes that in trauma, the ego, 'caught by surprise, is unprepared to master or control the impacting force'.[8] Running away is Simba's reaction to this demand for control, as he chooses self-enforced exile as a way of attempting to modify the pain inflicted upon him. However, despite this trauma, parental death adheres to the supposed natural order. If the death of the child is the thing that 'just can't be',[9] Canetti counters that a 'son finds it natural that his father should die before him'.[10] The death of the father not only can be but also has to be. The naturalness of the child outliving the parent relates not only to the logical progression of ageing but, according to Freud's Oedipal theories of the psyche, to the unconscious yet undeniable desire of the child to usurp the same-sex parent.[11] This comes to the fore in *The Lion King*, in which Simba has already expressed his desire to rule over the pridelands. Simba's exile, therefore, cannot be permitted to last forever.

The ambiguity with which Freud imbues the father–son relationship stems from this Oedipal tension, as the father's authority – symbolized through the threat of castration – sits uncomfortably alongside the son's feelings of defiance. In death, the father's power is diminished: 'One who was once all-powerful is now impotent, his strength extinguished and his lifeless remains at the disposal of the very being who was for many years weak, helpless and entirely in his power.'[12] The death of the father heralds the son's moment for supremacy, a chance to attain the power he has hitherto been denied. The desire to succeed the father – even though succession involves the latter's death – forms a crucial part of the unconscious in Oedipal terms. The 'fright', the trauma of the death, is not only a response to the loss but to the gain, and the guilt associated with the unconscious wish for the father's demise.

Canetti characterizes the death of the patriarch as the moment that a 'new régime' is established, whereby 'the breach between the old and the new is immense and irreparable'.[13] The father's reign is over; the son, in his place, exerts his authority by creating a new order that departs from that of his predecessor. This 'new régime' recalls Freud's contention that civilization itself stems from the death of the primal father. However, Freud maintains a link between fathers and sons beyond death. Fathers are never fully buried, and in eliminating him the sons only succeed in 'accomplish[ing] their identification with him'.[14] *The Lion King*, too, works to overcome the 'irreparable' breach. What is permitted to occur is not a break with the father but a continuation of him through the child, who internalizes the father at the point of death.

This notion of paternal continuation is encapsulated in *Phenomenon* (Jon Turteltaub, 1996), in which George (John Travolta) dies but only once he has become 'a happy father' to his girlfriend's children.[15] George, beleaguered by a freak acquisition of immense brainpower after being struck by lightning, cannot hope to survive. Instead, he invests his legacy in Al (David Gallagher) and Glory (Ashley Buccille). He uses an apple to illustrate immortality, instructing the children to 'take a bite' so that the apple, once devoured, will still be a part of them. This is reminiscent of the moment when Mufasa explains to Simba that when lions die, they become the grass, eaten by the antelopes that the lions then devour, placing them within a cycle of perpetual life. Similarly, George's demonstration acts as a form of reassurance in the face of death. It also reveals the process by which the patriarch both dies and does not die, enabling him to attain a future without bodily form. Through building a meaningful, paternal relationship with them, George becomes a part of the children and in doing so lives on. This is not so much the establishment of a 'new régime' as the reiteration of the value of the old one. If the death of the patriarch seems at first counter-intuitive to a discussion of his survival, then this is tempered by a persistent narrative impetus that resurrects him morally, physically and finally through the child. This resurrection confirms the father's power in the face of death. In filtering the male future through fatherhood, the reliance is on the promise of continuing to exist beyond the self through his progeny. Therefore, the on-screen death simply puts this existence-beyond in motion, rather than eliminating the father at the point of his mortal demise.

I just can't wait to be king: Desire, death and resurrection

Simba's reluctance to return to the pridelands and become king must be overcome in order to effect Mufasa's survival. Reviving that implicit rejection of queerness that Hollywood's investment in the father persistently enacts without acknowledgement, the film must also reject the queer potential embedded in Simba's pseudo-familial relationship with meerkat Timon (Nathan Lane) and warthog Pumbaa (Ernie Sabella). Simba must instead be reinserted into his own reproductive future, in which the paternal legacy is carried further forward by the birth of Simba's own cub at the end of the film.

Though the film is an animated production, with the characters rendered as African animals, Mufasa and Simba continue to reflect Hollywood's broader narrative of troubled white masculinity. Though Mufasa is voiced by black actor James Earl Jones, in appearance he and Simba (voiced by two white actors) are coded as white. Their light colouring and golden manes contrast with Scar's darker skin and black mane, as well as the grey and black colouring of the hyenas. The politics of representation in *The Lion King* have attracted much critical consideration, notably in the construction of Scar as an effeminate, '[stereotypically] gay' character and the ghettoization of the hyenas Shenzi (Whoopi Goldberg), Banzai (Cheech Marin) and Ed (Jim Cummings), whose savagery and violence is confined to the 'shadowlands' of the landscape.[16] Rafiki is likewise rendered an ancient, exotic Other. Against these characters, Mufasa and Simba can be read as anthropomorphized representatives of a white American father and son. Mufasa is a typical American '90s-style ... involved dad',[17] by turns playful and protective, and like his human counterparts is facing a two-dimensional version of the same underlying crisis, simply relocated to the savannah.

Unlike Hollywood's human dads, however, Mufasa is not only the patriarch–father but patriarch–king. *The Lion King* reimagines *Hamlet* and owes a considerable debt to the Oedipal complex, structural elements that are crucial to an understanding of how the film balances succession with constancy to cement the patriarchal myth.[18] The film opens with Simba being formally presented to the amassed animals (subjects) of the kingdom as Mufasa's son and heir. As a cub, Simba is by turns respectful and defiant, compelled to push the limits of his father's authority in a manifestation of the Oedipal conflict between affection and envy.[19] Until Mufasa's death at the end of the first half of *The Lion King*, the film is forced to balance the knowledge of the impending death with the conviction that he will not die. A belief in Mufasa's immortality as king must coincide with the reality of Simba's eventual succession.

Such an attitude is exemplified in the song 'I Just Can't Wait to Be King', in which Simba's desire to rule is expressed without ever consciously acknowledging the event that must precede this eventuality. For Simba to become king, 'free to do it all my way', Mufasa has to die. To Simba, being king simply means freedom ('no one saying do this / no one saying be here'), although the repeated reference to 'no one' is a reminder of the unspoken rules of his succession. The duality of knowing and not-knowing these rules is established in two conversations between cub and father. In the first, the two of them survey the kingdom in the early morning sun. Mufasa explains that his rule extends to 'everything the light touches', adding, 'one day, Simba, the sun will set on my time here and will rise with you as the new king.' Simba appears unperturbed, more eager to discover what he will become king of ('everything?') than the conditions of this inheritance. Later, however, his uncertainty is revealed. After Mufasa rescues Simba and Nala (Niketa Calame) from the hyenas, Simba wrestles with his dad under the stars, anxiously looking for reassurance: 'We'll always be together, right?' Despite his earlier bravado Simba remains subordinate to Mufasa, whose superior strength is evidenced both in the pair's wrestling and the defeat of the hyenas. The Oedipal structure is still intact, as Simba's physical and emotional immaturity prevent him from posing any significant threat to his father.

Such a structure, however, depends eventually on progression and succession. As Peter Blos observes, 'Every father has first been a son; arriving at fatherhood and having a son weaves his own sonship experience into the new context of a generational continuum.'[20] Mufasa evokes the same continuum as he tries to reassure Simba: 'Let me tell you something that my father told me. Look at the stars. The great kings of the past look down on us from those stars. So whenever you feel alone, just remember that those kings will always be there to guide you. And so will I.' Simba is therefore made aware of his place in this perpetual familial order, that same 'Circle of Life' made explicit in the film's soundtrack. This circle shapes *The Lion King*, bookended with two almost identical images of baptism and renewal, as first Mufasa, then Simba, reveal their cub to the waiting animals from atop Pride Rock, images that prioritize survival and inheritance over democracy.[21]

Rather than ensure the cycle's continuation, however, Mufasa's premature death ruptures it, as Simba's immaturity collides with Scar's devious plotting. The threat of Mufasa's more permanent erasure becomes the primary concern of the film's second half. As Scar – coded as a queer, and therefore potentially non-reproductive, figure – becomes king, Simba disappears into a homosocial exile with Timon and Pumbaa, a carefree existence modelled on their no-worries motto of 'hakuna matata'. Mufasa's legacy is now doubly threatened. Under Scar's reign, the once-fertile pridelands become barren and dry, a landscape in which 'morbidity persists', underlining the non-reproductivity for which the outcast brother stands.[22] Simba, too, risks his own reproductive future by ignoring his betrothal to Nala and revelling in the alternative family structure offered by a meerkat and a warthog, in which his wish of being 'free to run around all day' is fulfilled not by being king but by his relaxed jungle lifestyle.

That the symbolic link between Mufasa and Simba has been broken becomes clear in a scene in which Timon, Pumbaa and Simba discuss the origin of stars. Simba offers his own interpretation, only to immediately dismiss it. 'Somebody once told me that the great kings of the past are up there, watching over us,' he tells his new friends. 'Pretty dumb, huh?' This is Simba's 'my dad's a liar' moment, the equivalent of the discarded harmonica in *Jack Frost* (discussed below), and in his casual rejection of Mufasa's story lies the threat of a second, more permanent death.

The scene is thus set for an intervention, facilitated by Rafiki and Nala but led by the spirit of Mufasa, who has become an intangible figure, lost to time, memory and Simba's hidden guilt. *The Lion King* figures Mufasa's return as another form of rescue, this time saving Simba from himself and his (by now) self-indulgent exile. In fact, it might more accurately be understood as a rescue of Mufasa, whose own immortal survival is jeopardized by Scar, a pretender to the throne with no heir (and no regard for Mufasa's model of benevolent rule), and Simba, who is no longer enthralled by the prospect of being king. To save his father, adult Simba (Matthew Broderick) must be compelled to reject his carefree life, return to the pridelands and take back the kingdom for his own future offspring.

Enter adult Nala (Moira Kelly), who laments Simba's failure to be 'the king I know he is / the king I see inside' and sets the scene for Simba's rebirth as a responsible son and father-in-waiting. This rebirth is effected by Mufasa's image appearing in the clouds and speaking to his disbelieving son: 'You are more than what you have become. You must take your place in the circle of life. Remember who you are. Remember. Remember. Remember.' Simba, it transpires, cannot help but remember who he is. Rafiki, promising to show Simba his father, leads him to a pool of water where he sees only his reflection. The animation of adult Simba is already very close to that of Mufasa, but here Simba literally morphs into the image of his father. While Dundes and Dundes suggest that this is an indication of Simba being 'ready to replace' Mufasa, I argue that it is less a case of replacing him and more one of internalizing him.[23] Simba does not aim to mimic Mufasa but restore his memory within him, thus securing his father's survival as well as his own. Likewise, when Susan Mackey-Kallis identifies *The Lion King* as a 'father quest' film, in which Simba must 'find the father inside of him' to complete this quest, it is more accurate to suggest that Simba must find *his own* father inside of him, underlining what is truly at stake.[24] 'See? He lives in you,' Rafiki urges, as Simba looks on with some scepticism ('that's just my reflection'). But this is what Simba must accept. Much like Mufasa's metaphor of the antelopes and the grass, the father remains alive through the body of his son. His death is negated both by his ephemeral appearance in the sky and the assertion that he 'lives' on in Simba.

This doubling of Mufasa and Simba in the water's reflection has precedent. Earlier, when confronted by the hyenas, Simba attempts to ward them off with a roar, only to emit a pathetic, immature squeak. Trying again, he is gratified to find an immense roar issue from his mouth, only to realize the source is an unseen Mufasa, thundering to the rescue. This inadvertent lip-sync captures the essence of *The Lion King*, as Simba becomes the vessel through which Mufasa continues to exist, lending additional weight to Nala's suggestion that Simba is already a king 'inside'. Later, both Scar and Simba's mother mistake Simba for his father, the latter misrecognition reinforcing distinct Oedipal overtones as he 'nuzzles his mother before his mate Nala' following his battle with Scar.[25] Here, the Oedipal structure of *The Lion King* successfully comes full circle. Simba desires the kingdom but is unable to overpower his father; his father dies; Simba inherits the kingdom and gains power – including sexual power, as the head of the pride – over all the other lions, including his mother.

In Oedipal terms, Simba has usurped his father. Yet this usurpation retains the element of innocence. This is vital to Simba's construction as a hero, as it is innocence that underpins Simba's right to the throne. To be responsible for Mufasa's death (as Scar claims) would make the conditions of Simba's reign uncomfortably obvious.[26] The patricidal taboo is solved by displacing Mufasa's death onto Scar, thus ensuring that Simba can become king without guilt. The inevitability of succession is tempered by Simba's survival in the image of his father. Mufasa's death does not preclude the elder lion's future influence. Any 'new régime' is dismissed, whether Scar's reign of terror and apathy or Simba's carefree, egalitarian jungle life. Compelled by his father to 'remember who you are', this is not simply a call for Simba to return to the pridelands but a reminder that he must take his place in the generational, familial order to preserve his father's heritage. The Simba of 'hakuna matata' is no more permitted to be king than Scar is. Both are potentially queer, non-futuristic positions that do nothing to advance the paternal legacy that remains the structuring principle of the savannah.

In the film's closing scenes, Simba and Nala dominate the frame. It is only this mature, responsible Simba, on the brink of procreation, who can save both the kingdom and Mufasa from beyond the grave. In his work on narcissism as a cultural condition of late twentieth-century America, Christopher Lasch suggests that the narcissistic figure has little interest in the future and a parallel disregard for the past, the result of which is a loss of both 'continuity' and a 'sense of belonging to a succession of generations'.[27] Simba's jungle exile reveals these same narcissistic impulses. However, by the end of the film these are channelled towards a more fruitful form of narcissism, that of the illusion of immortality through reproduction. The success of Mufasa's own survival, dependent on this same model of 'strategically misrecognized' narcissism,[28] is captured in the final scene through the mirroring of the opening scene, confirming the 'circle of life'. This mirroring further reinforces the future as shaped by father, rather than son. Notably, Simba does not attempt to rebuild the kingdom in his own image or dismantle the hierarchies he has lived without in the jungle. Rather, he is bound to 'speak' as his father would have done. Restored atop Pride Rock, he lets out a roar. While he has no need for Mufasa's help on this occasion, the sound and image recall his (rightful) predecessor and firmly cement Simba as king, father and, most importantly, son.

Snow dad is better than no dad: The returning father in *Jack Frost*

The finality of Mufasa's death is undermined by his on-screen return, both in Simba's vision and in the visual and aural parallels between father and son. Mufasa's return may be comforting to young audiences because it signals the enduring presence of their loved ones, even in the case of death.[29] After the traumatic experience of losing the on-screen father figure too soon, the audience – like Simba – are ultimately reassured by his symbolic resurrection.

The Lion King is not the only family film that returns the father from the dead during the 1990s and in this repetition it is possible to see shades of the same quest for mastery discussed in previous chapters. As noted above, these films echo the model of paternal resurrection established in *Field of Dreams*, in which Ray Kinsella (Kevin Costner) is compelled by a disembodied voice to build a baseball diamond in his cornfield, promised that 'if you build it, he will come'. It is Ray's dead father John who eventually comes, his appearance healing old wounds as the two are finally granted their over-determined game of catch in a classic redemption story. Earlier, Ray laments their fraught relationship, of which his abiding memory is one of rejecting this quintessential bonding moment. 'Imagine, an American boy refusing to play catch with his father,' he marvels. When they do finally pull on their baseball gloves both Ray, as the angry son, and John, as the repressed father, are redeemed. In this moment, John's own legacy is revived. His physical resurrection is temporary, lasting just long enough to re-establish the link between himself and Ray and assure his future. Their game of catch becomes a literal act of a father 'passing the ball' to his son in a game of patriarchal continuance, as the distance between them becomes paradoxically shorter.[30] As with Mufasa and Simba, this is emphasized by a visual link between Ray and John as they walk side by side, their stride and their mannerisms mirroring each other's. By the end of the film, it is clear that John will survive through his son.

This same conceit of bringing back the father just long enough to set things right forms the basis of the poorly received family comedy *Ghost Dad* (Sidney Poitier, 1990), in which widowed father Elliot (Bill Cosby) dies in a car crash but remains behind as a ghost for three days until his life insurance policy becomes valid and his children's economic future is secured. Elliot's temporary reprieve from death allows him to fulfil his paternal duties of financial provision. He will be remembered as a good dad, gone too soon but having done the right thing before the end. If the death is inevitable, then the conditions of it are not. What all of these returned or resurrected fathers have in common is a quest to be remembered in such a way that they can be assured of a continued existence in memory and action.

In these films, *The Lion King* included, the father must impart one last piece of guidance, one more apology or one more act of care before he can rest. *Jack Frost* is the most overt instance of such a reverse father quest. Jack (Michael Keaton) must negate his careless approach to fatherhood from beyond the grave, returning as a magical snowman to impart crucial life lessons to his son Charlie (Joseph Cross). Like many of his Hollywood counterparts, Jack is casually disappointing as a dad, never capricious but oftentimes thoughtless. Though he loves his son, he continually neglects him in his pursuit of his musical career. This leads to a familiar raft of forgotten hockey games, missed bedtimes and unseen achievements, all borne with a weary stoicism on Charlie's part, until Jack finally decides to put his family first. On Christmas Day, having chosen to play a gig instead of accompanying his wife Gabby (Kelly Preston) and Charlie to their family's cabin, he changes his mind and turns back. Jack is killed by an oncoming truck on this return journey. One year later, he is resurrected in the front yard as a living, talking snowman, keen to put right the neglect of the past.

Figure 8 Resurrected as a snowman, Jack makes amends in *Jack Frost* (1998). Warner Bros.

Jack bears the markers of narcissistic behaviour outlined by Lasch, from his preoccupations with fame and his need for external validation to his belief that the rules do not apply to him, not least in his assumption that Charlie will continue to respect and look up to him despite his frequent paternal misdemeanours.[31] It is this narcissistic impulse that must be subdued, shifted from a focus on the present to an investment in the future. Lasch argues that the narcissist 'does nothing to provide himself with the traditional consolations of old age, the most important of which is the belief that future generations will in some sense carry on his life's work'.[32] Instead, he is relentlessly wedded to the moment. Jack must resist immediate self-gratification (in the shape of fame, fortune and recognition) in favour of the lasting consolation of fatherhood and symbolic immortality. To do this requires a literal rebirth.

Alive, Jack is a transient figure, most often seen leaving or arriving. This visual motif denies him any fixed paternal influence and instead Gabby takes on the stereotypically masculine role. She is the breadwinner with a steady job; she shovels snow from the driveway; she threatens to discipline Charlie if his school report is poor; and she fixes a leak under the sink, at which point Charlie, seeing only the flannel shirt, mistakes her for Jack in a damning moment of misrecognition. While Gabby fulfils the role of both male and female parent, Charlie is left with no discernible masculine influence within the home. This lack potentially threatens the young boy's development as he approaches adolescence. In Oedipal terms, he has a limited opportunity to separate from the mother and emulate the father, as his dad is hardly ever there.

Jack is thus framed as an inadequate provider, not simply because of his unstable financial contribution but his inability to guide Charlie towards maturity. His position is threatened on two fronts. When Gabby decorates the house for Christmas, it is Jack's best friend Mac (Mark Addy) who helps, while Jack is busy preparing for his gig. He is further displaced by Coach Gronic (Henry Rollins), who teaches Charlie how to take a winning shot in hockey. Jack promises to teach Charlie 'the J-shot', supposedly superior to Coach Gronic's shot, but never does. These stand-in father figures function much like the stepfathers discussed in Chapter 2, threatening the bond between father and son, while Jack remains oblivious to the ways in which he is failing Charlie.

Their bond is further damaged when Charlie, disillusioned by his dad's decision to miss Christmas at the cabin, returns Jack's harmonica. This harmonica is the symbolic paternal talisman of *Jack Frost*, akin to the snow globe Charlie Calvin uses to contact his dad in *The Santa Clause* or the toy plane in *Paradise*. Prized by Jack, it was bought the day of Charlie's birth. 'I walked out of hospital in a great mood, bought myself that harmonica,' he explains. 'Never had a harmonica that played better than that.' The instrument is linked explicitly to a celebration of Jack's fatherhood and his decision to pass it on to Charlie – much like John passing the ball to Ray – is meant to signify the unassailable generational link between them. Charlie ruptures this link, however, when he drops the harmonica in the snow. Jack protests – 'I gave this to you' – but Charlie is adamant. 'I don't want it,' he tells his father. It is a damning rejection, not least because Jack claims that if Charlie plays the harmonica, his father will 'always hear' him. Charlie, apparently sick of going unheard, strips it of its talismanic properties and leaves it lying at Jack's feet. Their fractured relationship is never afforded the opportunity to heal before Jack dies. It is this that must be rectified, both for Charlie's sake and for Jack's own chance of survival.

Reflecting Aronson and Kimmel's contention that the child is the saviour of the man, it must be Charlie who resurrects Jack. The Christmas that Jack dies, he and Charlie build a snowman together in a rare moment of bonding. The following year, Charlie embarks on the same project, accessorizing his snowman with Jack's old hat and scarf, found in a box alongside the discarded harmonica. In the year since Jack's death, Charlie has become withdrawn and dispirited, a boy lacking the presence of his father. Later he plays a few experimental notes on the harmonica, his longing for his father revealed as the source of his outward anger. On this occasion Jack does 'hear' Charlie, correcting the pattern of oblivious neglect established while he was alive and allowing him a temporary return that becomes the catalyst for rebuilding their relationship. It is also an opportunity for Jack to steer Charlie towards a responsible, purposeful adolescence. Only then can Jack die (melt) for a second time, safe in the knowledge that he has belatedly imbued his son with the values necessary to a meaningful adult life. Roger Ebert ridicules the film's lack of scope, as Charlie and the snowman's adventures are confined to beating the school bullies rather than anything more ambitious or otherworldly.[33] But this lack of scope is precisely the point. The true purpose of Jack's return is not to have a great adventure or unravel the meaning of life but to offer both guidance and an apology to the only person capable of continuing his legacy beyond himself. What appears to be an act of saving Charlie will be revealed as Jack's own redemption.

As the snowman, Jack thanks Charlie for 'giving me a second chance to be your dad', albeit the one that melts all over the kitchen floor, and in this second chance resides the possibility for forgiveness and an opportunity to be memorialized much more favourably than before. Much like Mufasa's return is only partially intended as an act of comfort for Simba, Jack's return is also bound up in a purpose beyond temporary solace. The bridge between father and son must be rebuilt and Jack must bestow on Charlie the necessary tools – physical and mental – for Charlie to become a man in his father's image, something that, given Jack's behaviour and the influence of Mac and Coach Gronic, is far from certain when Jack dies.

The dangers of father–son estrangement are hammered home in the shallow characterization of school bully Rory (Taylor Handley). Charlie begins the film willing to challenge Rory but after Jack's death is content to let Rory pelt younger children with snowballs without intervening. One boy notes that Charlie is 'no fun to pick on since his old man died', to which Rory opines that Charlie should 'get over it', adding, 'I never even met my old man.' The subtext here is clear. Rory is an unpleasant bully because he has no relationship with his father. It becomes imperative, therefore, that Charlie takes the opportunity to reconcile with Jack. As a suddenly sympathetic Rory suggests later, recognizing his own paternal loss, 'Snow dad is better than no dad.' Buried in this glib aside is the wider Hollywood project writ large. Imperfect though they may be, such fathers are worth the effort of rehabilitation, both for themselves and their sons.

Helping Charlie defeat Rory and the other school bullies is the first point on Jack's own map to paternal restoration. In the short time he has, he must turn Charlie back into the boy he was before. Crucially, this 'before' refers not only to Jack's death but also the period before Charlie's disillusionment with his father. Charlie must be restored to that hard-working member of the hockey team, a loyal friend and well-behaved son, but this time these qualities must be a direct result of his father's intervention, bestowed not by his coach, his mother or his dad's best friend but by Jack. The parameters of Jack and Charlie's adventures are necessarily narrow to ensure both get out of the encounter what they truly need. Rather than ignoring Rory, snowman-Jack (capable of hurling snowballs at a frightening pace) encourages Charlie to stay and fight. In defeating the bullies, Charlie once again learns the value of protecting his friends, this time with the help of his dad, who reinforces his son's masculine development by reigniting in him the desire to stand up and fight.

The second fix that Jack must perform is to finally teach Charlie the 'J-shot' and convince him to rejoin the hockey team. This not only restores Charlie's self-confidence but allows Jack to fulfil his failed promise to attend one of his hockey games. Teaching Charlie the 'J-shot' also displaces Coach Gronic's influence; the coach is further undermined when the sight of a walking, talking snowman frightens him into a nervous panic. Using the 'J-shot', Charlie scores his first goal, the one Gabby claimed Jack would miss if he continued to prioritize his own commitments. Two wrongs are thus righted. Charlie's success is now linked to his dad's influence and Jack has demonstrated the responsibility he was so sorely lacking while alive.

Like many Hollywood dads, Jack finally realizes the importance of the world beyond himself. This sense of responsibility must also be passed on to their sons. Jack's most emphatic lesson is one of maturity and obligation. He discusses with Charlie the importance of 'looking out for' his mother, reminding him that 'you've got responsibilities now, Charlie, and you've got to face them'. That Jack is the one who has inadvertently placed Charlie in this position is glossed over. Like Simba, Charlie must put his grief to one side and face up to his future as a man in the (belatedly constructed) image of his father.

This acceptance of responsibility is a key element of upholding the existing regime. What occurs in these films is the bridging of an existing gap between father and son. Faludi suggests that the break with the father, with which Simba and Charlie both grapple, is central to the shattered sense of masculinity that pervades contemporary culture. She deploys a similar bridge metaphor to that used repeatedly by President Clinton: 'Down the generations, the father wasn't simply a good sport who played backyard catch, took his son to ball games, or paid for his education. He was a human bridge connecting the boy to an adult life of public engagement and responsibility.'[34] It is crucial that this responsibility is both recognized and accepted by both father and son. Charlie must return to his engaged, ambitious former self. Simba cannot become king until he renounces his 'naïve and ego-driven' ways.[35] Yet in doing so, Simba simply trades one form of narcissism for another, that which Edelman characterizes as being 'from life-negating to vital'.[36] He renounces a selfish existence for one in which the interests of the kingdom are put first, ultimately replicating Mufasa's legacy and taking his own place in the immortal 'circle of life'. Likewise, Charlie's act of facing up to his looming adolescence enacts a similar sleight of hand. Rediscovering his love of hockey and his commitment to his mother and his friends channels his energy outwards, away from the self-indulgent anger and withdrawal of his grief. Yet it only invites a more acceptable, 'vital' narcissism in preparing Charlie for an adulthood in which his father's legacy will be secured. Rather than confining Jack to memory, Charlie is encouraged to imbue his own actions with Jack's guidance and reimagine his own future. The interest in the propagation of this future is what propels these narratives towards their conclusion.

Freud suggests that when an individual is grieving, eventually 'respect for reality gains the day'.[37] However, the tendency to deny the need to sever bonds with the lost object 'can be so intense that a turning away from reality takes place and a clinging to the object through the medium of a hallucinatory wishful psychosis'.³⁸ This melancholic wallowing in the past must be avoided if reality is to triumph, much as in those films discussed in Chapter 3. Confronted by the ghost of his dead father, Simba must face the reality of the ravaged pridelands, not dwell on the looming memory of Mufasa even as he acts in his name. Therefore, while reality is adjusted in order to effect the dead father's return, it is never suspended completely. The father's return must always be geared towards the good of the future rather than acting as a useless nostalgic bridge to the past.

Charlie, too, must look forward. Once Jack is sure he has instilled in his son the values that will make him an asset to his father's name, he melts away, this time for good. Gabby sees her dead husband for a matter of moments before he disappears, reinforcing Jack's primary need to fix his relationship with his son rather than see his wife. As he disappears, Jack tells Charlie, 'You're going to be a good man.' For Freud, this is the driving force behind the parent's narcissistic construction of the child: 'The child shall fulfil those wishful dreams of the parents which they never carried out – *the boy shall become a great man and a hero in his father's place*, and the girl shall marry a prince as a tardy compensation for her mother.'³⁹ These final words clarify the necessary outcome of Jack's return, the guarantee that Charlie will not just be a good boy but a good man. In an era where the fragility of masculinity was much debated, the father's return is an act of masculine reassurance, a salve against the fear that America's sons had been abandoned. At the end of the film, another Christmas on, a happy Charlie plays hockey in the front garden with his friends, all thoughts of building a magic snowman forgotten. He has moved on from mourning his father (the past) to living out the life his father has helped engineer (the future). Jack may be gone, but he will be remembered each time Charlie makes the 'J-shot', itself symbolic of Charlie's own future success.

More to life: The battle against meaninglessness

The previous chapters reveal wish-fulfilment as a recurring theme in Hollywood's father films. Children find their disinterested fathers transformed; their divorced parents suddenly on civil terms; against all the odds, their paternal disillusion is allayed. The father's return from the dead takes this wish-fulfilment one step further. While there is, of course, a Freudian aspect to this wish-fulfilment – a reversal of the unconscious desire to kill the father, powered by the son's guilt – the cultural context is also crucial to understanding the motivations of these films. Once again, the AIDS epidemic is an important touchstone. Pearl's work on 'reincarnation films', noted briefly in Chapter 3, is illuminating in this regard. Just as films depicting the death of a child can be understood as metaphorical AIDS narratives, reflecting contemporary anxieties around erasure and survival, the father's temporary on-screen return suggests similar fears. Pearl defines reincarnation films as those in which a dead character returns as a ghost, inhabits a new body, or occupies as existing one, framing these acts of reincarnation as 'attempts to give meaning to what is experienced in our Western culture as the unbearable meaninglessness of the virus that causes AIDS'.[40] The concept of meaninglessness refers first to the medical enigma of the virus, which resisted initial identification and subsequent treatment, and the sense of unfairness associated with any disease that impacts notably on young as well as old. Secondly, it disproportionately devastated communities of gay men across the United States, mere years after the emergence of the gay liberation movement, compounding this unfairness further. This sense of meaninglessness is further magnified by connotations of loss, (premature) death and 'abandonment', and it is these points of dread that the reincarnation narrative attempts to address and alleviate.[41] Pearl's suggestion of abandonment recalls Faludi's characterization of the father–son relationship at the end of the millennium, reinforcing the fact that at the heart of these fatherhood films lies a chronic dread of being left behind.

Reincarnation allows simultaneously for restoration and reassurance, a temporary abeyance of trauma. Pearl suggests that the 'primary anxiety' in such films is that of 'resolution: that ethereal love, but also concrete bodies, will be restored'.[42] The films discussed here share this anxiety, channelling it towards a restoration of meaning through the figure of the father, whose body remains unconcrete (he is vapour, ghost, snow, memory) and yet whose love and worth is assured. The son has not been abandoned after all. Reincarnation suggests that the apocalyptic event has not been entirely successful. There is still the possibility of being able to harness the future and reverse the meaninglessness that the father's loss threatens, restored order being the defence against a loss of meaning.

The restoration of meaning brings with it stability and continuance, that which Hollywood's men – much like the nation itself – were craving. Elsewhere, this is figured through a return to a reproductive future and the inherent survival it connotes. Just as an adult Simba is last seen presenting his progeny to the world, in the disaster-adventure film *Twister* and science-fiction drama *Contact* adult daughters who lost their fathers as children are propelled towards the formation of a stable heterosexual relationship as the most productive – and potentially *re*productive – method of paternal veneration. Both films are unusual in that they examine the father–daughter dynamic within the paradigm of father loss. Given the cultural context of masculine crisis, the consideration of the father's death in relation to the son is perhaps inevitable. The themes of a legacy being passed on and the inheritance of a paternally infused future likewise echo Oedipal assumptions of generational, patriarchal succession. However, *Twister* and *Contact* further illuminate the reproductive imperative in the battle against meaninglessness and anticipate the exchange of father for husband that so starkly marks the conclusion of *Armageddon*, discussed in Chapter 1.

'I thought it was just a metaphor': The reproductive imperative

Like *Armageddon*, *Twister* and *Contact* invest in the drive towards reproduction and family that promises the continued survival of the father. Dealing with scenarios of disaster and threat, they belong to that significant stable of pre-millennial disaster films that intertwine 'apocalyptic dread' with questions of the father's survival.[43] In all three films, the answer lies in the daughter's successful entry into a conventional heterosexual union. In *Twister* and *Contact*, she must also renounce her external preoccupations with unproductive and unknown forces of nature, towards that which maintains the illusion of being knowable; that is, reproduction.

In *Contact*, scientist Ellie (Jodie Foster) works in the field of the Search for Extra-Terrestrial Intelligence (SETI). Her mother died in childbirth, another example of the collateral damage inflicted by Hollywood's persistent marginalization of the mother. The opening scenes establish young Ellie's close relationship with her father Ted (David Morse), who encourages his daughter's love of science. Ellie plays constantly with a radio, keen to make contact with people across the country and beyond. 'Could we talk to Alaska?' she asks her father. 'Could we talk to the moon? Could we talk to Jupiter? Could we talk to Mom?' Though Ted is clear, gently telling Ellie, 'I don't think even the biggest radio could reach there', her quest is amplified once Ted suffers a heart attack and dies. After the funeral she desperately radios out: 'Dad, are you there? Dad, this is Ellie, come back?' This frantic plea recalls Simba crouching over Mufasa's body, trying to shake him awake, but while Simba flees, Ellie's adult life becomes a quest to resurrect Ted.[44] The film opens with a vision of the universe overlaid with snippets of music and speech representing events of the twentieth century, including the prominent announcement of JFK's assassination. Just as the youthful, Democratic spirit of JFK was resurrected in President Clinton (largely by Clinton himself[45]), whose image and voice is also used prominently in the film, so Ellie is tasked with bringing her father back to life.

This is most evident in Ellie's choice of career. Though she is mocked by her colleagues in her search for 'little green men', Ellie is spurred on by her father's belief that 'if we're the only ones out there, it seems like an awful waste of space'. Ted's influence triumphs over the beliefs of the wider scientific community, symbolizing Ellie's faith in, and commitment to, her dad and his memory. From him, she inherits her life's mission. When she does discover a communication from elsewhere in the universe, a vindicated Ellie is given the opportunity to venture into the unknown. On the mission, Ellie encounters an alien who takes the form of Ted and calls her by her childhood nickname, Sparks. The alien, as Ted, repeats his oft-used mantra, 'Small moves, Ellie. Small moves', as the two meet on a beach that resembles one of Ellie's childhood drawings. The encounter reveals Ellie's longing for her father and is suggestive of the extent to which her own quest in life is inherently bound to him.

Significantly, Ellie's own scientific legacy is eventually curtailed. *Jurassic Park* is clear that Alan Grant's monumental intervention into the field of palaeontology (recognizing the evolutionary relationship between dinosaurs and birds) is worth little compared to his discovery of fatherhood. Here, Ellie's mission report is received with lukewarm ambivalence. Her claims of interacting with an extra-terrestrial are disputed by her fellow scientists and her funding is cut. Ellie must instead be content with a more manageable, conceivable future. Of her scientific ambitions, the most significant survivor is Ted, who lives on in Ellie's teaching. At the end of the film she speaks to a

Figure 9 In *Contact* (1997), Ellie encounters an alien manifestation of her father. Warner Bros.

group of children about the universe, echoing her father's rationale for the existence of extra-terrestrials: 'If it's only us, it seems like a big waste of space.' In part, *Contact* is a meditation on faith and science, demonstrated in Ellie's continued faith in her father and in the veracity of her own alien encounter. Beyond this, the film also reinforces the value of an individual legacy over a collective one. Scientific rigour would demand that Ellie interrogates her experience with alien-Ted, questions their emotionally charged interaction and expose it to science. Instead, she chooses to hold onto her dad, another indication of the fallacy of the 'new régime'. The film's faith, like Ellie's, lies in the father.

That the film ends by echoing her father's speculative ethos regarding the universe reinforces the passing of the ball from Ted to Ellie, who cements the father's primacy even after death by voicing his beliefs to the next generation, the human equivalent of Simba's lip-synced roar. There is another facet to this act of living on, too. As well as a lack of funding, Ellie's scientific ventures are also modified by her relationship with Joss (Matthew McConaughey), who challenges her view of science as inherently good, essentially undermining the one point of stability in Ellie's life. *Contact* thus sets up a scenario in which Ellie must look for stability elsewhere. This comes in the form of Ted's legacy and her future relationship with Joss. It is not enough that Ellie immortalize her father through words. By the end of the film, the rapprochement between Ellie and Joss points towards a more productive future for Ellie, one in which the conventions of a heterosexual union may offer a more concrete future not only for herself but for the continued memory of her father.

Released a year before *Contact*, *Twister* was the second-highest grossing film of 1996, attracting huge audiences with its narrative of Midwestern natural disaster, family-friendly adventure and a prickly romantic subplot between its leads, Jo (Helen Hunt) and Bill (Bill Paxton). Like *Contact*, it begins with a young girl experiencing the death of her father. Five-year-old Jo sees her dad (Richard Lineback) swept away by a tornado metres from the entrance of their storm cellar after attempting to rescue the family dog. Like Ellie, Jo channels this traumatic moment into her chosen career. She becomes a meteorologist and 'tornado chaser', designing equipment that can be deposited inside a tornado to reveal its inner workings. As with Ellie, there is a desire for mastery through science. Just as Ellie hopes to prove contact with the world beyond is possible and so bridge the chasm opened up by Ted's death, Jo is driven by a compulsion to understand the mechanisms of the tornado and demystify the loss of her dad.

Jo is a dedicated scientist and a pioneering researcher, but her singular commitment to the cause is characterized as a destructive force that must be channelled, yet again, towards something more productive. Even more so than *Contact*, *Twister* maintains a concerted focus on the establishment of a romantic relationship for its female lead. Jo must reconcile with Bill, her estranged husband and fellow tornado chaser. At the beginning of the film, while Jo chases a tornado, Bill chases Jo in a bid to get her to sign their divorce papers.

Thrown together by an outbreak of tornadoes, the two eventually and inevitably re-establish a romantic relationship.

Twister presents Jo's current life as being as hollow as the tornadoes she pursues. The future she might have had with Bill is dangled in front of her in the form of Bill's new fiancée Melissa (Jami Gertz). It is further mocked through the monitoring equipment Jo has designed and named 'Dorothy', an overt reference to *The Wizard of Oz* but also a sterile stand-in for a child, made and named but ultimately marked for destruction. Jo's crusade to explain – and, in some way, negate – her father's death is the wrong kind of paternal survival quest, and this must be corrected. It is Bill who presents Jo with the stark choice she faces, telling her, 'Killing yourself won't bring your dad back … You've got to move on. Stop living in the past and look what you've got right in front of you. Me, Jo.'

Jo's career is one way of foregrounding the father and working towards his survival, in this case through the wish fulfilment of reversing his death through scientific discovery. Yet overtaking this is Jo's own contribution to the next generation, in which her father's future, and her own, can be continued indefinitely. To successfully honour her father, Jo must move beyond her single-minded quest to understand his death and instead focus on generating life. Christening the tornado monitoring equipment is not enough. Jo and Bill's reconciliation is the first step towards their own shared reproductive future, a more fruitful extension of both Jo's life and that of her late father. It is worth noting that Dorothy was the original creation of both Jo and Bill, further emphasizing its metaphorical value as a surrogate child. The sterile scientific equipment consuming Jo's life cannot be allowed to supersede what Freud calls 'the extension of individual life into that of the species'; Jo must accept her place within, rather than at the end of, the generational continuum.[46]

That Jo and Ellie are both scientists, working in predominantly male fields, is interesting not least because by the end of both films, their commitment to their profession has been shaken. They must not lose sight of their true purpose as women, daughters and sole carriers of their father's legacy. While those films focusing on the surviving son reflect an Oedipal desire to both overcome and yet venerate the father, these father–daughter scenarios speak to another facet of the same psychoanalytic theory, the young girl's need to renounce her attachment to her father in favour of a healthy (read: heteronormative) adult relationship. The images of a young Ellie and a young Jo as a precursor to the main action of *Contact* and *Twister* reinforce such an early attachment to the father. This must be tempered later by their attachment to a different man. In *Armageddon*, when faced with death Harry gives his blessing to Grace and A.J.'s relationship and is rewarded by being prominently memorialized at the scene of their wedding. In all three films, the father is still a structuring force, but his influence is diminished just enough that he survives without jeopardizing the next generation.

Conclusion: The father's ultimate victory

In P.D. James's novel *The Children of Men*, protagonist Theodore reiterates the illusion of immortality embedded in the figure of the child, that 'we being dead yet live'.[47] This, after all, is the project of generational succession. Children offer the promise of a future even within a reality in which death is inevitable. Canetti observes knowledge as a crucial aspect of survival, where to 'know' that one has lived on is the point of power: 'When he is no longer there, then his name must continue.'[48] Not only that, it must be a name of which the child can be proud, a name they will willingly carry into their own future and beyond.

Canetti's reflections on survival inevitably coalesce with ideas of power and victory, the latter being 'one and the same' as survival in man's eyes.[49] This perception of power informs an understanding of Hollywood's scenarios of paternal death. The death of the father once again reflects deep-seated anxieties regarding the absent or inadequate father and the apparent demise of the reliable, strong patriarch. But in his survival – either through resurrection, the child's renewed commitment to the future, or both – power is realized. He is restored, he is remembered, he is proven right. His name will live on. If what he craves is 'a feeling of invulnerability', then this can be found in the 'pleasure' of knowing his legacy will continue.[50] Much like the new man, who appears to relinquish power in a bid to acquire more, here the dead father is ostensibly gone and yet retains his grip and influence on the future.

This goes some way to explaining why Hollywood's dead fathers are so often relatively young. In the films discussed here only Ray is an adult at the time of his dad's death, and *Field of Dreams* makes much of the fact that John was already lost to Ray at a much younger age. The loss is suffered by a child, again recalling the cultural trauma of paternal abandonment. Moreover, in this way the father never suffers the indignity of old age, the cause of much 'intense fear' in western culture.[51] His death will not be a gradual fading out. He is spared the moment in which his child loses complete faith in him (*Jack Frost* perhaps walks this tightrope more precariously than most). In youth is inherent power – it is no accident that John Kinsella returns as a young man – and so in dying prematurely the father paradoxically retains an element of victory. Counterintuitive though it may at first seem, in its explorations of the death of the father Hollywood reveals less disillusion than hope, shoring up his power through these narratives of resurrection, rehabilitation and reproduction.

5

Guys that say goodnight: Gay fatherhood and the quest for legitimacy

In November 1998, *The New York Times Magazine* ran a series on status. Representatives of various demographics, including psychiatrists, Arab immigrants, trailer park residents, CEOs and vegetarians, held forth on the thing that, to them, could be considered an ultimate sign of status. Journalist and activist Dan Savage, latterly of the It Gets Better movement, made his own definitive statement on behalf of gay men: 'The Baby'.[1] As the millennium approached, an alternative future for gay men began to enter the cultural consciousness, one far removed from the trauma of the HIV/AIDS epidemic. Fatherhood promised fulfilment, commitment and, above all, survival. No wonder, then, that Hollywood took up the cause of gay fathers with some enthusiasm.

By the mid-1990s, against a backdrop of improving HIV/AIDS treatment, expanding options for alternative reproduction and gay rights' campaigns for marriage and parenting equality, mainstream popular culture tentatively turned its attention to portrayals of same-sex parents. Most often, the focus was on two mothers, reflecting the persistent cultural association of motherhood with a natural female impulse. *Friends* (1994–2004), which routinely attracted more than twenty million viewers across the United States, introduced lesbian mothers Carol (Jane Sibbett) and Susan (Jessica Hecht), with whom Ross Geller (David Schwimmer) begrudgingly co-parented son Ben. Though Ross's attitude was frequently hostile, Carol and Susan were portrayed positively as parents. Other television shows, including *NYPD Blue* (1993–2005), *ER* (1994–2009) and *The Wire* (2002–8), continued this trend into the early 2000s. Gay men, on the other hand, were still most likely to be portrayed as hedonistic, selfish and/ or tragic figures, precluding their depiction as fathers, for whom responsibility remains a key defining factor. In the 1990s, however, three Hollywood films emerge, which explore gay fatherhood: *The Birdcage*, a remake of Eduoard Molinaro's *La Cage Aux Folles* (1978); romantic comedy-drama *The Object of My Affection*; and *The Next Best Thing*, briefly discussed in Chapter 2. This chapter explores the representation of gay fatherhood within the broader project of masculinity, paternity and survival embarked upon in Hollywood during this period.

As I have argued, the potency of a future through fatherhood and its ability to save American men should not be underestimated, particularly in a period of ostensible masculine crisis. Moreover, the power of this survival is particularly pronounced when the men in question are gay, given the proximity to the AIDS crisis. Tying the future to fatherhood and reproduction takes on increased significance after fifteen years of witnessing the devastation of the virus and its ability to curtail the very future now being offered (tentatively, perhaps, but proffered nonetheless). If Hollywood's father quest is characterized primarily by significant anxiety, manifested in disaster, legal wrangling, illness, absence and death, these films suggest a creeping sense of hope and progress by the latter part of the 1990s. Looking back is no longer an option. Instead, these men look forward to a future in which fatherhood will bring them lasting fulfilment and meaning. Whether Hollywood achieves this progressive vision is dubious, but the fatherhood-as-saving-mechanism model finds no greater advocacy than in its images of gay dads in the 1990s, in which men may be saved from decadence, emptiness and death by their commitment to a new life.

Of the films explored in this book, *The Birdcage*, *The Object of My Affection* and *The Next Best Thing* are perhaps the most closely examined by critics and theorists.[2] In particular, James Keller's analysis is instructive in revealing their paradoxical nature, in which a socially progressive motivation does not preclude the 'bleak picture of gay parental rights' observable on closer viewing.[3] My own analysis examines a different yet related paradox. It considers how fatherhood is constructed as a site of survival for gay men in a determinedly post-AIDS American landscape, an escape from the meaninglessness connoted by the loss of a future. However, underlying this optimistic project is a raft of conditions that render this survival problematic.

Though Keller claims all three films as queer, this designation is based on the willingness to insert gay characters into the narrative rather than the more radical queerness expounded by Edelman. If queerness 'names the side of those *not* "fighting for the children"' and marks out a space of resistance to the 'unquestioned good' of futurity, these films are resoundingly not queer.[4] Their entire mission is one of fetishizing the future, often to the detriment of the gay men at their centre. Fatherhood is routinely bestowed only on those men willing to undergo a significant erasure of identity and sexuality, a sacrifice of the self for the chance of a more symbolic form of survival.

This is not to argue that gay men must adhere to Edelman's vision of queer resistance to the future any more than any other men. Indeed, Edelman reinforces the fact that 'nothing intrinsic to the constitution of those identifying as lesbian, gay, bisexual, transgendered, transsexual, or queer predisposes them to resist the appeal of futurity, to refuse the temptation to reproduce'.[5] That the films discussed here uncouple the desire for a child from heterosexuality is welcome. What is more problematic is the way in which they also uncouple 'father' from 'gay man' in such a way that the two facets of identity become almost incompatible. Desiring fatherhood is permitted, but negotiating the identity of 'gay father' ultimately encourages the elimination of one or other element, harnessing the future to a version of the self that adheres to a heteronormative vision of paternal masculinity. Survival thus becomes conditional, apt to be modified or denied if the sacrifice underwriting the promise of paternity is not sufficiently enacted. It is in light of this underlying tension that all three films are subsequently explored.

Survival and its limitations in a 'post-AIDS' landscape

In the United States, the 1990s marked a period of debate and change around gay rights, particularly concerning family, marriage and parenthood. It was also a site of continued battle – and considerable progress – against HIV/AIDS, both medically and politically. While gay men may have seen their 'horizons of possibility … severely diminished by the AIDS epidemic', gradually campaigns emerged in which other possibilities, intrinsically linked to an expansion of opportunity – including legal rights to kinship, marriage and adoption – entered the equation.[6] Gay parenting and the construction of queer families was nothing new, but the legal, political and wider social acknowledgement was novel. This was a decade in which the threat of erasure met the promise of recognition. It is this collision that informs Hollywood's images of gay fatherhood.

Bersani acknowledges the tension between HIV/AIDS and the rights campaigns that focus implicitly on the future, observing, 'We [gay men] demand a future without discrimination even as AIDS makes us wonder how much of a future we have.'[7] There is power in being able to conceive of a future, as Savage emphasizes. He employs fatherhood, specifically, as a way of drawing a line under the devastation wrought by AIDS. 'At its darkest hour,' Savage suggests, 'AIDS seemed as if it would swallow all of us up. But now, thanks to those wonder cocktails, gay men, with H.I.V. and without, can imagine our lives going on and on – provided we stay the hell out of Wyoming.'[8] The allusion to Matthew Shepard, the young gay man brutally beaten and killed in Laramie, Wyoming, in October 1998, is a reminder that while violence and death still pose a significant threat to gay men, medical advancement (for those who could access it) is such that the threat of HIV/AIDS is now second to personal attack. Savage encapsulates neatly the idea that fatherhood not only opens up a future for gay men, through which their lives may go 'on and on', but also acts as a salve on the trauma caused by the AIDS epidemic.

Here AIDS is both relegated to the past and to a space outside the family, recalling the frequent and problematic designation of AIDS as other to the (assumed heterosexual) family.[9] Savage reveals an ostensibly post-AIDS landscape that must be understood as being informed by financial, medical and geographical privilege. The notion that there is an 'end' of AIDS[10] ignores its continued presence in the lives of millions around the world. His claims root this future-through-fatherhood in a particular American temporality, not only in the passing reference to Wyoming but also in the assumption that the 'darkest hour' of the AIDS epidemic has passed, with the United States benefiting from the availability of highly active antiretroviral therapy (HAART) by the mid-1990s.[11] With reference to his and his partner's adoption of a son, Savage suggests that 'considering what the last 15 years were like, perhaps that future is the ultimate status item for gay men'.[12] This demarcation of 'the last 15 years' as the boundary of the threat of AIDS, beyond which it cannot reach, places AIDS firmly in the past and children firmly in the future. As a result, fatherhood becomes the underlying structural element of this future, not just for straight men but for gay men too. Edelman, in highlighting Savage's commitment to 'compulsory reproduction', observes that parenthood is cast in opposition to 'the lethal counterweight of narcissism, AIDS, and death'.[13] The narcissism that has historically been equated with homosexuality is derided as selfish, while the parental narcissism threaded through the very fabric of reproductive futurism paves the way for cultural acceptance. Fatherhood promises a sense of immortality, a form of completion that works against the erasure of death.

This attitude of parenthood as progress, of fatherhood as the key with which to unlock the door of a meaningful future, is embedded within the narratives of the films discussed here. While the representation of gay fatherhood is encouraging, however, the execution reveals some significant limitations on the autonomy of the men in question. In *The Object of My Affection*, pregnant Nina (Jennifer Aniston) is adamant that 'none of the old rules apply' as she asks her gay best friend and roommate George (Paul Rudd) to co-parent her baby. Nina and the film are ostensibly progressive in their outlook. 'We can make it up for ourselves,' she tells a sceptical George, in a move that appears to transcend biology and expectation in favour of a more inclusive form of family. Her offer suggests a broadening of paternal horizons that allow George, as a gay man, to be situated within – rather than outside – the family. However, there remains a continued reliance upon heterosexual genital reproduction, in which George's opportunity to become a father relies on Nina's prior relationship with Vince (John Pankow). George's reduced autonomy is exacerbated by a continued reliance upon a visualization of the family within a heteronormative nuclear paradigm, rejecting same-sex parenting in favour of limiting gay fatherhood to an arrangement with a straight woman. While Nina is actively choosing this version of family, for George this constitutes something of a best – and final – offer.

When Nina states that 'none of the old rules apply', it recalls Edelman's argument that reproductive futurism is so pervasive and inarguable as to be almost invisible, structuring the political order to such a degree that it is impossible to be for or against it, as everyone is already assumed to be on the same side. This dismissal of the 'old rules' does not go so far as dismissing the one overarching rule, that meaning is sought in the future and that this future is to be achieved through the child. The renewed availability of a future within a period so close temporally to the AIDS epidemic is no doubt promising. However, funnelling the promise of survival through fatherhood becomes problematic when it is the only option made available, particularly when cast as a pure alternative to an empty, hedonistic existence, as in both *Object* and *The Next Best Thing*. Fatherhood has long been articulated as involving a significant amount of self-sacrifice. In the case of George, as with Hollywood's other gay dads, this sacrifice bleeds much further into his personal and political life than it does for his straight counterparts, so that at best, 'gay' and 'father' remain uncomfortable consorts. On closer inspection, what exist as the antithesis of AIDS and death – the child and the future – involve a significant death of self in order to achieve realization.

Bersani addresses the issue of 'self-erasure' in a discussion regarding assimilation, suggesting that in attempting to achieve distance from an 'enforced identity',

> we are reduced to playing subversively with normative identities – attempting, for example, to 'resignify' the family for communities that defy the usual assumptions about what constitutes a family. These efforts, while valuable, can have assimilative rather than subversive consequences; having de-gayed themselves, gays melt into the culture they like to think of themselves as undermining.[14]

For Bersani, 'De-gaying gayness ... accomplishes in its own way the principal aim of homophobia: the elimination of gays', observing that the 'consequence of self-erasure is ... self-erasure'.[15] Constructing fatherhood through a heteronormative lens, and bestowing the label of 'father' only on those men willing to, as Bersani would have it, 'de-gay' themselves (along sexual, political and social lines), welcomes gay fathers only at the point of significant self-sacrifice, a survival based on a paradoxical erasure of the self.

Bad equations and logical families

This demand for sacrifice is obscured by the narratives of choice that underpin these films. Both *Object* and *The Next Best Thing* are structured around a close friendship between a gay man and a straight woman. Such screen pairings were increasingly common in the 1990s and early 2000s,[16] and Baz Dreisinger suggests that gay male friends represent 'a new incarnation of the perfect man', chosen by straight women as a viable and appealing alternative to disappointing straight men.[17] This notion of choice is significant inasmuch as it reflects the fundamental feature of what author Armistead Maupin calls the 'logical family',[18] built not on obligation or blood relation but on choice and acceptance. A 'logical', 'chosen'[19] or 'queer'[20] family suggests a myriad of possible kinship patterns, free of the limitations imposed by the socio-political rhetoric of a nuclear, biological family that 'understands biological parents as inherently superior'.[21] Nina and Abbie's move beyond these narrow definitions of family are a deliberate and active attempt to choose a different, potentially more fulfilling path. As Nina tells George, she and Vince are a 'bad equation'. In George, she glimpses a better future for herself and her child.

To justify Nina's invocation of personal choice over biological prerogative, the characterization of George and Vince is crucial. Vince is just boorish enough that Nina's aversion is understandable to the audience, while George must represent a significantly better choice to ensure Nina is not demonized for her dismissal of the biological father. Cast in the role of romantic lead despite his sexuality, George occupies the space of the 'right partner', positioned to 'save' the heroine from an ill-advised commitment.[22] Like other on-screen gay best friends, he is attentive and sensitive. He willingly accompanies Nina to dance classes and stays up late to eat ice cream and discuss their failed relationships. Moreover, his job as an enthusiastic primary school teacher ensures his credentials as a father are sound. In choosing George, the restrictive logic of the nuclear family is subjugated by the freedom to choose your own family.

Considering Nina's offer, George too is given a choice. Choice is crucial to the visualization of gay fatherhood in these films. It connotes activity and privilege, not least in the very act of being offered the option in the first place. The fact that George can choose fatherhood at all plays into the notion of western entitlement and a particular Americanized viewpoint, especially when considering the contemporary presence of AIDS and the discrimination faced by gay men worldwide. George is a product of a time and place that allows his future to be visualized through the lens of fatherhood; that in fact allows it to be visualized at all.

Ingrained in this privileged position, however, is a distinct passivity that characterizes George's entire relationship to his potential fatherhood. The 1990s witnessed frequent and often heated debate regarding gay parental equality and recognition. Legally, the status of gay parents remained uncertain, particularly when no biological relationship existed between parent and child. While some states moved towards explicit legal recognition of second-parent or joint adoption, others enacted prohibitive laws.[23] Many more states retained ambiguous legislation, with decisions often decided on a case-by-case basis.[24] From the 1980s onwards, gay women could opt for alternative insemination or in vitro fertilization, while gay men were more often reliant upon surrogacy and adoption.[25] These options, however, require both time and money.[26] As a result, fatherhood was more readily an option for middle-class, affluent, established couples. For George, a single man on a teacher's salary, the film perhaps reflects the reality that an informal arrangement with a friend may be one of the more accessible routes to fatherhood. However, it also neatly sidesteps any engagement with how individuals or same-sex couples can and do choose to have children. Neither does the film engage with the politics of George's desire to be a father. Instead, it relies on a model of accidental fatherhood via a straightforward case of heterosexual genital reproduction. For George, the prospect of fatherhood is a surprising one, characterized by his realization that 'I don't always have to be the one watching [the children] leave.' If fatherhood is understood as a form of active masculine survival, the passivity with which George is offered this role has implications for the realization of his own future. A space in which gay men can be imagined as fathers emerges, yet its projection through a heteronormative framework determines that they remain beholden to the actions and choices of others. Here, in contradistinction to Canetti's declaration that '[t]he moment of *survival* is the moment of power' is the concept of survival without power, a shadowy, accidental fatherhood offered as a simulacrum of the real thing.[27]

The Next Best Thing is similarly constructed around a gay male/straight female relationship, with one crucial variation. Robert believes, erroneously, that he is Sam's biological father, resulting from a drunken one-night stand with Abbie. His fatherhood is therefore characterized less by passivity than George's, yet it is still predicated upon an act of heterosexual genital reproduction. Fatherhood is again narrowed to a heteronormative framework, as the film fails to acknowledge any other way in which Robert might become a father. This is encapsulated in a conversation between Robert and his mother Helen (Lynn Redgrave), who suggests, 'It's an opportunity that's come up. It won't come up again.' Helen believes that Robert's only chance at fatherhood is through the accidental impregnation of his best friend. Robert, accepting Abbie's co-parenting proposal, explains, 'I don't want to be some gay uncle who lives on the other side of the tracks with his roommate Bruce, who no one's supposed to talk to. I want to be the baby's father, forever and always.' He, it seems, agrees with his mother. The possibility of Robert and the fictional Bruce having a child together is left unacknowledged. Robert either has a child with Abbie or is consigned to a shady, unfulfilling existence as 'uncle'.

The Birdcage does portray two men, Albert (Nathan Lane) and Armand Goldman (Robin Williams), as co-parents. The difference here is that their son Val (Dan Futterman) is an adult and so little in the way of active, hands-on parenting is necessary. This effectively eliminates any image of two gay men bringing up a young child, which has often attracted unwarranted unease among homophobic campaigners based on erroneous notions of paedophilia. There is also a preoccupation with the missing biological parent, Val's birth mother Katherine (Christine Baranski), foregrounding biological reproduction at the expense of the actual labour of co-parenting, creating a tacit hierarchy of parenthood.[28] Armand, as biological and custodial father, enjoys a clearly defined and accepted role denied to Albert. Katherine's self-confessed lack of maternal instinct and non-existent involvement in Val's upbringing does not preclude her necessary inclusion both in the narrative of the film and in the Goldmans' shambolic family dinner, thrown to appease the conservative relatives of Val's fiancée Barbara (Calista Flockhart). When Albert mourns the fact that they won't have more children, Armand responds, 'Not without a miracle.' The 'miracle' required for Armand and Albert to become parents again highlights Val's conception as a one-time-only deal, just as Robert and George perceive their own chances of becoming Dad. Once again, a straight woman is required to facilitate gay fatherhood.

In all these scenarios, the 'chosen' family is subjugated to the primacy of heterosexual genital reproduction. Reproduction outside of this model is often perceived as being unnatural, and alternative reproductive technologies commonly retain connotations of artificiality. Sylviane Agacinski refers to the perception that 'It takes a certain "violence," if one is homosexual, to want a child,'[29] and this violence is reflected in scenes preceding Abbie and Robert's one-night stand, in which furniture is overturned, lamps are smashed and glasses and vases are broken in a 'disorienting and destructive brawl'.[30] In choosing to ignore the various ways in which gay men may become fathers beyond heterosexual genital reproduction, these films limit the autonomy of gay men who must instead rely on happy accidents and 'miracles'.

For George, Robert and Albert, denying a biological relationship between father and child bestows a kind of passive impotency and suggests a desire to disassociate the child from a blood relation to gay men, blood (and semen) being implicated in the threat of HIV/AIDS. In court, Robert argues that biology has no bearing on his parenting ability and refers to blood 'getting bad', alluding further to this unease. Denying Robert's biological relation to Sam disrupts Robert's survival, however, as it becomes clear that for the court, blood does matter. Once again, the court's narrow definition of fatherhood penalizes the wrong man. There is a continued cultural approximation of homosexuality with sterility, emphasized through suggestions of unnaturalness and non-reproductivity.[31] Sue Ellen Case sums up this perceived dichotomy in two opposing equations, 'hetero=sex=life' and 'homo=sex=unlife'.[32] While Nina may dismiss Vince, the baby and herself as a 'bad equation', in the end the equations that prevail are those proposed by Case. If they are to access the future staked to their potential fatherhood, George and Robert must do so on someone else's terms. The failure to choose this future, restricted as it is, propels them back to the realms of the 'unlife', the antithesis of survival.

'Like a family': Authenticity and imitation

When Nina clarifies her vision of future family life, she explains to George, 'I thought we could keep living together. Like a family.' The choice of words is telling. Nina envisages them living 'like', not 'as' a family, and this subtle distinction becomes a fault line in the image. It suggests both an assimilationist desire for imitation ('like') and an acknowledgement that there remains a space between this imitation and the monogamous, nuclear, heteronormative 'family' to which it aspires ('as'). Nina's vision is further undermined as childish and naive through the visual composition of the scene in which Nina first proposes her co-parenting plan to George. This scene takes place at a fairground as they both ride the children's rollercoaster, surrounded by gaudy lights. Male homosexuality has long been associated pejoratively with assumptions of 'arrested development' and 'perpetual adolescence', and cramming George's body into the tiny rollercoaster seat only perpetuates these associations.[33] The setting subverts the wisdom of Nina's proposition. It is as if she and George are simply playing at families, only one step removed from the playhouses and dolls of childhood.

Figure 10 Nina and George discuss parenthood in *The Object of My Affection* (1998). 20th Century Fox.

This lack of authenticity dogs Hollywood's representations of gay fatherhood, in which allusions to performance persist. George appears on stage at the beginning and end of the film, bookending his role in not-quite-real terms, while Robert frequently engages in elaborate play and performance. Performativity has long been a preoccupation of gender and queer studies, revealing the constructed nature of gender and sexuality.[34] Here, however, these references to performance act not as critique but to reinforce a sense of masculine inadequacy and unnaturalness. To place gay fathers persistently in performative roles retains connotations of femininity, essentially refusing authoritatively masculine positions to gay fathers and rooting masculine parenting in heterosexuality.[35] In one scene, George watches a father and son play baseball and is consequently convinced to accept Nina's offer. But George's placement outside the playground's perimeter, removed from the site of father–son bonding by a metal fence, hints at a lingering unease surrounding George's ability to be a masculine father. By applying various caveats – peripheral, feminine, infantile – to its imagining of gay fatherhood, *Object* circumscribes the survival of George's identity and his capacity to perform masculine fatherhood even as it advances the hopeful possibility of the future.

Robert, too, is frequently visualized in a performative role. In one scene, he and Sam play in the garden, dressed in homemade spaceship costumes. Robert also creates the 'Adventures of Princess Tinyfuse' by pretending to read books upside down to reveal hidden stories. When Abbie dispatches Robert to retrieve her keys from her hostile ex, he does not assume a display of authority, or threaten violence; rather, he dresses flamboyantly and embarrasses Kevin (Michael Vartan) into returning the keys by pretending (in front of Kevin's friends) that they are ex-lovers. Underlining the link between heterosexuality, masculinity and authentic fatherhood, Yvonne Tasker observes a definite distinction between Robert and Abbie's new partner Ben (Benjamin Bratt). At the beach, Ben runs through the surf with Sam on his shoulders, displaying a masculine 'ease', while Robert is isolated in the foreground, sitting on a blanket, a fragile and forlorn figure.[36]

George's speech to Nina, in which he accepts her offer to co-parent, plays on this notion of genuine fatherhood as a masculine privilege. 'I always thought that I could teach other people's children,' he begins,

> but someone else, you know, a real guy like Vince gets to take them home. Then I thought, I don't always have to be the one watching them leave. I don't always have to be the one who waits for twilight to pass. For the first time I thought, I could be the guy who says goodnight.

Here, George demonstrates two things: one, the realization that a future, through fatherhood, is available to him ('I could be'); and two, that fatherhood is anchored to a particular version of masculinity, as embodied in 'a real guy' like Vince. In this moment, fatherhood is not so much available to George, as available to George-as-imitation-of-Vince. Eve Kosofsky Sedgwick suggests that 'the healthy homosexual' (i.e. a gay man who finds acceptance in mainstream culture) is 'a) one who is already grown up and b) acts masculine'.[37] George's acceptance as a father is thus tempered by suggestions regarding his childishness and his unmanliness. It taps into that conservative demand that gay men 'grow up and become responsible citizens' to be accepted by mainstream culture.[38] Such labels similarly attach themselves to Robert and to Albert, who is prone to throwing histrionic tantrums and is described by Armand at one point as being 'practically a breast'. To take Sedgwick's term, if George is not strictly 'a healthy homosexual', by these criteria he is unhealthy (again inviting parallels with AIDS) and potentially Other to the family. By presenting fractured and incomplete images of George and Robert as 'real' (mature, masculine, heterosexual) men the films ensure that their status as 'father' remains uncertain. Imitation becomes a necessary condition of fatherhood and yet the performance of this imitation brings its own limitations.

Essentially, as these films attempt to mount an assimilative vision of the family that includes gay men in a paternal role, an elision occurs whereby the man is both awarded and not awarded fatherhood. In binding him to such a heteronormative vision of the family, his potentially queer (non-straight) sexuality is neutralized, yet the potential of this queerness is never fully erased, thus threatening to disrupt the future that is, in theory, on offer. Rather than actively choosing the future, or indeed no future, George and Robert occupy a passive in-between space that connotes a weakened, de-masculinized, sort-of fatherhood.

This 'sort-of' fatherhood is linked directly to the faltering illusion of a heteronormative family. For the first five years of Sam's life he, Robert and Abbie live together as a family, albeit with Robert and Abbie occupying different bedrooms. When Sam, troubled by the teasing of his peers, questions this arrangement, his parents are uncomfortable with providing the answer. There is palpable discomfort with acknowledging their unconventional – yet functional – parenting arrangement. Even as Robert and Abbie find a solution that seems to work for them, expectations intrude. That their arrangement breaks down when they meet other romantic partners reveals the fragility of their family set-up, a model that depends on imitation to hold together. As such, the progressive implications of such alternative arrangements are undermined by the reality: such models have little flexibility, particularly for the gay men working within them, convinced that this is their only opportunity to be a dad.

Likewise, George and Nina's first forays into their impending parenthood are giddy and idyllic. They live harmoniously in their shared apartment. They attend ultrasound appointments, where George is visibly rapturous, moved not only by his awe of human reproduction but also his location within its midst. In another scene they go shopping, arm in arm, for baby paraphernalia. 'Do you think most married couples are as happy as we are?' George asks as they browse. Though this scene – and this line – is intended to confirm the superiority of their chosen future, it is further indicative of imitation, of aspiration to a more traditional model. George's suggestion relies on the assumption that (heterosexual) marital bliss is still the standard that they will measure themselves by. To legitimize their own arrangement they must not only match but also exceed the happiness experienced by 'most married couples'. George and Nina, as a result, are more inclined to imitate and aspire to a heterosexual relationship than they are to carve out any recognizable alternative, an aspiration that enfolds Nina's own attraction to George. Once again, however, romance conspires to reveal the fragility of this arrangement. Moments after George smugly reflects on their happiness, he comes face to face with an ex. As they flirt, Nina looks on, troubled, a precursor of what will come later when George meets Paul (Amo Gulinello) and tries to balance his impending fatherhood with a new relationship. George and Nina's version of family crumbles under the weight of romantic and sexual fulfilment, bearing out its imitative quality and the restrictions placed on George as an active gay man who also wishes to be a father. That Nina can take away her offer of fatherhood because she is uncomfortable with George 'fucking a man in the next room' affirms the disingenuous nature of her original proposal.

Analysing both films, Stella Bruzzi proposes the idea of a 'domestic "third term"',[39] recalling Marjorie Garber's 'third term', referring to the unique space occupied by cross-dressing individuals in relation to binary definitions of gender.[40] Bruzzi's adaptation of the term to cover domestic arrangements further recalls Valerie Lehr's extensive work on queer kinship, in which '[t]he ability of gays and lesbians to play a role in constructing … an alternative narrative [of family] requires that we reject making arguments about our worth as citizens on the basis of our ability to copy, albeit with some modification, the sexual family'.[41] Lehr's contention that imitation should be abandoned in favour of forging genuinely alternative forms of family resonates in

Bruzzi's 'third term', which dictates that the union formed between a straight woman, gay man and child, 'should not be subsumed into and understood as being either heterosexual marriage or a gay relationship' but rather afforded its own space.[42] Karin Quimby makes a similar claim regarding the relationship between the titular characters in *Will & Grace* (1998–2006), suggesting that they 'are navigating their way through a relationship that has no prescribed model in our culture'.[43] There is an echo of Michel Foucault's question at the root of this third term: 'What relations, through homosexuality, can be established, invented, multiplied and modulated?'[44] Nina's belief that 'none of the old rules apply' suggests the beginning of an answer to this question. She theoretically establishes a space in which it is possible to form a more desirable image of family within previously uncharted territory, a space where such a 'domestic "third term"' can be imagined.

Though it is a compelling reading, within the narratives of both films it remains little more than a fallacy, however. Judith Butler suggests that there are spaces – what she terms 'nonplaces' – where it is possible for alternative forms of kinship to operate, perhaps along the lines of such a 'third term'.[45] Yet to exist in these 'nonplaces' is to elude recognition from others, as well as self-recognition. George and Nina may believe that they have discovered something superior in their attempt to establish one such 'nonplace', yet their attempts to define it within the already available lexicon of kinship ('like' a marriage, 'like' a family) ensures that this 'third term', or 'nonplace', remains elusive.

The end of *Object* compounds its unease with a truly alternative vision of family. On the surface, it appears fully committed to the joyfully complicated parameters of the family it has created, at the centre of which stands Nina's daughter Molly (Sarah Hyland), appearing in a school play orchestrated by George, now the school's principal. This, too, is a reflection of the film's progressive intent, as fears over gay teachers routinely stoked discriminatory campaigns in the 1970s and 1980s, notably Anita Bryant's Save Our Children crusade in Florida and the so-called Briggs Initiative in California.[46] In the audience, watching Molly, are the players that make up Nina's rule-defying family: Nina, Vince, Nina's new partner Louis (Kevin Carroll), her stepsister Constance (Allison Janney), Constance's husband (Alan Alda) and teenage daughter Sally (Paz de la Huerta), Paul and Paul's former lover and mentor, Rodney (Nigel Hawthorne), now ersatz grandfather to Molly. Afterwards, Molly is thrilled to report that she had 'more people come see me than anyone', to which Nina responds, 'Honey, you're just the luckiest little girl.'[47] Such an inclusive image of the family appears to validate Nina's advocacy of the chosen family. Yet this was not the family that Nina envisaged originally, and even these final scenes end with the gradual dispersal of all these characters until only George, Nina and Molly are left. While the audience are aware that Nina and George are no longer a 'couple' in the way they once were, the final shot immortalizes them as a heterosexual family unit, walking down the street together with Molly between them. Though George and Nina both have men waiting for them at home, this is elided in favour of one final glimpse of the 'right' couple. Molly's chosen family is collapsed into the traditional image of mother, father and child, freezing George's fatherhood (such as it exists at this point) within a heteronormative framework at the film's end.

Ultimately, the choice facing Robert and George is neither expansive nor accommodating. Robert, powerless, must watch from the sidelines as Abbie attempts to build a more conventional family with Ben and excise Robert from the narrative. George must face Nina's cruel ultimatum, to choose between her (and thus the baby) and Paul. This all-or-nothing approach circumscribes both men's experience of fatherhood to such a degree that any aberration from a normative model of the family ensures a regression back to 'uncle'. This withholding of legitimacy has important ramifications. Survival is based upon the ability to imitate straight men, first and foremost. This imitation, furthermore, must take place within a relationship that mimics a monogamous, heterosexual one. Any deviation from this framework results in a cessation of fatherhood. Robert insists in court that he is both 'a father' and 'a homosexual man', yet these films in fact rest on the incompatibility of these two markers of identity. Similarly, George can be an active father or an active gay man, but in *Object*'s vision of 'like a family' only one is permissible at once. The conditions of fatherhood are, ultimately, rooted in a form of self-erasure for both men.

'Just for tonight': Morality and masquerade in *The Birdcage*

Themes of authenticity, imitation and masquerade also permeate *The Birdcage*. Here legitimacy overtly relies on performance, though the film is at least open in its critique of this state of affairs. However, a similar problem remains. Despite its commitment to confirming Armand and Albert's great worth as fathers, *The Birdcage* cannot escape from the primacy of the white, normative heterosexual family unit in the shape of the Keeleys, Val's future in-laws. When Val announces his engagement to Barbara, his singular concern is how to pass off his unconventional family as acceptable to Senator Keeley (Gene Hackman), a conservative Republican, and his wife Louise (Dianne Wiest).

In this context, Val's misgivings are understandable. Armand is the flamboyant owner of a South Beach drag club; Albert, as Starina, is the club's star act. The two live above the club in a cheerful, well-worn apartment with their eccentric Guatemalan housekeeper Agador (Hank Azaria). In contrast, the staid Keeleys occupy a faceless, lavishly decorated mansion, and their interactions are stiff and reserved.

When Val tells Armand he is engaged, Armand is quick to embrace him, even as he expresses mild disapproval. Barbara, however, faces an interrogation as to the Goldmans' social and financial credentials. These two scenes lay the groundwork for a favourable comparison between the Goldmans, who value the love of a family, and the Keeleys, who value its appearance. Only when the senator wishes to detract from the scandal of his running mate being found dead in the bed of an underage black prostitute does the marriage become appealing as a way of restoring the family's public image. 'A wedding is hope,' Louise declares, 'and a white wedding is family and morality and tradition.' For the Keeleys, the wedding symbolizes the triumph of 'love and optimism' over 'cynicism and sex', the irony being that it is the Keeleys who are engaging in a cynical piece of misdirection from a sex scandal, while it is the Goldmans who promise love (if not exactly optimism).

Like the previously discussed films, *The Birdcage* sets up its queer family as ostensibly preferable to its straight counterpart. Armand and Albert are undoubtedly the more desirable parents. Yet this recognition does not translate into legitimacy. Instead, they must contort their loving, supportive family into a version that appeases the Keeleys, a version that relies on the enduring appearance of heteronormativity and the erasure of the autonomy of its members, with the exception of Val, notably the only straight man. True to *La Cage*, the film has tremendous fun with these contortions, as Armand and Albert mount a complicated masquerade to fool the Keeleys and ensure their son's happiness. Beneath this mischievous pleasure, however, lies a web of sacrifice and concession, a demand that is not made of the Keeleys. To save Val's future, the Goldmans must change their name, their home, their appearance and, in Albert's case, their gender, in order to pacify a couple who would rather they did not exist.

Originally, Armand is adamant that Val will not dictate such changes. When Val suggests that Armand should be 'a little less obvious', his father is unimpressed: 'Yes, I wear foundation. Yes, I live with a man. Yes, I'm a middle-aged fag. But I know who I am, Val. It took me twenty years to get here and I'm not going to let some idiot senator destroy that. Fuck the senator.' Soon after, however, Armand capitulates. He submerges twenty years of struggle beneath a façade designed to avoid jeopardizing Val's chances of a successful heterosexual partnership, within which 'fucking' retains the prospect of reproduction, so long as Armand doesn't 'fuck the senator' first. The success of the heterosexual romance is paramount in *The Birdcage*, 'constructed on the bent backs of gay fathers (proving their love through self-abnegation and denial), and the arrogant shoulders of straight sons (proving their privilege through requesting the denial)'.[48] The Goldmans comply because to deny Val would be to bring into question the primacy of their fatherhood. Val, meanwhile, feels secure in the knowledge that he will be obeyed. This peculiar reversal of father–son relations works once again to infantilize the gay father, as Armand is chastised for his excessive and 'obvious' choices.

A comprehensive makeover replaces the apartment's cheerful flamboyance and numerous phallic sculptures with a more austere interior design, while a dark, formal suit is substituted for Armand's patterned shirts and colourful accessories. Val reminds Armand that at school, he was permitted to tell the teacher his father was a 'businessman', without elaboration. When Armand bristles, reminding Val he is no longer a child, Val is quick to remind him petulantly, 'I could still get hurt'. That Val's marriage is based on the Keeleys' acceptance of his family is not interrogated; the wedding's importance supersedes the 'dignity' of Albert and Armand.[49] Moreover, the potential 'hurt' to which Val may be exposed displaces the actual hurt experienced by Albert, who is excluded from the dinner after he fails to present as authentically straight. 'It's just for tonight,' Val placates, but Albert is under no illusion: 'I understand. It's just while people are

Figure 11 The Goldmans reinvent themselves as the Colemans in *The Birdcage* (1996). United Artists.

here.' Prior to the dinner, Armand gives Albert a palimony agreement, telling him, 'You own half of my life and I own half of yours. There's only one place in the world I call home and it's because you're there.' That Armand lets Val modify this home – both the physical home and the home that Armand locates within his relationship with Albert – becomes a stark suppression of one love for the realization of another.

Val's request for subjugation continues, extending beyond clothing and interior design to another pillar of the family's identity: their Jewishness. In an act of Jewish 'passing', inviting parallels between Jewish and homosexual persecution, the gay Goldmans become the straight Colemans.[50] Comedy is derived from Senator Keeley's misrecognition of the elephant in the room, exclaiming 'You're Jewish?' as the masquerade is revealed, where an audience might expect, 'You're gay?' This deflection only serves to further highlight the cultural assumptions of what a legitimate American family looks like. A straight, white, conservative Christian identity is reinforced as being synonymous with a normative 'American' identity, raising questions about exactly who is deemed worthy of inheriting the very American future so at stake in millennial Hollywood.

The masquerade of Christianity is one thing, but to be authentic in the eyes of the Keeleys, what the Goldmans really need is a mother. To this end an aggrieved Albert, banished from the party after failing to heed Armand's lessons in masculinity, creates the role of Mrs Coleman for himself. Mrs Coleman is a model conservative housewife, espousing the benefits of a 'stricter moral code' and charming the Senator while Armand and Val look on with horror. Comedy aside, Albert's appearance as Mrs Coleman is a bid for the recognition due to him as a parent, but the fact that Albert has actively mothered (and fathered) Val *as himself* matters little in this scenario. The Keeleys, as the 'ordinary' family, must be placated, while Albert only risks further admonishment. Val's birth mother Katherine, meanwhile, endures the reverse, as she is co-opted into performing 'mother' for the benefit of Val's future. Katherine must conceal her own identity as not-wife ('I'm between husbands,' she reveals earlier) and not-mother ('I'm not exactly maternal') for Val's sake. As a woman bound neither by marriage nor children, Katherine is just as threatening to the heteronormative family as two gay men, adopting the queer position against reproductive futurism as she rejects parenthood, and she too is compelled to perform.

As the charade unravels and Val realizes he has done his fathers a disservice, he reveals Albert's true identity, prompting Senator Keeley to ask 'just how many mothers' Val has. 'Just one,' he replies, removing Albert's wig. Albert's parenthood and Katherine's non-maternal identity are belatedly acknowledged. Yet Val stops short of referring to Albert as his father. In his own analysis, Keller observes that Armand and Albert 'represent positions within the traditional gender hierarchy of marriage' and chooses to refer to Albert using female pronouns.[51] However, this obscures the reality of two men parenting together. It conflates maternal traits with motherhood and denies the parental model of two fathers bringing up a child, instead relying on a traditional image that is performed rather than challenged. Even in its revealed unconventionality, Val ensures that his family conforms to the same nuclear framework that dictates the structure of George and Robert's not-so-queer families. Once again, authenticity is paradoxically suggested through performance and imitation.

Sex, politics and sacrifice

The big reveal comes too late for the Goldmans, none of whom (except Val) escape having to perform roles that require a comprehensive modification of identity. The Keeleys may be constructed as the poor equivalent of a truly loving family, but their right to their sense of self is never questioned. This sacrifice dilutes the very future offered through fatherhood. It is no longer Armand and Albert who survive, in this version of events, but rather a facsimile of themselves that undermines the very notion of survival.

Sacrifice is inherent in the cultural construction of fatherhood. Time, money, sleep, freedom and personal fulfilment: giving up any or all of these is routinely framed as a requirement of becoming a parent. The implicit reward for such sacrifice is the particular and exclusive joy of fatherhood. One sacrifices a part of himself to the next generation and gains in return that illusion of immortality, a trade that is understood culturally as venerable and selfless. But the sacrifice imagined in these films goes beyond this, demanding the renunciation of identity, politics and sexuality in exchange for a future. These visions of gay fatherhood obscure 'gay' in favour of 'father' until this obfuscation of gay identity is disrupted and fatherhood is curtailed as a result. What emerges, therefore, is not an image of fatherhood that plays a part in alleviating masculine crisis – as it does in the case of straight men during the same period – but one that involves a severe limiting of autonomy and thus calls into question the very concept of masculine survival.

Political erasure is crucial in maintaining gay men as unthreatening to a mainstream audience. In the 1990s, two threads of gay political activism dominated. One centred on politicized AIDS campaigns, led by groups such as the AIDS Coalition to Unleash Power (ACT UP). ACT UP mounted direct-action initiatives and adopted the slogan Silence = Death, fighting for political recognition of AIDS, access to improved medical funding and treatment and legislative change. The other saw rights campaigns emerge around marriage equality, parental rights, access to healthcare benefits and anti-discrimination legislation, spearheaded by organizations such as the Human Rights Campaign. Curiously, these films fail to engage with either strand of political visibility. Despite being transplanted to 1990s Florida, *The Birdcage* is hardly a daring update of its parent. Armand may own a drag club, but there is little sense that either he or Albert is engaged with a wider, contemporary gay community. Senator Keeley's right-wing 'family values' policies confirm that Reagan–Bush conservatism has made it to Florida, which only makes the omission of gay rights and AIDS activism more noticeable. Criticism of this conservative family values rhetoric is woven through the film, but it remains gentle and more or less forgiving. Even when Armand presents Albert with the palimony agreement, the moment is personal – Armand is essentially apologizing for taking Albert for granted – rather than political. That this scene takes place in a bus shelter also separates it from the rest of the film, rendering it of little consequence and almost apologetic in its inclusion.

This sense of apology, of not wanting to intrude on the privilege of their straight counterparts, characterizes the conditions of gay fatherhood in these films. Writing about lesbian motherhood, Nancy Polikoff argues that separating the two elements is 'politically devastating'.[52] Nevertheless, an apolitical pursuit of parenthood must triumph, one in which fatherhood becomes a private endeavour, not a political action. In *Object* Vince, a socialist lawyer (or 'Bolshevik', as Constance declares), suggests that George should be teaching in a public school rather than a private academy, standing up for other 'disenfranchised' people. George, however, rejects this label. As Vince chastises him, Nina and George share a weary, knowing look that invites the audience to dismiss Vince along with the two of them. This rejection underpins an apolitical gay identity, in which George – a white, professional, American gay man – has little discernible interest in the concept of disenfranchisement. Here is a gay man who is not likely to disrupt proceedings with any seizure of rights or privileges. 'Vince can really fill a room,' Nina reflects with embarrassment, to which the subtext is surely that George cannot, and furthermore has no interest in doing so. George, instead, will occupy the corner of the room, waiting to be invited to the table.

The insistence on an apolitical identity reinforces the desire to construct these characters as safe and unthreatening. Legitimacy and survival are, once again, reliant on a lack of difference. These films rely on the notion of characters who are nominally gay but untainted by any kind of political involvement, recalling Andrea Weiss's '"happen to be gay" syndrome', whereby a character is 'sexually "gay"' but otherwise 'straight', so that their sexuality 'doesn't touch on other aspects of their lives'.[53] This recalls Bersani's notion of '[d]e-gaying gayness' and his contention that such assimilation threatens erasure, whereby the silence of a suppressed gay identity equals a different kind of death. Yet in Hollywood such silence is rewarded with survival. Only by erasing any trace of political concerns with equal rights or AIDS activism can survival be assured to these men, as their fatherhood is mortgaged to such a modification of identity.

Crucially, a lack of political involvement allows for a disavowal of both HIV/AIDS and AIDS activism. AIDS was undeniably part of the reality of being a gay man in 1990s America, not only for those men who contracted HIV but the men who were their friends, their lovers and their community.[54] As a virus, HIV/AIDS does not discriminate along the lines of sexuality or gender – it is, as Nadel points out, a disease 'transmitted by fluids, not by types of people' – but in the United States its most overt devastation was reserved for men who had sex with men.[55] It is notable, therefore, that as an out and active gay man in New York, an epicentre of the epidemic in the 1980s, George has a negligible relationship with AIDs and people with AIDS. Three years before the events of *Object*, AIDS was the leading cause of death for men in George's age demographic; it seems disingenuous to imagine George inhabits a world that AIDS has not impacted. *The Next Best Thing* goes a little further, beginning with the funeral of David's (Neil Patrick Harris) partner Joe and later showing David's collection of pill bottles, acknowledging his own ongoing treatment. This depiction, however, remains at the margins. If AIDS can be related to 'a future which constantly diminishes',[56] then the insistence that AIDS belongs in the past and to other, less responsible men, is necessary in order to pave the way for George and Robert to be constructed as gay men with a future.

Along with political sacrifice, then, is an attendant sexual sacrifice that must also be understood within the framework of AIDS. These films present remarkably sexless images of fatherhood, of straight women and of gay men. This manifests first in the unease surrounding the biological relationship between gay father and child. The disengagement of fatherhood from reproduction may be identified as a positive disambiguation, a re-articulation of fatherhood along the lines of social rather than biological function. However, in these films it only serves to undermine the gay father and relegate him to a secondary role. Secondly, there is a persistent lack of sex, rendering gay fathers 'safe' through their apparent de-eroticization.

The chasteness of many of the films discussed in this book has been noted in previous chapters, reflecting both the importance of the family audience to Hollywood studios and a lingering unease around sex triggered by the threat of AIDS. Indeed, a lack of sex even characterizes the decade's biggest political scandal, as Clinton famously and defiantly claimed that he 'did not have sexual relations with that woman ... Miss Lewinsky', in a televised speech to the American public. Here, a lack of sex is originally filtered through the straight female characters. Nina declares confidently that 'sex is no big deal', while Abbie tells Robert that she is 'over' sex and all its complications. This post-sexual approach ensures that the companionable benefits of a relationship are saved, while the 'detriments' of a sexual relationship are avoided; what Dreisinger characterizes as a privileging of 'the warm and fuzzy over the orgasmic'.[57] Abbie's friends, meanwhile, lament their own sexless marriages and express envy for Abbie and Robert's superior companionship, reinforcing Quimby's assertion that these gay man/straight woman partnerships are designed to address 'straight women's dissatisfactions with traditional – marital – definitions of male-female love, commitment, and desire', offering an appealing – if non-sexual – alternative.[58]

This is what Dreisinger refers to as a 'safe eroticism', as the audience is rewarded with a frisson of sexual attraction between the leads that is ultimately left unconsummated.[59] Safe-sex campaigns were a vital part of AIDS activism in the 1980s and 1990s, promoting condom use and non-penetrative sexual activity. Here, 'safe' becomes synonymous with an affectionate, yet ultimately abstemious, bond. At a point when gay male sex was associated with annihilation and death (what Bersani characterizes as 'an unquenchable appetite for destruction'), survival becomes the privilege of those who abstain.[60] De-sexualization is the price of a future, even when that future is imagined through a child, which in these films remains undeniably the product of a sexual union.

Where two gay men are seen parenting together, the solution is to remain bound to a 'queenly, asexual' stereotype that limits any display of physical intimacy, as in *The Birdcage*.⁶¹ For George and Robert, sex with other men becomes an unfulfilling, shadowy endeavour. Newly single, George has a disastrous date with a man who arrives dressed fully in leather, swiftly tarnishing gay sex with fetishistic connotations. The same man is later revealed to be an uncle of one of George's schoolchildren, a reminder of the status Robert and George can be relegated to should they fail to conform. Deterred, George resigns himself to the single bed in Nina's spare room, exchanging romantic and sexual satisfaction for the promise of parental fulfilment. This decision is portrayed as both logical and uniquely viable against a backdrop of empty alternatives, represented by George's ex Joley (Tim Daly). Joley leaves his 'twin-bedded friendship' with George for a younger man and a red sports car, a decision that only serves to reinforce the wisdom of George's choice. Devoid of the same paternal epiphany, Joley loses both George – the 'right' romantic partner – and the chance at fatherhood that George, in his willingness to overlook sex, is rewarded with. That Joley later tries to rekindle a relationship with George further suggests the folly of being distracted by a new man.

Fatherhood stands in opposition to frivolity and becomes the acceptable face of grown-up narcissism. In *The Next Best Thing*, it is David – last seen at his partner's funeral, now surrounded by medication – who expresses scepticism at Robert's decision. 'I'm bored of it all,' Robert counters. 'I'm bored of the parties, I'm bored of the drugs, I'm bored of the body obsession. It's not a sacrifice, you know, it's an opportunity.' This echoes Savage's self-satisfied proclamation that 'many of us have decided we want to fill our time with something more meaningful than sit-ups, circuit parties and designer drugs'.⁶² Not only is Robert on track for a future – and a survival – that David is not, but once again the only viable gay future is explicitly structured against that stereotypically narcissistic imagining of gay male life, an empty, self-centred existence that can only be imagined, in this context, as singularly destructive and reckless. Robert's other gay friends, Vernon and Ashby, are an aging, musical-obsessed couple who are 'maniacs about their stuff', from their elaborate garden to their lavish home and its contents. In the absence of anything else to occupy their time, Vernon and Ashby pursue the empty pleasures of consumerism. Amidst these examples it is implied that Robert, in choosing fatherhood, is making a lucky escape.

His fundamental error, however, is misunderstanding that the 'opportunity' to be a dad is the opposite of 'sacrifice'. Robert, like George, will only be castigated for his attempts to balance fatherhood with a relationship, in this case with an unnamed cardiologist (Mark Valley). Despite the implied seriousness of this relationship, the two men appear on screen together only once, when they break up. In bed, Robert rejects his partner's embrace and turns away, expressing his concern over Sam's impending first day at school. His boyfriend, exasperated, suggests that Robert's heart is no longer in their relationship. Here, Robert's fatherhood directly opposes his capacity for a fulfilling relationship. In contrast, Abbie's relationship with Ben – named and visible – suffers no such fate. While Ben is seen frequently interacting with Sam, Robert's boyfriend has no such involvement and he is conspicuously absent at Sam's well-attended birthday party. Confining their relationship to one unhappy bedroom scene simply reinforces the association between gay men, sex and an ultimate lack of fulfilment.

In the end, only capitulation to a sexless, apolitical identity is compatible with fatherhood. Even then, it is not guaranteed, as Robert discovers. Though he is belatedly reunited with Sam, this does not negate the heartless and unnecessary fact of their separation. These films should not be misunderstood as reflections simply on the sacrifices inherent in parenthood. They are, explicitly, narratives of gay fatherhood that remain uncomfortable with the proximity of a gay identity to a paternal one, narratives in which the only meaningful future is harnessed to a child who can always be denied, or who can deny his parents. For gay men, this future becomes available only in the denial of any kind of active gay identity and the acceptance of a resolutely heteronormative model of family.

Conclusion: All of the old rules apply

Hollywood's project of saving men through fatherhood extends into new territory by the second half of the 1990s. Visualizing gay men as fathers suggests a concerted effort to envisage a future far removed from the stereotypes of narcissistic loneliness or AIDS-induced destruction. In this sense, Hollywood's efforts suggest progress and a willingness to engage with the new horizons of an ostensibly post-AIDS culture, in which survival was once again a reality. No surprise, then, that Hollywood would bind this survival to fatherhood, given its wider preoccupations with such themes during the decade.

The issue remains, however, that this vision of survival remains proscriptive. Rather than adhering to Nina's suggestion that 'none of the old rules apply' these films in fact reiterate familiar models: of the primacy of the white, American, heteronormative family; of the incompatibility of homosexuality with parenthood; of self-modification as a necessary condition of legitimacy. Entry into the realm of the family is predicated upon an apolitical, asexual, ahistorical reimagining of gay male identity, in which to deviate is to risk losing this familial privilege.

Never mind that this denies the myriad and creative ways in which chosen families have been, and are, constructed; what is more pernicious in these films is that fatherhood becomes the *only* form of salvation, meaning or, indeed, happiness. The one rule that does still apply is the iron-clad rule of reproductive futurism. For Armand and Albert to declare their son selfish and refuse his demands, or for

George and Robert to turn down the offers of sort-of fatherhood: this is narratively inconceivable. In case they were in any doubt, other, peripheral gay characters come to signify the dead ends to be avoided, whether these be routes of promiscuity, narcissism, empty extravagance or death.

The linking of fatherhood to the future, then, becomes increasingly problematic when viewed through the lens of gay fatherhood in 1990s Hollywood. Though fatherhood is, technically, a role available to any man – this is, after all, the fundamental basis of its ability to 'save' men in a period of masculine uncertainty – it becomes clear that certain constructions of fatherhood and of masculinity are still required for this survival to be realized. Gay men, who as Savage claims may have more of a conscious desire than most for such a survival, are offered a less-than-fatherhood that fractures their own identity. At the same time, it denies their ability to imagine an existence outside of the normative constraints of the nuclear family and outside of reproductive futurism, without regressing back to the equation of 'homo=sex=unlife'.

Conclusion

To characterize a decade as possessing particular characteristics that can be confined to a ten-year period on the calendar is fraught with difficulty, not least because social and cultural conditions rarely observe these neat temporal designations. The 1990s, however, is broadly coherent as a period of contrast, one part optimism to one part trepidation, one part progressive intent to one part existential crisis. The definite end point of the 1990s – the turn of the millennium – helps to qualify this sense of crisis, anchored as it is to an underlying fear that with the end of the 'American century' would come the end of the United States' own political and cultural dominance. Laura Mulvey identifies an 'indistinct sense of foreboding [belonging] to the year 2000', and it is this pervasive uncertainty that leaves its mark on Hollywood during this same period.[1] Contradiction was rife. Bill Clinton's presidency was rooted in the apparent irreconcilability of youth with political experience and of libido with responsibility. The family was both a site of disintegration and the only cure to a wide variety of social problems. The father, likewise, was both problem and solution. Straight, white men – for so long the universal subject – were undergoing an apparent crisis, as traditional images of masculinity came under scrutiny and the pluralization of masculine identities revealed the inherent constructedness of gendered assumptions of power and dominance.

The same contradictions that imbue these political, familial and social debates are woven through the decade and imprinted on its popular culture. Was the United States a nation looking eagerly towards a bright future, or a nation experiencing significant anxiety as the millennium approached? Were those aforementioned American men still experiencing the power and privilege their fathers had implicitly promised them, or were they facing an uncertain new world in which crisis was a defining condition? On the Hollywood screen, another new world was dawning, one of special effects, swiftly developing digital technology and the growing importance of auxiliary products, augmented by the continued rise of increasingly global conglomerates and the opportunity and competition provided by the home entertainment market.[2] Its narratives, meanwhile, absorbed these nascent anxieties and projected them back at an audience apparently eager for images of upheaval, destruction and destabilization.

As the previous chapters have revealed, Hollywood's solution to this destabilization is to reshape its men into responsible father figures. Their commitment to the next generation and the renunciation of ostensibly selfish or self-centred impulses paves the way for their survival regardless of the uncertainty attached to the future and, in particular, their future as men. Reflecting contemporaneous concerns surrounding fatherhood, families, male role models (both domestic and political) and shifting gender relations, Hollywood links masculine triumph to paternal success and places its faith firmly in Dad – or the man who would be Dad – as the key to ensuring its male protagonists could confidently cross that mythical bridge into the millennium and beyond.

The persistence of these narratives of redemptive fatherhood across genres, enfolding a variety of audiences and running the gamut from blockbuster to semi-independent art-house films, emphasizes the universality of concerns over erasure and continuation. That so many of the films discussed hinge on loss – the loss of the child (whether symbolic or actual), the loss of the father, the loss of the nation – is testament to what is at stake. In this case, it is nothing more or less than the future, brought into stark relief by the symbolic temporality of the millennium. Edelman's work on reproductive futurism is illuminating when used to deconstruct these films for precisely this reason, as it reveals the collective political and social illusion of futurity as the antithesis of death and meaninglessness. With the future under threat, the child becomes the salvific figure, the one capable of delivering wayward men into a more secure existence. In the end, fatherhood is revealed as the saving mechanism capable of allaying the uncertainties of post-millennial masculinity and redirecting adrift men into a reassuringly productive existence. In productivity – and re-productivity – Hollywood stakes the conditions of meaning and therefore survival.

If fatherhood is the persistent thread in these otherwise often disparate films, then a second unifying factor can also be determined. There is, regardless of genre, budget or audience, a desire for mastery embedded in these narratives of paternal redemption. Freud's work on the pleasure principle argues that though humans have a tendency towards pleasure, this is tempered by an opposite tendency towards 'the postponement of satisfaction', the result of which is the 'temporary toleration of unpleasure as a step on the long indirect road to pleasure'.[3] Hollywood cinema is an ideal arena in which to exercise this temporarily delayed quest for pleasure, given the implicit promise of resolution. During the decade, scenarios of upheaval found a natural home on the big screen, as audiences experienced moments of unpleasure with the anticipation of eventual relief. To focus so resolutely on disaster, apocalypse, domestic turmoil and loss clearly illuminates the fears and concerns underlying many of these films, reflective of the anxious cultural moment within which they emerge. However, to persistently re-enact these scenarios on screen – both in a domestic and national context – becomes an elaborate, cinematic game of *fort-da*. The end is glimpsed and then postponed, envisaged only to be delayed or reversed. This is the same whether it is an asteroid being diverted, a father being reinvited into the family home, a bereaved man being given a second chance at fatherhood or a gay man whose reward for subjugating his own identity is the right to be called 'Dad'. That unconscious desire for the end, embedded in the death drive, is temporarily indulged and then rescinded as order is restored.

Fatherhood, then, becomes Hollywood's ultimate tool in this game of mastery. All those existential fears surrounding the millennium and the crisis of masculinity can be reduced, in the end, to a fear of meaninglessness. The rise of male-oriented rights movements during the 1990s, chief among them the men's movement and the fathers' rights movement, incorporate a fear of obsolescence into their rhetoric. The men's movement encouraged men to return to nature, to reconsider their identity as men and re-evaluate their capacity for dominance and power. Men, they suggested, were not defunct but merely lost. Though the fathers' rights movement is in many ways more concerned with tangible issues such as custody and access, it maintains a similar quest for recognition and restoration. Many fathers' rights narratives are characterized by an anxious refutation of any suggestion that fathers are no longer crucial to the family and to their children. Fears over a loss of substance – that 'man' or 'father' may be losing currency – are echoed in those significant political issues of the decade, from the shattered sense of meaning triggered by the AIDS epidemic to the questions over the president's continued ability to speak for the nation. Against all of this, fatherhood is established as an anchor, capable of bestowing worth and meaning on all men. Crucially, it is a route by which the future can be accessed and survival can be assured through an implicit link to the next generation.

It is also a role that is, theoretically, available to any man who might choose to pursue it. Fathers, Hollywood emphasized, came in all shapes and sizes. This is part of its enduring appeal as a solution to men in crisis. Fathers, as portrayed in numerous roles by a common screen presence such as Robin Williams, might be hirsute and funny; they might be neglectful but ultimately well-meaning, like Jim Carrey and Tim Allen's dads; they might be domestically inept, besmirched by weakness, work too hard (or not enough) or reluctant to grow up. They are, frequently, resolutely ordinary, impacted by tragedy or disaster not of their own making. In all cases, the challenge of fatherhood is reassuring surmountable. These are, in the end, narratives of responsibility and investment, recalling that neoliberal ideology so ingrained in US society and politics by the end of the century. This was survival but the kind that men could engineer themselves with a little commitment, some reprioritizing and a dose of paternal love.

Of course, an obstinate focus on survival suggests that there is something from which to survive, in this case the contemporary crisis of masculinity, understood here as an amalgamation of scrutiny over the construction of masculine identity and the perception (if not the reality) of lost power. Though in reality the crisis of masculinity is an exaggeration of persistent – rather than unique – unease regarding men's roles, Hollywood wholeheartedly adopts the crisis and its attendant anxieties regarding erasure and continuance during the 1990s, seeking a solution in the figure of the father and the promise of reproductive futurism. Amidst a preoccupation with apocalypse and destruction in the build-up to the millennium, rendered through cataclysmic scenarios on the big screen, Hollywood constructs a domestic apocalypse in which fatherhood becomes the one solution powerful enough to negate extinction for men struggling to define a coherent masculine identity.

Second chances are common in these scenarios, allowing men who have temporarily failed their children, or who have not considered the benefits of fatherhood, to be redeemed. Redemption is central to this Hollywood project of paternal restoration, an acknowledgement of disappointment that can be rectified. It follows, however, that something must be done about those men who do not take the opportunity for redemption. In constructing fatherhood as such a prominent and unremitting solution to these perceptions of crisis and upheaval, inevitably there must be an acknowledgement of the fate of those men who do not embrace their fatherhood (or who are prevented from doing so), or else who remain wedded to an outdated or unworkable vision of paternity. Often, this is figured as a literal death, frequently at the hands of the 'good' father. Crisp, whose pursuit of his son is based not on fatherly love but possessive vindictiveness in *Kindergarten Cop*, is killed by Kimble, who replaces him as the ideal father figure (and so takes his own second chance). Bowden, in *Cape Fear*, sees off Cady and in doing so glimpses the possibility of his own delayed redemption. In *Falling Down*, Bill's inability to reconfigure his expectations of fatherhood and manhood seals his fate, as Prendergast's fatal shot sends him falling off the end of the pier into the Pacific Ocean. Prendergast, whose own young daughter is dead, is possessed of the valuable knowledge that Bill has refused to internalize: fatherhood is a privilege, not a right to be exploited.

There are, of course, those men who simply fail to see the potential in fatherhood and so reject it: Sean, in *Nine Months*, for example, or Joley (*The Object of My Affection*) and David (*The Next Best Thing*), men who are punished for rejecting parenthood with loneliness, emptiness or death. Here lies the uncomfortable underside of Hollywood's restoration of the father. To refuse to capitulate to the demands of fatherhood and of reproduction becomes increasingly unthinkable. Most overt in representations of gay fatherhood, in which a curtailment of identity becomes a requirement of legitimizing their parenthood, there remains a determined focus not on pluralizing images of masculinity and shattering the dominance of hegemonic constructions of manhood but on shifting the boundaries of power just enough to offer the illusion of progress. The shift from physical, muscular heroics to a more domesticated, emotional, family-oriented model of masculinity undoubtedly marks a significant change in Hollywood's leading men. It opens up a space in which ordinary men might too be heroes of a kind. But beyond this new-found inclusivity an exclusion zone still exists.

Unspoken but inbuilt in these films is the fear of that exclusion zone, a potentially queer space outside of the reproductive familial order and outside of (hetero)normalized expectations. In battling against erasure, these films, and the men within them, are also battling against the realization of that 'other side' that Edelman identifies as being almost invisible and incomprehensible.[4] The 'almost' is important here, because this queer, non-reproductive space – this space in which it is possible to question the value of the future – is glimpsed through the cracks in these films, a manifestation of the anxiety that coalesces around the failure to harness this waiting future. It is displaced, with subdued but unmistakable hysteria, onto melancholic mothers, hedonistic bachelors, divorced fathers and tragic gay men. That there might be another form of masculine survival (indeed, that the value of survival may even be questioned) is suppressed in favour of a wholesale investment in the father as the hero and fatherhood as the saviour. Such is the power of that 'fantasmatic' future and the fear of being left behind.[5]

As a unique temporal occurrence, the millennium provides the backdrop to this futuristic preoccupation. However, Hollywood's – and the nation's – concept of survival underwent a fundamental re-evaluation in the early part of the new century. The solution to the various ostensible crises of the 1990s – of masculinity, of fatherhood, of the presidency – that is, a determined rehabilitation of the father, faltered as a much more tangible, physical crisis engulfed the nation. One year and nine months after the year 2000 dawned and just eight months after Clinton, the president that encapsulated the complexities and contradictions of the pre-millennial moment, left office, the United States experienced a domestic catastrophe with global implications. The 9/11 terrorist attacks on the World Trade Center and the Pentagon brought not only mass death and injury but also a more profound sense of uncertainty. This was not an individual crisis but a national crisis, one that struck at the heart of the United States' sense of itself, its strength and its place in the world. It ensured that 'collective fantasies of the national image were – if not shattered – then radically reframed'.[6]

Where the nation goes, Hollywood inevitably follows, holding up its big screen mirror to the preoccupations of its audiences. And so by the mid-2000s, masculine heroism was once again channelled towards a larger project of protection and defiance, often via a raft of re-emerging superheroes, including *Spider-Man* (Sam Raimi, 2002), *X2: X-Men United* (Bryan Singer, 2003), *Fantastic Four* (Tim Story, 2005), *Superman Returns* (Bryan Singer, 2006) and another reiteration of Batman on the big screen in Christopher Nolan's *Dark Knight* trilogy (2005–12). The focus was once again on saving the nation, whether from supervillains, terrorists or the ever-present threat of natural disaster (*The Day after Tomorrow* [Roland Emmerich, 2004]; *2012* [Emmerich, 2009]). The resurgence of the superhero, in particular, demonstrates a reorientation back towards 'spectacular achievement' as a visual confirmation of American heroism.[7]

There are, however, lingering shades of the paternal project still to be glimpsed in post-millennial Hollywood. Steven Spielberg's *War of the Worlds* (2005), for instance, underpins its post-9/11 adaptation of H. G. Wells's sci-fi invasion narrative with a subplot featuring a disengaged, divorced father. Ray Ferrier (Tom Cruise) must rise to the challenge of shepherding his daughter Rachel (Dakota Fanning) and his angry teenage son Robbie (Justin Chatwin) to a safe place after alien tripods invade the United States. The allusions to 9/11 are clear enough, but what is striking is that *War of the Worlds* would not feel out of place in 1990s Hollywood, with its collection of displaced men rediscovering their fatherhood and, with it, the triumph of survival, whether literal or symbolic. What is significant, however, is the way in which *War of the Worlds* falls short of guaranteeing Ray's survival. This has less to do with whether he lives or dies and everything to do with the precarious note on which his fatherhood still rests at the end of the film. *War of the Worlds* becomes a distorted cousin of *Jurassic Park*. Spielberg employs the same tactic of suggesting that the protagonist's future can be realized through a paternal commitment. Once again, the concept of survival has very real implications, as dinosaurs are replaced by machines focused on destruction. Like Alan Grant, Ray's battle against the monstrous enemy is intertwined with a realization of paternal responsibility. Yet by the end of the film, Ray has not succeeded in fully reconciling with Robbie. While he and Rachel have forged a renewed bond in their struggle for survival, Robbie makes his own way to his grandparents' house in Boston, arriving before his father and sister. The father–son reunion is muted rather than triumphant. Though all the ingredients are there for a rehabilitated father and a more secure future, the reality is less edifying. The scenario ultimately fails, leaving an unbridgeable gap and thus a future that once again remains unsure.

The political landscape post-2001 was dominated by 9/11, overshadowing the presidency of George W. Bush. Though all presidents face inevitable crises, Bush Jr's were more pronounced than many of his predecessors. The terrorist attacks and the aftermath of the wars in Iraq and Afghanistan, the domestic policy that followed (such as the controversial Patriot Act, which expanded laws around the surveillance and monitoring of citizens), the devastation of (and delayed response to) Hurricane Katrina (2005) and the financial crisis (2008) are the resounding legacies of Bush's two terms in office. But in the case of Bush, the question of presidential legacies goes even further. The ascension of Bush Jr to the executive office is an act of paternal restoration at the highest level. His own father, George H. W. Bush, served only one term as president, four years that largely underwhelmed the American public after the perceived coherence of Reagan's time in office. Bush Sr ran against Clinton in 1992 and lost; for all the Republicans' sniping at Clinton's age, experience, education and war record, Clinton promised a youthful optimism that chimed with the nation's vision of the future. Bush Jr's bid to follow in his father's footsteps echoes the statement made by Charlie at the end of *The Santa Clause* that marks his reconciliation with his father and thus the assurance of Scott's own future: 'I'm going into the family business.' For the Bush men, the presidency becomes the family business through which their own project of paternal rehabilitation can take place. For Bush Jr to succeed Clinton and defeat Al Gore – barely, necessitating a recount in Florida – and put another Bush back in the Oval Office felt almost like an act of vindication, a return to something familiar. A return to Father.

In his 2001 inaugural address, Bush Jr began by inserting himself into the 'generational continuum' of presidents: 'I am honoured and humbled to stand here where so many of America's leaders have come before me, and so many will follow.' Though he made no overt reference to his father (choosing, instead, to invoke God, the ultimate symbolic father), in acknowledging his place in the line of presidents – those chosen fathers of the nation – Bush Jr invoked the father–son line of succession, adding, 'now we must choose if the example of our fathers and mothers will inspire us or condemn us.'[8] This act of restoration, of course, was dealt a blow only a few months in to Bush Jr's presidency. Any hope of continuing his father's terminated legacy was put on hold as the nation appeared to unravel. The father's redemption, it seemed, would have to wait, though Bush Jr did oversee the Second Gulf War in a mirroring of his father's own incursion into Iraq and Kuwait. (In the same Gallup poll that confirms Clinton's continued popularity with the American public, George H. W. Bush is remembered now as a better president than his son; neither inspire widespread veneration.) And so here, once again, the

American presidency reflects the broader paternal landscape. In the 1980s, Americans were compelled – in society and in Hollywood – to (as Robin Wood has it) 'trust Father'.⁹ In the 1990s, this trust wavered but was ultimately rewarded; Americans, it seemed, still wanted their 'daddy'.¹⁰ But in the 2000s, this faith was shaken more significantly. Post-9/11, not even Dad could make things right again.

This same break occurs in Hollywood. The optimism inherent in the images of fatherhood that 1990s Hollywood presents, of fatherhood as the key to the future, fails to guard fully against such a near-shattering of identity and meaning. The apocalyptic images inherent in 1990s cinema exist in part to be neutralized, to prove the ability of men to overcome the threat of annihilation; 9/11, conversely, becomes the apocalypse that cannot be averted. Fatherhood in post-9/11 Hollywood is, as a result, much more unstable. The ability of fatherhood to save the man is no longer guaranteed. Ray, in *War of the Worlds*, goes through the motions of adopting a more responsible paternal persona and shepherding his children to safety, but he is left lingering on the doorstep of a house that is not his own by the end of the film. Ray and the children are safe, but this is not an uncomplicated or triumphant conclusion.

The Weather Man (Gore Verbinski, 2005) similarly revisits some common themes, including the impact of divorce on a man's ability to be an involved father and the spectre of the dying father. Dave Spritz (Nicolas Cage) is a Chicago television weatherman, outwardly successful but in reality depressed and struggling to be a good father to his wayward son Mike (Nicholas Hoult) and disrespectful daughter Shelly (Gemmenne de la Peña), who live with his ex-wife Noreen (Hope Davis) and her new partner Russ (Michael Rispoli). When Dave's father Robert (Michael Caine), with whom he has a difficult relationship, is diagnosed with a terminal illness, Dave's depression only deepens. Robert insists on having a 'living funeral', at which his family and friends gather to celebrate his life before he dies. The symbolic implications of a 'living funeral' for the patriarch – marking his demise even as he still lives – further underline the loss of faith in the father that occurs after the millennium. True to form, the dying father does attempt to impart some wisdom on his son before he dies, but this wisdom is often banal. Robert suggests that Dave, as a 'grown man', should carry more than a dollar in change. He instructs him to speak to Shelly about her clothing, as her peers have dubbed her 'Camel Toe'. More substantially, he hints that Dave should focus more on his family than his work (when Dave gets a better job with a better salary, Robert congratulates him on a 'very American accomplishment'). Though Dave does appear to take this latter advice to heart, not least in punching his son's therapist after the therapist makes inappropriate advances on Mike, by the end of the film he is still alone. Triumph is reduced to the fact that passers-by no longer throw fast food at Dave when they recognize him from the television. Dave's redemption contains little of the optimism of those adrift Hollywood dads of the 1990s. Undermined by Mike's therapist and by Russ, Dave ponders whether it would be easier to leave the parenting to Noreen and Russ. *The Weather Man* borrows one symbol of paternal restoration from *Mrs. Doubtfire* – seeing her ex-husband on the screen in his new role, Noreen does not turn off the television – but by this point Dave is already in another city and his ongoing relationship with his children is far from resolved. Like *War of the Worlds*, *The Weather Man* imitates the journey of the redeemed father only to leave as many questions as answers by the end of the film.

Not all post-2000s Hollywood films concerning the father take this same subdued tone. Two of the decade's most successful family films are *Cheaper by the Dozen* (Shawn Levy, 2003) and its sequel, *Cheaper by the Dozen 2* (Adam Shankman, 2005), starring Steve Martin as Tom Baker, a father of twelve children. Yvonne Tasker describes *Cheaper by the Dozen* as a 'celebration of fecundity, family and fatherly commitment', as Tom engages with the common dichotomy of work and family and embraces the responsibility that comes with fatherhood.[11] In their sunny, optimistic nature, the *Cheaper by the Dozen* films have much in common with those father-driven comedy vehicles of the 1990s, with one evident difference. It is no longer enough that Tom is a father; he must be father to a vast number of children and coach a whole football team besides. The Bakers' 'fecundity' is an anxious manifestation of that belief in fatherhood as a saving mechanism. Tom now has a dozen links to his own immortal survival, a fact that emphasizes the fragility of this survival through a sheer investment in numbers.

Despite their underlying uncertainties and the revelations of fears around longevity, value and influence, Hollywood's fatherhood films of the 1990s retain a sense of optimism that does not survive intact beyond the millennium. It is this optimism, above all, that characterizes those narratives of fatherhood lost and rediscovered, re-evaluated and redeemed, examined in the chapters of this book. To be sure, on the surface this optimism is often difficult to glimpse among the tales of death, destruction and familial disintegration, but it remains as the guiding point of all these films, which in the end reward audiences with the triumphant image of the restored father. What often begins as a knowing eye roll at the typically disappointing father – he is selfish, or disinterested, or ungrateful, or else so difficult to fathom that the son has simply stopped trying – inevitably becomes a gaze of veneration, a realization that father knows best after all. Investment in the father halts the apocalyptic erasure of masculinity by restoring certainty to a world perpetually threatened by crisis. The drive towards renewal and rehabilitation is broadly successful: the father is restored in time, avoiding the previously threatened eradication.

This, above all, is the story of masculinity in 1990s Hollywood. The construction of fatherhood as a saving mechanism for anxious men does not begin and end with the decade, but it is during this period – sandwiched between the muscular, hard-bodied heroes of the 1980s and the patriotic superheroes of the 2000s – that the father becomes a persistent figure of hope and redemption. The 1990s is a unique period in that it embodies a great deal of upheaval and anxiety while existing on the brink of a momentous temporal occasion that casts a patina of optimism across the nation. The future was not yet written. And if this future felt out of reach – if America's men felt adrift from the promise of that metaphorical 'bridge' – then Hollywood was busy constructing the solution in the shape of fatherhood. And, for a while, it worked. The message is ultimately one of hope: by anchoring himself to the figure of the child, the American man took responsibility not only for the child but for his own survival, transcending the shifting sands of family, work, community and masculinity and staking his future on the illusive certainties of fatherhood as the nation raced towards its millennial reckoning.

Notes

Introduction

1. Jimmy Carter, 'Address to the nation on energy and national goals: The "Malaise Speech"', 15 July 1979. Available at http://www.presidency.ucsb.edu/ws/?pid=32596 (accessed 3 August 2018).
2. William J. Clinton, 'Address before a joint session of Congress on the state of the Union', 4 February 1997. Available at http://www.presidency.ucsb.edu/ws/index.php?pid=53358 (accessed 3 August 2018).
3. William J. Clinton, 'Address before a joint session of Congress on the state of the Union', 19 January 1999. Available at http://www.presidency.ucsb.edu/ws/index.php?pid=57577 (accessed 3 August 2018).
4. US Census Bureau, 'We the American Women', *We the Americans Report* 8 (1993), 4–6.
5. Michael Kimmel, *Manhood in America: A Cultural History* (Oxford: Oxford University Press, 2012); Brenton J. Malin, *American Masculinity under Clinton: Popular Media and the Nineties Crisis of Masculinity* (New York: Peter Lang, 2005); Sally Robinson, *Marked Men: White Masculinity in Crisis* (New York: Columbia University Press, 2000); Susan Faludi, *Stiffed: The Betrayal of the Modern Man* (London: Chatto & Windus, 1999); E. Anthony Rotundo, *American Manhood: Transformations in Masculinity from the Revolution to the Modern Era* (New York: Basic Books, 1993); Antony Easthope, *What a Man's Gotta Do: The Masculine Myth in Popular Culture* (London: Routledge, 1992).
6. Kimmel, *Manhood in America*, 216.
7. For example, Susan Faludi observes in *Stiffed* that the loss of a sports team that moves cross-country, erasing the social community around it, often contributes to a sense of loss and bewilderment.
8. Fintan Walsh, *Male Trouble: Masculinity and the Performance of Crisis* (Basingstoke: Palgrave Macmillan, 2010); Raewyn Connell, *Masculinities* (Berkeley: University of California Press, 1993); Judith Butler, *Gender Trouble: Feminism and the Subversion of Identity* (London: Routledge, 1990).

9   Raewyn Connell and James W. Messerschmidt, 'Hegemonic masculinity: Rethinking the concept', *Gender & Society* 19, no. 6 (2005), 832–3.
10 Kimmel, *Manhood in America*, 1.
11 Donna Peberdy, *Masculinity and Film Performance: Male Angst in Contemporary American Cinema* (Basingstoke: Palgrave Macmillan, 2013), 44.
12 Faludi, *Stiffed*, 6.
13 John Beynon, *Masculinities and Culture* (Buckingham: Open University Press, 2002); Rowena Chapman, 'The great pretender: Variations on the new man theme', in *Male Order: Unwrapping Masculinity*, ed. Rowena Chapman and Jonathan Rutherford (London: Lawrence and Wishart, 1988), 225–48.
14 Helene Shugart, 'Managing masculinities: The metrosexual moment', *Communication and Critical/Cultural Studies* 5, no. 3 (2008), 280–300; Mark Simpson, 'Here come the mirror men: Why the future is metrosexual', *The Independent*, 15 November 1994.
15 Susan Jeffords, *Hard Bodies: Hollywood Masculinity in the Reagan Era* (New Brunswick: Rutgers University Press, 1994), 143.
16 Peter Krämer, 'Would you take your child to see this film? The cultural and social work of the family adventure movie', in *Contemporary Hollywood Cinema*, ed. Steve Neale and Murray Smith (London: Routledge, 1998).
17 Murray Pomerance (ed.), *A Family Affair: Cinema Calls Home* (London: Wallflower, 2008), 1.
18 Robert C. Allen, 'Home alone together: Hollywood and the "family film"', in *Identifying Hollywood's Audiences: Cultural Identity and the Movies*, ed. Melvyn Stokes and Richard Maltby (London: BFI, 1999), 114.
19 Tino Balio, 'A major presence in all of the world's important markets: The globalization of Hollywood in the 1990s', in *Contemporary Hollywood Cinema*, ed. Steve Neale and Murray Smith (London: Routledge, 1998).
20 Ibid., 65.
21 Tom Bierbaum, 'Booming 80s behind it, vid faces uncertainty', *Variety*, 10 January 1990.

22 Chuck Kleinhans, '1993: Movies and the new economics of blockbusters and indies', in *American Cinema of the 1990s: Themes and Variations*, ed. Chris Holmund (New Brunswick: Rutgers University Press, 2008); Wheeler Winston Dixon, 'Twenty-five reasons why it's all over', in *The End of Cinema as We Know It: American Film in the Nineties*, ed. Jon Lewis (New York: New York University Press, 2001); Steve Neale and Murray Smith (eds), *Contemporary Hollywood Cinema* (London: Routledge, 1998).

23 Noel Brown, *The Hollywood Family Film: A History, from Shirley Temple to Harry Potter* (London: I.B. Tauris, 2012); Allen, 'Home alone together'; Krämer, 'Would you take your child'.

24 Amy Aronson and Michael Kimmel, 'The saviors and the saved: Masculine redemption in contemporary films', in *Masculinity: Bodies, Movies, Culture*, ed. Peter Lehman (London: Routledge, 2001), 44.

25 Stella Bruzzi, *Bringing Up Daddy: Fatherhood and Masculinity in Post-War Hollywood* (London: BFI, 2005); Hannah Hamad, *Postfeminism and Paternity in Contemporary U.S. Film* (London: Routledge, 2014).

26 Rebecca Feasey, *Mothers on Mothers: Maternal Readings of Popular Television* (Oxford: Peter Lang, 2016); Heather Addison, Mary Kate Goodwin-Kelly and Elaine Roth, *Motherhood Misconceived: Representing the Maternal in U.S. Films* (Albany: State University of New York Press, 2009); Lucy Fischer, *Cinematernity: Film, Motherhood, Genre* (Princeton: Princeton University Press, 1996); E. Ann Kaplan, *Motherhood and Representation: The Mother in Popular Culture and Melodrama* (London: Routledge, 1992).

27 Claire Jenkins, *Home Movies: The American Family in Contemporary Hollywood* (London: I.B.Tauris, 2015); Pomerance, *A Family Affair*; Mike Chopra-Gant, *Hollywood Genres and Postwar America: Masculinity, Family and Nation in Popular Movies and Film Noir* (London: I.B. Tauris, 2005); Sarah Harwood, *Family Fictions: Representations of the Family in 1980s Hollywood Cinema* (Basingstoke: Macmillan, 1997).

28 Yvonne Tasker, 'Practically perfect people: Postfeminism, masculinity and male parenting in contemporary cinema', in *A Family Affair: Cinema Calls Home*, ed. Murray Pomerance

(London: Wallflower, 2008); Fred Pfeil, *White Guys: Studies in Postmodern Domination and Difference* (London: Verso, 1995); Susan Jeffords, *Hard Bodies: Hollywood Masculinity in the Reagan Era* (New Brunswick: Rutgers University Press, 1994); Tania Modleski, *Feminism without Women: Culture and Criticism in a 'Postfeminist' Age* (London: Routledge, 1991).

29 Hamad, *Postfeminism and Paternity*, 1.
30 Lynne Joyrich, *Re-Viewing Reception: Television, Gender and Postmodern Culture* (Bloomington: Indiana University Press, 1996), 106. For further discussion of the marginalized mother, see Berit Åström (ed.), *The Absent Mother in the Cultural Imagination: Missing, Presumed Dead* (Basingstoke: Palgrave Macmillan, 2017).
31 Bruzzi, *Bringing Up Daddy*, 153.
32 Terence McSweeney (ed.), *American Cinema in the Shadow of 9/11* (Edinburgh: Edinburgh University Press, 2017); Christina Hellmich and Lisa Purse (eds), *Disappearing War: Interdisciplinary Perspectives on Cinema and Erasure in the Post-9/11 World* (Edinburgh: Edinburgh University Press, 2017); Guy Westwell, *Parallel Lines: Post-9/11 American Cinema* (London: Wallflower Press, 2014); John Markert, *Post-9/11 Cinema: Through a Lens Darkly* (Lanham: Scarecrow Press, 2011).
33 Sigmund Freud, 'The future of an illusion', in *The Standard Edition of the Complete Psychological Works of Sigmund Freud*, vol. 21, trans. James Strachey (London: Hogarth Press, 1961), 19.
34 Sigmund Freud, 'On narcissism', in *The Standard Edition of the Complete Psychological Works of Sigmund Freud*, vol. 14, trans. James Strachey (London: Hogarth Press, 1955), 91.
35 Peter Blos, *Son and Father: Before and Beyond the Oedipus Complex* (London: The Free Press, 1985), 6.
36 Åström (ed.), *The Absent Mother*.
37 Lee Edelman, *No Future: Queer Theory and the Death Drive* (Durham: Duke University Press, 2004).
38 Ibid., 44.
39 Ibid., 3.
40 Ibid., 33.
41 Ibid., 112.

42 Freud, 'On narcissism', 91.
43 Edelman, *No Future*, 33.
44 Elias Canetti, *Crowds and Power*, trans. Carol Stewart (London: Penguin, 1992), 227.
45 Freud, 'On narcissism', 91.
46 Ronald Reagan, 'Inaugural address', 20 January 1981. Available at http://www.presidency.ucsb.edu/ws/?pid=43130 (accessed 3 August 2018).
47 William J. Clinton, 'Address before a joint session of Congress on administration goals', 17 February 1993. Available at http://www.presidency.ucsb.edu/ws/?pid=47232 (accessed 3 August 2018).
48 Edelman, *No Future*, 13.
49 Canetti, *Crowds and Power*, 227.
50 Jeffords, *Hard Bodies*, 141.
51 Ibid., 166.
52 Iain Robert Smith and Constantine Verevis, *Transnational Film Remakes* (Edinburgh: Edinburgh University Press, 2017); Constantine Verevis, *Film Remakes* (Edinburgh: Edinburgh University Press, 2005); Jennifer Forrest and Leonards R. Koos, *Dead Ringers: The Remake in Theory and Practice* (Albany: State University of New York Press, 2002).
53 Kirsten Moana Thompson, *Apocalyptic Dread: American Film at the Turn of the Millennium* (Albany: State University of New York Press, 2007), 40.
54 Allen, 'Home alone together', 125.
55 Joseph Natoli, *Hauntings: Popular Film and American Culture 1990–1992* (Albany: State University of New York Press, 1994), 42.
56 Thompson, *Apocalyptic Dread*, 33.
57 Robin Wood, *Hollywood from Vietnam to Reagan ... and Beyond* (New York: Columbia University Press, 2003), 154–5.
58 Kimmel, *Manhood in America*, 215.
59 Faludi, *Stiffed*, 407.
60 Robin Lakoff, quoted in Margaret Dowd, 'Of knights and presidents: Race of mythic proportions', *New York Times*, 10 October 1992.
61 Robert Bly, *Iron John: A Book about Men* (Shaftesbury: Element, 1992), 92.

62 Peberdy, *Masculinity and Film Performance*, 126.
63 Kimmel, *Manhood in America*, 215.
64 Malin, *American Masculinity under Clinton*, 16–17.
65 Ibid., 7.
66 Faludi, *Stiffed*, 6. Emphasis in original.
67 Ibid., 407.
68 Colin Campbell and Bert A. Rockman, *The Clinton Legacy* (New York: Seven Bridges Press, 2000), xii.
69 Roxane Roberts, '16 Candles for Chelsea', *Washington Post*, 27 February 1997.
70 Dick Morris, *Behind the Oval Office: Winning the Presidency in the Nineties* (New York: Random House, 1997), 181.
71 Peter Rubin, 'Family man: Bill Clinton, national dad', *New Republic*, 27 April 1998, 12.
72 Andrew Dugan and Frank Newport, 'Americans rate JFK as top modern president'. Available at https://news.gallup.com/poll/165902/americans-rate-jfk-top-modern-president.aspx (accessed 17 July 2018).
73 US Census Bureau, *Statistical Abstract of the United States 2012* (Washington, DC, 2011), 840.
74 US Census Bureau, *Living Arrangements of Children 1996* (Washington, DC, 2001), 5.
75 Judith Seltzer, 'Relationships between fathers and children who live apart: The father's role after separation', *Journal of Marriage and Family* 53, no. 1 (1991), 86.
76 Joanna L. Grossman and Lawrence M. Friedman, *Inside the Castle: Law and the Family in 20th Century America* (Princeton: Princeton University Press, 2011), 214.
77 David Blankenhorn, *Fatherless America: Confronting Our Most Urgent Social Problem* (New York: Harper Perennial, 1996); see also Stephen Baskerville, 'The politics of fatherhood', *PS: Political Science and Politics* 35, no. 4 (2002), 695–9.
78 Tamar Lewin, 'Father's vanishing act called common drama', *New York Times*, 4 June 1990; Anon., 'Single-parent families' father deficit', *Chicago Tribune*, 15 January 1995.
79 Anon., 'A world without fathers', *Newsweek*, 30 August 1993.
80 Colbert I. King, 'Where are the fathers?', *Washington Post*, 10 July 1999.

81 Jocelyn E. Crowley, 'Organizational responses to the fatherhood crisis: The case of fathers' rights groups in the United States', *Marriage and Family Review* 39, nos 1–2 (2006), 99–120.
82 Jessica and Richard were ultimately returned to their biological fathers; Emily remained with her adoptive family. See Andrew S. Rosenman, 'Babies Jessica, Richard and Emily: The need for legislative reform of adoption laws', in *Chicago-Kent Law Review* 70, no. 4 (1995), 1851–96.
83 Robert L. Griswold, *Fatherhood in America: A History* (New York: Basic Books, 1993), 9.
84 Grossman and Friedman, *Inside the Castle*, 288.
85 Canetti, *Crowds and Power*, 227.
86 Faludi, *Stiffed*, 6.

1 Fathers of the future: Extinction, survival and apocalyptic narratives

1 Adrian Schober and Debbie Olson, *Children in the Films of Steven Spielberg* (Lanham: Lexington Books, 2016); Karen B. Mann, 'Lost boys and girls in Spielberg's *Minority Report*', *Journal of Narrative Theory* 35, no. 2 (2005), 196–217; Robin Wood, *Hollywood from Vietnam to Reagan ... and Beyond* (New York: Columbia University Press, 2003).
2 Spielberg's narrative preoccupation with paternal rescue and redemption can be seen across his body of work, including *Sugarland Express* (1974), *Schindler's List* (1993), *Catch Me If You Can* (2002), *The BFG* (2017), *Ready Player One* (2018) and the *Indiana Jones* series (1981–2008), and is often attributed to his own childhood experience of his parents' divorce.
3 Joanna L. Grossman and Lawrence M. Friedman, *Inside the Castle: Law and the Family in 20th Century America* (Princeton: Princeton University Press, 2011), 58–9.
4 Robert L. Griswold, *Fatherhood in America: A History* (New York: Basic Books, 1993).
5 Grossman and Friedman, *Inside the Castle*, 4.
6 Ibid., 5.

7 Susan Sontag, 'The imagination of disaster', in *Against Interpretation and Other Essays*, ed. Susan Sontag (New York: Picador, 1966), 209–10.
8 Noel Brown, *The Hollywood Family Film: A History, from Shirley Temple to Harry Potter* (London: I.B. Tauris, 2012), 5.
9 Sontag, 'The imagination of disaster', 220.
10 Ibid., 225.
11 J. Hoberman, '*Nashville* contra *Jaws*, or "The imagination of disaster" revisited', in *The Last Great American Picture Show*, ed. Thomas Elsaesser, Alexander Horwath and Noel King (Amsterdam: Amsterdam University Press, 2004), 198.
12 Michael Kimmel, *Manhood in America: A Cultural History* (Oxford: Oxford University Press, 2012), 215.
13 Reagan/Bush Campaign, 'Peace through strength', 1980. Available at http://www.livingroomcandidate.org/commercials/1980/peace-republican#4072 (accessed 3 August 2018).
14 Sigmund Freud, 'Beyond the pleasure principle', in *The Standard Edition of the Complete Psychological Works of Sigmund Freud*, vol. 18, trans. James Strachey (London: Hogarth Press, 1955), 15.
15 Theodor Adorno, *Minima Moralia* (London: Verso, 1978), 109.
16 Freud, 'Beyond the pleasure principle', 36. Emphasis in original.
17 Christopher Sharrett (ed.), *Crisis Cinema: The Apocalyptic Idea in Postmodern Narrative Film* (Washington, DC: Maisonneuve Press, 1993), 1.
18 Wheeler Winston Dixon, *Visions of the Apocalypse: Spectacles of Destruction in American Cinema* (London: Wallflower, 2003), 71.
19 Elias Canetti, *Crowds and Power*, trans. Carol Stewart (London: Penguin, 1992), 265.
20 Sigmund Freud, 'On narcissism', in *The Standard Edition of the Complete Psychological Works of Sigmund Freud*, vol. 14, trans. James Strachey (London: Hogarth Press, 1955), 91.
21 Elena Woolley, 'The end of all things: Overcoming the end of the world in American cinema', *Cineaction* 95 (2015), 29.
22 Liv Tyler was raised by Todd Rundgren, whom she believed to be her biological father.
23 Dixon, *Visions of the Apocalypse*, 1–2.
24 Freud, 'Beyond the pleasure principle', 15.

25 Ibid., 35.
26 Woolley, 'The end of all things', 30.

2 Dad versus the state: Hollywood's courtroom battles

1 Susan Faludi, *Stiffed: The Betrayal of the Modern Man* (London: Chatto & Windus, 1999), 6.
2 Arthur J. Norton and Louisa F. Miller, 'Marriage, divorce and remarriage in the 1990s', *Current Population Reports (U.S. Bureau of the Census)* 23, no. 180 (1992), 1.
3 Center for Disease Control, 'Births, marriages, divorces, and deaths: Provisional data for January–December 2000', *National Vital Statistics Report* 49, no. 6 (2001), 1.
4 Mary Ann Mason, *From Father's Property to Children's Rights: The History of Child Custody in the United States* (New York: Columbia University Press, 1994), xix.
5 Lynne Joyrich, *Re-Viewing Reception: Television, Gender and Postmodern Culture* (Bloomington: Indiana University Press, 1996), 106.
6 Glenda Riley, *Divorce: An American Tradition* (Oxford: Oxford University Press, 1991), 162.
7 Pauline Irit Erera and Nehami Baum, 'Chat-room voices of divorced non-residential fathers', *Journal of Sociology and Social Welfare* 36, no. 2 (2009), 63–83; Sharona Mandel and Shlomo A. Sharlin, 'The non-custodial father: His involvement in his children's lives and the connection between his role and the ex-wife's, child's and father's perception of that role', *Journal of Divorce and Remarriage* 45 (2006), 79–95.
8 Erera and Baum, 'Chat-room voices', 67.
9 The 'tender years' doctrine assumes that young children should remain with their mothers after divorce or separation, unless she is proven to be an unfit parent.
10 Paul Bergman and Michael Asimow, *Reel Justice: The Courtroom Goes to the Movies* (Kansas City: Andrews and McMeel, 1996).

11 Richard Collier, *Masculinity, Law and the Family* (London: Routledge, 1996), 70.
12 Robert C. Allen, 'Home alone together: Hollywood and the "family film"', in *Identifying Hollywood's Audiences: Cultural Identity and the Movies*, ed. Melvyn Stokes and Richard Maltby (London: BFI, 1999), 125.
13 Martha Fineman, 'The politics of custody and gender: Child advocacy and the transformation of custody decision making in the USA', in *Child Custody and the Politics of Gender*, ed. Carol Smart and Selma Sevenhuijsen (London: Routledge, 1989), 33.
14 Stephen Baskerville, 'Is there really a fatherhood crisis?' in *The Independent Review* 8, no. 4 (2004), 486–8.
15 Dana Mack, *Assault on Parenthood: How Our Culture Undermines Parenthood* (San Francisco: Encounter, 1997), 304.
16 Martha Fineman, *The Autonomy Myth* (New York: New Press, 2004).
17 Jonathan Herring, 'Relational autonomy and family law', in *Rights, Gender and Family Law*, ed. Julie Wallbank, Shazia Choudhry and Jonathan Herring (New York: Routledge, 2010), 257–75.
18 Andrew Horton, 'Is it a wonderful life? Families and laughter in American film comedies', in *A Family Affair: Cinema Calls Home*, ed. Murray Pomerance (London: Wallflower, 2008), 51.
19 Steven K. Wisensale, *Family Leave Policy: The Political Economy of Work and Family in America* (London: Routledge, 2015).
20 David Blankenhorn, *Fatherless America: Confronting Our Most Urgent Social Problem* (New York: Harper Perennial, 1996), 124.
21 William J. Clinton, 'Address before a joint session of the Congress on the state of the Union', 25 January 1994. Available at http://www.presidency.ucsb.edu/ws/index.php?pid=50409 (accessed 3 August 2018).
22 William J. Clinton, 'Address accepting the presidential nomination at the Democratic National Convention in New York', 16 July 1992. Available at http://www.presidency.ucsb.edu/ws/index.php?pid=25958 (accessed 3 August 2018).
23 William J. Clinton, 'Presidential proclamation 6701: Father's Day 1994', 14 June 1994. Available at http://www.presidency.ucsb.edu/ws/index.php?pid=50336 (accessed 3 August 2018).

24 Nancy E. Dowd, *Redefining Fatherhood* (New York: New York University Press, 2000).
25 Richard Collier, 'Fatherhood, law and fathers' rights: Rethinking the relationship between gender and welfare', in *Rights, Gender and Family Law*, ed. Julie Wallbank, Shazia Choudhry and Jonathan Herring (New York: Routledge, 2010), 119–43; Erera and Baum, 'Chat-room voices'; Mandel and Sharlin, 'The non-custodial father'; Jocelyn E. Crowley, 'Organizational responses to the fatherhood crisis: The case of fathers' rights groups in the United States', *Marriage and Family Review* 39, nos 1–2 (2006), 99–120.
26 Jude Davies, 'I'm the bad guy?: *Falling Down* and white masculinity in 1990s Hollywood', *Journal of Gender Studies* 4, no. 2 (1995), 145–52.
27 Angela Melville and Rosemary Hunter, '"As everybody knows": Countering myths of gender bias in family law', *Griffith Law Review* 10 (2001), 127.
28 Carol Smart, 'Power and the politics of child custody', in *Child Custody and the Politics of Gender*, ed. Carol Smart and Selma Sevenhuijsen (London: Routledge, 1989), 1–26.
29 Michael Flood, 'Separated fathers and the "fathers' rights" movement', *Journal of Family Studies* 18, nos 2–3 (2012), 235–45; Molly Dragiewicz, 'Patriarchy reasserted: Fathers' rights and anti-VAWA activism', *Feminist Criminology* 3, no. 2 (2008), 121–44.
30 Jude Davies and Carol R. Smith, *Gender, Ethnicity and Sexuality in Contemporary American Film* (Edinburgh: Keele University Press, 1997), 37.
31 David Ray Papke, 'Peace between the sexes: Law and gender in *Kramer vs. Kramer*', *University of San Francisco Law Review* 30 (1996), 1200.
32 Smart, 'Power and the politics', 1.
33 Margaret F. Brinig and Douglas W. Allen, 'These boots are made for walking: Why most divorce filers are women', *American Law and Economics Review* 2, no. 1 (2000), 136.
34 Blankenhorn, *Fatherless America*, 148.
35 Michael Asimow, 'Embodiment of evil: Law firms in the movies', *UCLA Law Review* 48 (2001), 1341.
36 Smart, 'Power and the politics', 1.

37 Stephen Baskerville, 'The politics of fatherhood', *PS: Political Science and Politics* 35, no. 4 (2002), 695–9.
38 Asimow, 'Embodiment of evil', 1357.
39 Other examples of the workaholic father include *Kramer vs. Kramer*, *Regarding Henry*, *Hook* (Steven Spielberg, 1991), *Jingle All the Way*, *Jungle 2 Jungle* (John Pasquin, 1997), *Jack Frost* and *The Shaggy Dog* (Brian Robbins, 2006).
40 Amy Lawrence, *Echo and Narcissus: Women's Voices in Classical Hollywood Cinema* (Berkeley: University of California Press, 1991), 180.
41 Davies, 'I'm the bad guy?' 150.
42 Rowena Chapman, 'The great pretender: Variations on the new man theme', in *Male Order: Unwrapping Masculinity*, ed. Rowena Chapman and Jonathan Rutherford (London: Lawrence and Wishart, 1988), 225–48.
43 Katie Barnett, 'Any closer and you'd be Mom: The limits of postfeminist paternity in the films of Robin Williams', in *Screening Images of American Masculinity in the Age of Postfeminism*, ed. Elizabeth Abele and John Gronbeck-Tedesco (Lanham: Lexington Books, 2016), 19–34.
44 Blankenhorn, *Fatherless America*, 185.
45 Jonathan Pettigrew, '"I'll take what I can get": Identity development in the case of a stepfather', *Journal of Divorce and Remarriage* 51, no. 1 (2013), 25–42.
46 Sigmund Freud, 'Totem and taboo', in *The Standard Edition of the Complete Psychological Works of Sigmund Freud*, vol. 13, trans. James Strachey (London: Hogarth Press, 1955), 129. Emphasis in original.
47 Joshua M. Gold and Oluwatoyin Adeyemi, 'Stepfathers and noncustodial fathers: Two men, one role', *The Family Journal: Counseling and Therapy for Couples and Families* 21, no. 1 (2013), 100–1.
48 Robert Bly, *Iron John: A Book about Men* (Shaftesbury: Element, 1992), 93.

3 Boys, interrupted: Fathers, sons and loss

1 Vicky Lebeau, *Childhood and Cinema* (London: Reaktion, 2008), 149.
2 Lee Edelman, *No Future: Queer Theory and the Death Drive* (Durham: Duke University Press, 2004), 11.

3 Mick Broderick, 'Heroic apocalypse: *Mad Max*, mythology and the millennium', in *Crisis Cinema: The Apocalyptic Idea in Postmodern Narrative Film*, ed. Christopher Sharrett (Washington, DC: Maisonneuve Press, 1993), 256. Emphasis in original.
4 Kay Talbot, *What Forever Means after the Death of a Child: Transcending the Trauma, Living with the Loss* (New York: Brunner-Routledge, 2002), 48.
5 Edelman, *No Future*, 12.
6 Dominic W. Lennard, 'All fun and games ... Children's culture in the horror film, from *Deep Red* (1975) to *Child's Play* (1988)', *Continuum: Journal of Media and Cultural Studies* 26, no. 1 (2012), 133–42; Julian Petley, 'The monstrous child', in *The Body's Perilous Pleasures: Dangerous Desires and Contemporary Culture*, ed. Michele Aaron (Edinburgh: Edinburgh University Press, 1999), 87–107; David J. Hogan, *Dark Romance: Sexuality in the Horror Film* (Jefferson: McFarland, 1997).
7 Neil Sinyard, *Children in the Movies* (London: B. T. Batsford, 1992), 9.
8 Frances Gateward and Murray Pomerance, *Where the Boys Are: Cinemas of Masculinity and Youth* (Detroit: Wayne State University Press, 2005), 2.
9 For example, *Lord of the Flies* (Peter Brook, 1963; Harry Hook, 1990), *E.T. the Extra-Terrestrial* (Steven Spielberg, 1982), *Stand By Me* (Rob Reiner, 1986), *Dead Poets Society* (Peter Weir, 1989) and *Mean Creek* (Jacob Aaron Estes, 2004).
10 Ellen Handler Spitz, *Illuminating Childhood: Portraits in Fiction, Film, and Drama* (Ann Arbor: University of Michigan Press, 2011), 176.
11 George Toles, 'Film death and the failure to signify: The curious case of Warni Hazard', *New Review of Film and Television Studies* 15, no. 2 (2017), 216; see also Michele Aaron, *Death and the Moving Image: Ideology, Iconography and I* (Edinburgh: Edinburgh University Press, 2014); Emma Wilson, *Love, Mortality and the Moving Image* (Basingstoke: Palgrave Macmillan, 2012); Boaz Hagin, *Death in Classical Hollywood Cinema* (Basingstoke: Palgrave Macmillan, 2010).
12 Laura Mulvey, *Death 24x a Second: Stillness and the Moving Image* (London: Reaktion, 2006), 31.

13 Geoffrey Gorer, *Death, Grief and Mourning in Contemporary Britain* (London: The Cresset Press, 1965).
14 Jacque Lynn Foltyn, 'Dead sexy: Why death is the new sex', in *Making Sense of Death, Dying and Bereavement: An Anthology*, ed. Sarah Earle, Caroline Bartholomew and Carol Komaromy (London: Sage, 2009), 47–51.
15 Toles, 'Film death', 217.
16 John O. Thompson, 'Reflexions on dead children in the cinema and why there are not more of them', in *Representations of Child Death*, ed. Gillian Avery and Kimberley Reynolds (Basingstoke: Macmillan, 2003), 211.
17 François Truffaut, *Hitchcock* (London: Simon & Schuster, 1985), 109.
18 Celia Hindmarch, *On the Death of a Child* (Abingdon: Radcliffe Medical Press, 2000), 44.
19 In 1997, the US infant mortality rate (deaths under 1 year per 1,000 births) stood at 7.0, down from 7.2 in 1996 and 7.6 in 1995. See Center for Disease Control, 'Births, Marriages, Divorces, and Deaths for 1997', *Monthly Vital Statistics Report* 46, no. 12 (1998), 4.
20 Emma Wilson, *Cinema's Missing Children* (London: Wallflower, 2003).
21 Serge Leclaire, *A Child Is Being Killed: On Primary Narcissism and the Death Drive*, trans. Marie-Claude Hays (Stanford: Stanford University Press, 1998), 2.
22 Ibid.
23 Sigmund Freud, 'Beyond the pleasure principle', in *The Standard Edition of the Complete Psychological Works of Sigmund Freud*, vol. 18, trans. James Strachey (London: Hogarth Press, 1955), 36–9.
24 Lebeau, *Childhood and Cinema*, 137.
25 William B. Rizzo, 'Lorenzo's oil: Hope and disappointment', *The New England Journal of Medicine* 329, no. 11 (1993), 802. The same criticism was levelled at the Odones by the medical establishment, who charged them with 'preferring a Hollywood ending', as recorded in Augusto Odone's obituary. See Peter Stanford, 'Augusto Odone obituary', *The Guardian*, 1 November 2013.
26 Jennifer L. Buckle and Stephen J. Fleming, *Parenting after the Death of a Child* (London: Taylor and Francis, 2011); Talbot, *What Forever Means*; Reiko Schwab, 'Gender differences in parental grief', *Death*

Studies 20 (1996), 103–14; W. C. Fish, 'Differences of grief intensity in bereaved parents', in *Parental Loss of a Child*, ed. Therese A. Rando (Illinois: Research Press Company, 1986), 415–28.

27 Wendy Simonds and Barbara Katz Rothman, *Centuries of Solace: Expressions of Maternal Grief in Popular Literature* (Philadelphia: Temple University Press, 1992), 2.
28 Larry G. Peppers and Ronald J. Knapp, *Motherhood and Mourning: Perinatal Death* (London: Praeger, 1980), 47.
29 Hindmarch, *On the Death of a Child*, 45.
30 Talbot, *What Forever Means*, 202.
31 Cynthia Bach Hughes and Judith Page-Lieberman, 'Fathers experiencing a perinatal loss', *Death Studies* 13 (1989), 537–56.
32 Hindmarch, *On the Death of a Child*, 45.
33 Frederick Mandell, Elizabeth McAnulty and Robert M. Reece, 'Observations of paternal response to sudden unanticipated infant death', *Pediatrics* 65, no. 2 (1980), 221–5.
34 Sigmund Freud, 'Mourning and melancholia', in *The Standard Edition of the Complete Psychological Works of Sigmund Freud*, vol. 14, trans. James Strachey (London: Hogarth Press, 1955), 246.
35 Leo Bersani, *Is the Rectum a Grave? And Other Essays* (Chicago: University of Chicago Press, 2010); see also Ann Cvetkovich, *Depression: A Public Feeling* (Durham: Duke University Press, 2012) and Douglas Crimp, *Melancholia and Moralism: Essays on AIDS and Queer Politics* (Cambridge: MIT Press, 2002).
36 Barron H. Lerner, 'The art of medicine: Complicated lessons: Lorenzo Odone and medical miracles', *The Lancet* 373, no. 9667 (2002), 888.
37 Augusto Odone died in 2013, outliving his son by five years.
38 Cathy Caruth, *Unclaimed Experience: Trauma, Narrative, and History* (Baltimore: Johns Hopkins University Press, 1996), 60. Emphasis in original.
39 Tom Gliatto, 'Running away with the box office by staying Home Alone, Macaulay Culkin is Hollywood's newest little big man', *People*, 17 December 1990, 128.
40 Judy Quinn, 'The mighty munchkin: Macaulay Culkin', *Incentive* 166, no. 12 (1992), 13.

41 Jane O'Connor, 'From Jackie Coogan to Michael Jackson: What child stars can tell us about ideologies of childhood', *Journal of Children and Media* 5, no. 3 (2011), 293.
42 Susan Faludi, *Stiffed: The Betrayal of the Modern Man* (London: Chatto & Windus, 1999), 598.
43 Ibid., 597.
44 Elias Canetti, *Crowds and Power*, trans. Carol Stewart (London: Penguin, 1992), 230.
45 Freud, 'Mourning and melancholia', 246.
46 Faludi, *Stiffed*, 41.
47 Buckle and Fleming, *Parenting after the Death of a Child,* 64; Ariella Lang and Laurie Gottlieb, 'Parental grief reactions and marital intimacy in bereaved and non-bereaved couples: A comparative study', in *Children and Death*, ed. Danai Papadatou and Constantine Papadatos (Washington, DC: Hemisphere, 1991), 267–75; Fish, 'Differences of grief intensity'.
48 For further discussion of these films, see Katie Barnett, 'The once and future king: Negotiating the survival of boys in 1990s Hollywood', *Boyhood Studies* 8, no. 2 (2015), 25–42.
49 Marita Sturken, '*Affliction*: When paranoid male narratives fail', in *The End of Cinema as We Know It: American Film in the Nineties*, ed. Jon Lewis (New York: New York University Press, 2001), 204.
50 Faludi, *Stiffed*, 596.
51 Center for Disease Control, 'HIV and AIDS – United States, 1981–2000', *Morbidity and Mortality Weekly Report* 50, no. 21 (2001), 434.
52 Center for Disease Control, 'Update: Mortality attributable to HIV infection among persons aged 25–44 years – United States, 1991 and 1992', *Morbidity and Mortality Weekly Report* 42, no. 45 (1993), 869.
53 Center for Disease Control, 'Annual summary of births, marriages, divorces, and deaths: United States, 1994', *Monthly Vital Statistics Report* 43, no. 13 (1995), 6.
54 Marita Sturken, *Tangled Memories: The Vietnam War, The AIDS Epidemic, and the Politics of Remembering* (Berkeley: University of California Press, 1997), 147.
55 Monica Pearl, 'Symptoms of AIDS in contemporary film: Mortal anxiety in an age of sexual panic', in *The Body's Perilous Pleasures: Dangerous*

Desires and Contemporary Culture, ed. Michele Aaron (Edinburgh: Edinburgh University Press, 1999), 219.
56 Harry M. Benshoff, *Monsters in the Closet: Homosexuality and the Horror Film* (Manchester: Manchester University Press, 1997).
57 Alan Nadel, *Flatlining of the Field of Dreams: Cultural Narratives in the Films of President Reagan's America* (New Brunswick: Rutgers University Press, 1997), 176.
58 Simon Watney, *Policing Desire: Pornography, AIDS and the Media* (London: Cassell, 1997), 102.
59 Wilson, *Cinema's Missing Children*, 2.
60 Edelman, *No Future*, 4.

4 Return of the (lion) king: Fatherhood beyond death

1 Wendy Simonds and Barbara Katz Rothman, *Centuries of Solace: Expressions of Maternal Grief in Popular Literature* (Philadelphia: Temple University Press, 1992), 172.
2 Wheeler Winston Dixon, *Hollywood in Crisis or: The Collapse of the Real* (Basingstoke: Palgrave Macmillan, 2016), 13.
3 Peter Blos, *Son and Father: Before and Beyond the Oedipus Complex* (London: The Free Press, 1985), 6.
4 Matt Roth, '*The Lion King*: A short history of Disney-fascism', *Jump Cut: A Review of Contemporary Media* 40 (1996), 15.
5 Sigmund Freud, 'Beyond the pleasure principle', in *The Standard Edition of the Complete Psychological Works of Sigmund Freud*, vol. 18, trans. James Strachey (London: Hogarth Press, 1955), 12.
6 Boaz Hagin, *Death in Classical Hollywood Cinema* (Basingstoke: Palgrave Macmillan, 2010), 45.
7 Freud, 'Beyond the pleasure principle', 31.
8 Teresa de Lauretis, *Freud's Drive: Psychoanalysis, Literature and Film* (Basingstoke: Palgrave Macmillan, 2010), 5.
9 Serge Leclaire, *A Child Is Being Killed: On Primary Narcissism and the Death Drive*, trans. Marie-Claude Hays (Stanford: Stanford University Press, 1998), 2.

10 Elias Canetti, *Crowds and Power*, trans. Carol Stewart (London: Penguin, 1992), 289.
11 Sigmund Freud, *An Outline of Psycho-analysis*, trans. James Strachey (London: Hogarth Press, 1979), 46.
12 Canetti, *Crowds and Power*, 289–90.
13 Ibid., 290.
14 Sigmund Freud, 'Totem and taboo', in *The Standard Edition of the Complete Psychological Works of Sigmund Freud*, vol. 13, trans. James Strachey (London: Hogarth Press, 1955), 142.
15 Brenton J. Malin, *American Masculinity under Clinton: Popular Media and the Nineties Crisis of Masculinity* (New York: Peter Lang, 2005), 91.
16 Annalee R. Ward, *Mouse Morality: The Rhetoric of Animated Disney Film* (Austin: University of Texas Press, 2002), 28.
17 Perri Klass, 'A Bambi for the 90s, via Shakespeare', *New York Times*, 19 June 1994.
18 Lauren Dundes and Alan Dundes, 'Young hero Simba defeats old villain Scar: Oedipus wrecks the Lyin' King', *The Social Science Journal* 43 (2006), 479–85.
19 Freud, 'Totem and taboo', 129.
20 Blos, *Son and Father*, 6.
21 Dundes and Dundes, 'Young hero Simba', 480.
22 Lee Edelman, *No Future: Queer Theory and the Death Drive* (Durham: Duke University Press, 2004), 170, n.51.
23 Dundes and Dundes, 'Young hero Simba', 483.
24 Susan Mackey-Kallis, *The Hero and the Perennial Journey Home in American Film* (Philadelphia: University of Pennsylvania Press, 2001), 92.
25 Dundes and Dundes, 'Young hero Simba', 483.
26 Robert A. Paul, 'Cultural narratives and the succession scenario: *Slumdog Millionaire* and other popular films and fictions', *The International Journal of Psychoanalysis* 92, no. 2 (2011), 457.
27 Christopher Lasch, *The Culture of Narcissism: American Life in an Age of Diminishing Expectations* (New York: W. W. Norton, 1991), 5.
28 Edelman, *No Future*, 13.
29 Meredith Cox, Erin Garrett and James A. Graham, 'Death in Disney films: Implications for children's understanding of death', *Omega: Journal of Death and Dying* 50, no. 4 (2004–5), 277.

30 Mary K. Kirtz, 'Canadian book, American film: Shoeless Joe transfigured on a *Field of Dreams*', *Literature/Film Quarterly* 23 (1995), 29.
31 Lasch, *The Culture of Narcissism*, p. 210.
32 Ibid.
33 Roger Ebert, 'Jack Frost', *Chicago Sun-Times*, 11 December 1998.
34 Susan Faludi, *Stiffed: The Betrayal of the Modern Man* (London: Chatto & Windus, 1999), 596.
35 Mackey-Kallis, *The Hero*, 98.
36 Edelman, *No Future*, 53.
37 Sigmund Freud, 'Mourning and melancholia', in *The Standard Edition of the Complete Psychological Works of Sigmund Freud*, vol. 14, trans. James Strachey (London: Hogarth Press, 1955), 244.
38 Ibid.
39 Sigmund Freud, 'On narcissism', in *The Standard Edition of the Complete Psychological Works of Sigmund Freud*, vol. 14, trans. James Strachey (London: Hogarth Press, 1955), 91. Emphasis added.
40 Monica B. Pearl, 'Symptoms of AIDS in contemporary film: Mortal anxiety in an age of sexual panic', in *The Body's Perilous Pleasures: Dangerous Desires and Contemporary Culture*, ed. Michele Aaron (Edinburgh: Edinburgh University Press, 1999), 219.
41 Ibid., 211.
42 Ibid., 213.
43 Kirsten Moana Thompson, *Apocalyptic Dread: American Film at the Turn of the Millennium* (Albany: State University of New York Press, 2007), 1.
44 Philip Strick, 'Contact', *Sight and Sound* 7, no. 10 (October 1997), 44–6.
45 Clinton frequently recalled meeting Kennedy as a young boy, a moment immortalized in a photograph. This encounter suggested a different kind of legacy in which Clinton, years later, ascended to the same office as the man who had inspired him – a fatherless boy – at a young age.
46 Freud, 'On narcissism', 78.
47 P. D. James, *The Children of Men* (London: Faber and Faber, 1992), 13; Edelman, *No Future*, 12.
48 Canetti, *Crowds and Power*, 227.
49 Ibid.
50 Ibid., 230.
51 Lasch, *The Culture of Narcissism*, 33.

5 Guys that say goodnight: Gay fatherhood and the quest for legitimacy

1. Dan Savage, 'Status is … for gay men; the baby', *New York Times Magazine*, 15 November 1998.
2. Yvonne Tasker, 'Practically perfect people: Postfeminism, masculinity and male parenting in contemporary cinema', in *A Family Affair: Cinema Calls Home*, ed. Murray Pomerance (London: Wallflower, 2008), 175–87; James R. Keller, *Queer (Un)Friendly Film and Television* (Jefferson, NC: McFarland, 2002); Stella Bruzzi, *Bringing Up Daddy: Fatherhood and Masculinity in Post-War Hollywood* (London: BFI, 2005); Suzanna Danuta Walters, *All the Rage: The Story of Gay Visibility in America* (Chicago: University of Chicago Press, 2001).
3. Keller, *Queer (Un)Friendly*, 173.
4. Lee Edelman, *No Future: Queer Theory and the Death Drive* (Durham: Duke University Press, 2004), 3. Emphasis in original.
5. Ibid., 17.
6. J. Jack Halberstam, *In a Queer Time and Place: Transgender Bodies, Subcultural Lives* (New York: New York University Press, 2005), 2.
7. Leo Bersani, *Homos* (London: Harvard University Press, 1995), 20.
8. Savage, 'Status is …', 95.
9. Simon Watney, 'The spectacle of AIDS', in *AIDS: Cultural Analysis / Cultural Activism*, ed. Douglas Crimp (London: MIT/October Magazine, 1996), 75.
10. Andrew Sullivan, 'When plagues end', *New York Times Magazine*, 10 November 1996.
11. Tony Barnett and Alan Whiteside, *AIDS in the Twenty-First Century: Disease and Globalization* (Basingstoke: Palgrave Macmillan, 2002), 338–9.
12. Savage, 'Status is …', 95. Savage subsequently documented their journey to fatherhood in *The Kid: What Happened after My Boyfriend and I Decided to Go Get Pregnant* (New York: Penguin, 2000).
13. Edelman, *No Future*, 75.
14. Bersani, *Homos*, 5.
15. Ibid.

16 For example *Tales of the City* (Channel 4/PBS, 1993), *Will and Grace* (NBC, 1998–2006; 2017–), *Sex and the City* (HBO, 1998–2004), *Clueless* (Amy Heckerling, 1995), *My Best Friend's Wedding* (P. J. Hogan, 1997), *Mean Girls* (Mark Waters, 2004).
17 Baz Dresinger, 'The queen in shining armor: Safe eroticism and the gay friend', *Journal of Popular Film and Television* 28, no. 1 (2000), 7.
18 Armistead Maupin, *Michael Tolliver Lives* (London: Black Swan, 2008), 88.
19 Kath Weston, *Families We Choose: Lesbians, Gays, Kinship* (New York: Columbia University Press, 1991), 110.
20 Valerie Lehr, *Queer Family Values: Debunking the Myth of the Nuclear Family* (Philadelphia: Temple University Press, 1999), 3.
21 Ibid.
22 Steve Neale, 'The big romance or something wild? Romantic comedy today', *Screen* 33, no. 3 (1992), 290.
23 American Civil Liberties Union, 'States where same-sex couples are able to get joint and/or second parent adoptions statewide'. Available at http://www.aclu.org/files/assets/aclu_map4.pdf (accessed 3 August 2018).
24 Susan Chira, 'Gay parents become increasingly visible', *New York Times*, 30 September 1993.
25 Joanna L. Grossman and Lawrence M. Friedman, *Inside the Castle: Law and the Family in 20th Century America* (Princeton: Princeton University Press, 2011), 322.
26 Arlene Istar Lev, 'Gay dads: Choosing surrogacy', *Lesbian and Gay Psychology Review* 7, no. 1 (2006), 74.
27 Elias Canetti, *Crowds and Power*, trans. Carol Stewart (London: Penguin, 1992), 265. Emphasis in original.
28 See also *The Kids Are All Right* (Lisa Cholodenko, 2010), where the parenting of Jules (Julianne Moore) and Nic (Annette Bening) is overshadowed by their children's discovery of their biological dad.
29 Sylviane Agacinski, quoted in Judith Butler, 'Is kinship always already heterosexual?', *Differences: A Journal of Feminist Cultural Studies* 13, no. 1 (2002), 29.
30 Tasker, 'Practically perfect people', 184.

31 Nikki Sullivan, *A Critical Introduction to Queer Theory* (Edinburgh: Edinburgh University Press, 2003), 52.
32 Sue Ellen Case, 'Tracking the vampire', *Differences: A Journal of Feminist Cultural Studies* 3, no. 2 (1991), 4.
33 Martin Hoffman, quoted in Weston, *Families We Choose*, 154.
34 Judith Butler, *Gender Trouble: Feminism and the Subversion of Identity* (London: Routledge, 1990).
35 Tasker, 'Practically perfect people', 185.
36 Ibid.
37 Eve Kosofsky Sedgwick, 'How to bring your kids up gay', in *Fear of a Queer Planet: Queer Politics and Social Theory*, ed. Michael Warner (Minneapolis: University of Minnesota Press, 1993), 71.
38 Tina Takemoto, 'The melancholia of AIDS: Interview with Douglas Crimp', *Art Journal* 62, no. 4 (2003), 88.
39 Bruzzi, *Bringing Up Daddy*, 175.
40 Marjorie Garber, *Vested Interests: Cross-Dressing and Cultural Anxiety* (London: Penguin, 1993), 11.
41 Lehr, *Queer Family Values*, 107.
42 Bruzzi, *Bringing Up Daddy*, 175.
43 Karin Quimby, 'Will & Grace: Negotiating (gay) marriage on prime-time television', *Journal of Popular Culture* 38, no. 4 (2005), 714.
44 Michel Foucault, 'Friendship as a way of life', in *Foucault Live: Interviews, 1961–1984*, ed. Sylvere Lotringer, trans. Lysa Hochroth and John Johnston (New York: Semiotext(e), 1996), 308.
45 Butler, 'Is kinship always already heterosexual?', 20.
46 California Proposition 6, commonly known as the Briggs Initiative, proposed banning gay men and lesbians from teaching in California public schools. It was defeated in 1978 after prominent campaigns on both sides.
47 Similarly, following Ben's birth in *Friends*, Phoebe (Lisa Kudrow) opines that Ben is 'the luckiest baby in the whole world' to have three parents.
48 Walters, *All the Rage*, 141.
49 Harry M. Benshoff, 'Queers and families in film: From problems to parents', in *A Family Affair: Cinema Calls Home*, ed. Murray Pomerance (London: Wallflower, 2008), 226.
50 Keller, *Queer (Un)Friendly*, 160.

51 Ibid., 156.
52 Nancy D. Polikoff, 'Lesbians choosing children: The personal is political revisited', in *Politics of the Heart: A Lesbian Parenting Anthology*, ed. Sandra Pollack and Jeanne Vaughn (Ithaca: Firebrand, 1987), 52.
53 Andrea Weiss, 'From the margins: New images of gays in the cinema', *Cineaste* 15, no. 1 (1986), 5.
54 Simon Watney, *Policing Desire: Pornography, AIDS and the Media* (London: Cassell, 1997), 102.
55 Alan Nadel, *Flatlining of the Field of Dreams: Cultural Narratives in the Films of President Reagan's America* (New Brunswick: Rutgers University Press, 1997), 189.
56 Mark Doty, *Heaven's Coast: A Memoir* (London: Jonathan Cape, 1996), 4.
57 Dreisinger, 'The queen in shining armor', 7.
58 Quimby, 'Will & Grace', 713.
59 Dreisinger, 'The queen in shining armor', 6.
60 Leo Bersani, *Is the Rectum a Grave? And Other Essays* (Chicago: University of Chicago Press, 2010), 18.
61 David Ansen, 'Gay films are a drag', *Newsweek*, 18 March 1996, 71.
62 Savage, 'Status is …', 95.

Conclusion

1 Laura Mulvey, *Death 24x a Second: Stillness and the Moving Image* (London: Reaktion, 2006), 23.
2 Wheeler Winston Dixon, 'Twenty-five reasons why it's all over', in *The End of Cinema as We Know It: American Film in the Nineties*, ed. Jon Lewis (New York: New York University Press, 2001), 356–9.
3 Sigmund Freud, 'Beyond the pleasure principle', in *The Standard Edition of the Complete Psychological Works of Sigmund Freud*, vol. 18, trans. James Strachey (London: Hogarth Press, 1955), 9–10.
4 Lee Edelman, *No Future: Queer Theory and the Death Drive* (Durham: Duke University Press, 2004), 3.
5 Ibid., 112.

6 Sharon Willis, 'Movies and melancholy', in *American Cinema of the 2000s: Themes and Variations*, ed. Timothy Corrigan (New Brunswick: Rutgers University Press, 2012), 61.
7 Susan Jeffords, *Hard Bodies: Hollywood Masculinity in the Reagan Era* (New Brunswick: Rutgers University Press, 1994), 166.
8 George W. Bush, 'Inaugural address', 20 January 2001. Available at http://www.presidency.ucsb.edu/ws/index.php?pid=25853 (accessed 3 August 2018).
9 Robin Wood, *Hollywood from Vietnam to Reagan ... and Beyond* (New York: Columbia University Press, 2003), 155.
10 Robin Lakoff, quoted in Margaret Dowd, 'Of knights and presidents: Race of mythic proportions', *New York Times*, 10 October 1992.
11 Yvonne Tasker, 'Practically perfect people: Postfeminism, masculinity and male parenting in contemporary cinema', in *A Family Affair: Cinema Calls Home*, ed. Murray Pomerance (London: Wallflower, 2008), 182.

Bibliography

Aaron, Michele. *Death and the Moving Image: Ideology, Iconography and I.* Edinburgh: Edinburgh University Press, 2014.

Addison, Heather, Mary Kate Goodwin-Kelly and Elaine Roth. *Motherhood Misconceived: Representing the Maternal in U.S. Films.* Albany: State University of New York Press, 2009.

Adorno, Theodor. *Minima Moralia.* London: Verso, 1978.

Allen, Robert C. 'Home alone together: Hollywood and the "family film"'. In *Identifying Hollywood's Audiences: Cultural Identity and the Movies,* edited by Melvyn Stokes and Richard Maltby, 109–34. London: BFI, 1999.

American Civil Liberties Union. 'States where same-sex couples are able to get joint and/or second parent adoptions statewide'. Available at http://www.aclu.org/files/assets/aclu_map4.pdf (accessed 3 August 2018).

Anon. 'America's worst deadbeat dad'. *People Weekly,* 4 September 1995.

Anon. 'A world without fathers: The struggle to save the black family'. *Newsweek,* 30 August 1993.

Anon. 'Single-parent families' father deficit'. *Chicago Tribune,* 15 January 1995.

Ansen, David. 'Gay films are a drag'. *Newsweek,* 18 March 1996.

Aronson, Amy, and Michael Kimmel. 'The saviors and the saved: Masculine redemption in contemporary films'. In *Masculinity: Bodies, Movies, Culture,* edited by Peter Lehman, 43–50. London: Routledge, 2001.

Asimow, Michael. 'Embodiment of evil: Law firms in the movies'. *UCLA Law Review* 48 (2001): 1339–92.

Åström, Berit, ed. *The Absent Mother in the Cultural Imagination: Missing, Presumed Dead.* Basingstoke: Palgrave Macmillan, 2017.

Balio, Tino. 'A major presence in all of the world's important markets: The globalization of Hollywood in the 1990s'. In *Contemporary Hollywood Cinema,* edited by Steve Neale and Murray Smith, 58–73. London: Routledge, 1998.

Barnett, Katie. 'Any closer and you'd be Mom: The limits of postfeminist paternity in the films of Robin Williams'. In *Screening Images of American Masculinity in the Age of Postfeminism*, edited by Elizabeth Abele and John Gronbeck-Tedesco, 19–34. Lanham: Lexington Books, 2016.

Barnett, Katie. 'The once and future king: Negotiating the survival of boys in 1990s Hollywood'. *Boyhood Studies* 8, no. 2 (2015): 25–42.

Barnett, Tony, and Alan Whiteside. *AIDS in the Twenty-First Century: Disease and Globalization*. Basingstoke: Palgrave Macmillan, 2002.

Baskerville, Stephen. 'Is there really a fatherhood crisis?' *The Independent Review* 8, no. 4 (2004): 485–508.

Baskerville, Stephen. 'The politics of fatherhood'. *PS: Political Science and Politics* 35, no. 4 (2002): 695–99.

Benshoff, Harry M. *Monsters in the Closet: Homosexuality and the Horror Film*. Manchester: Manchester University Press, 1997.

Benshoff, Harry M. 'Queers and families in film: From problems to parents'. In *A Family Affair: Cinema Calls Home*, edited by Murray Pomerance, 223–33. London: Wallflower, 2008.

Bergman, Paul and Michael Asimow. *Reel Justice: The Courtroom Goes to the Movies*. Kansas City: Andrews and McMeel, 1996.

Bersani, Leo. *Homos*. London: Harvard University Press, 1995.

Bersani, Leo. *Is the Rectum a Grave? And Other Essays*. Chicago: University of Chicago Press, 2010.

Beynon, John. *Masculinities and Culture*. Buckingham: Open University Press, 2002.

Bierbaum, Tom. 'Booming 80s behind it, vid faces uncertainty'. *Variety*, 10 January 1990.

Blankenhorn, David. *Fatherless America: Confronting Our Most Urgent Social Problem*. New York: Harper Perennial, 1996.

Blos, Peter. *Son and Father: Before and Beyond the Oedipus Complex*. London: The Free Press, 1985.

Bly, Robert. *Iron John: A Book about Men*. Shaftesbury: Element, 1992.

Brinig, Margaret F., and Douglas W. Allen. 'These boots are made for walking: Why most divorce filers are women'. *American Law and Economics Review* 2, no. 1 (2000): 126–69.

Broderick, Mick. 'Heroic apocalypse: *Mad Max*, mythology and the millennium'. In *Crisis Cinema: The Apocalyptic Idea in Postmodern Narrative Film*, edited by Christopher Sharrett, 251–72. Washington, DC: Maisonneuve Press, 1993.

Brown, Noel. *The Hollywood Family Film: A History, from Shirley Temple to Harry Potter*. London: I.B. Tauris, 2012.

Bruzzi, Stella. *Bringing Up Daddy: Fatherhood and Masculinity in Post-War Hollywood*. London: BFI, 2005.

Buckle, Jennifer L., and Stephen J. Fleming. *Parenting after the Death of a Child*. London: Taylor and Francis, 2011.

Bush, George W. 'Inaugural address', 20 January 2001. Available at http://www.presidency.ucsb.edu/ws/index.php?pid=25853 (accessed 3 August 2018).

Butler, Judith. *Gender Trouble: Feminism and the Subversion of Identity*. London: Routledge, 1990.

Butler, Judith. 'Is kinship always already heterosexual?' *Differences: A Journal of Feminist Cultural Studies* 13, no. 1 (2002): 14–44.

Campbell, Colin, and Bert A. Rockman. *The Clinton Legacy*. New York: Seven Bridges Press, 2000.

Canetti, Elias. *Crowds and Power*. Translated by Carol Stewart. London: Penguin, 1992.

Carter, Jimmy. 'Address to the nation on energy and national goals: The "Malaise Speech"', 15 July 1979. Available at http://www.presidency.ucsb.edu/ws/?pid=32596 (accessed 3 August 2018).

Caruth, Cathy. *Unclaimed Experience: Trauma, Narrative, and History*. Baltimore: Johns Hopkins University Press, 1996.

Case, Sue Ellen. 'Tracking the vampire'. *Differences: A Journal of Feminist Cultural Studies* 3, no. 2 (1991): 1–20.

Center for Disease Control. 'Annual summary of births, marriages, divorces, and deaths: United States, 1994'. *Monthly Vital Statistics Report* 43, no. 13 (1995): 1–44.

Center for Disease Control. 'Births, marriages, divorces, and deaths for 1997'. *Monthly Vital Statistics Report* 46, no. 12 (1998): 1–20.

Center for Disease Control. 'Births, marriages, divorces, and deaths: Provisional data for January–December 2000'. *National Vital Statistics Report* 49, no. 6 (2001): 1–8.

Center for Disease Control. 'HIV and AIDS – United States, 1981–2000'. *Morbidity and Mortality Weekly Report* 50, no. 21 (2001): 430–4.

Center for Disease Control. 'Report of final mortality statistics: 1995'. *Monthly Vital Statistics Report* 45, no. 11 (1997): 1–80.

Center for Disease Control. 'Update: Mortality attributable to HIV infection among persons aged 25–44 years – United States, 1991 and 1992'. *Morbidity and Mortality Weekly Report* 42, no. 45 (1993): 869–72.

Chapman, Rowena. 'The great pretender: Variations on the new man theme'. In *Male Order: Unwrapping Masculinity*, edited by Rowena Chapman and Jonathan Rutherford, 225–48. London: Lawrence and Wishart, 1988.

Chira, Susan. 'Gay parents become increasingly visible'. *New York Times*, 30 September 1993.

Chopra-Gant, Mike. *Hollywood Genres and Postwar America: Masculinity, Family and Nation in Popular Movies and Film Noir*. London: I.B. Tauris, 2005.

Clinton, William J. 'Address accepting the presidential nomination at the Democratic National Convention in New York', 16 July 1992. Available at http://www.presidency.ucsb.edu/ws/index.php?pid=25958 (accessed 3 August 2018).

Clinton, William J. 'Address before a joint session of Congress on administration goals', 17 February 1993. Available at http://www.presidency.ucsb.edu/ws/?pid=47232 (accessed 3 August 2018).

Clinton, William J. 'Address before a joint session of Congress on the state of the Union', 19 January 1999. Available at http://www.presidency.ucsb.edu/ws/index.php?pid=57577 (accessed 3 August 2018).

Clinton, William J. 'Address before a joint session of the Congress on the state of the Union', 25 January 1994. Available at http://www.presidency.ucsb.edu/ws/index.php?pid=50409 (accessed 3 August 2018).

Clinton, William J. 'Address before a joint session of Congress on the state of the Union', 4 February 1997. Available at http://www.presidency.ucsb.edu/ws/index.php?pid=53358 (accessed 3 August 2018).

Clinton, William J. 'Presidential proclamation 6701: Father's Day 1994', 14 June 1994. Available at http://www.presidency.ucsb.edu/ws/index.php?pid=50336 (accessed 3 August 2018).

Collier, Richard. 'Fatherhood, law and fathers' rights: Rethinking the relationship between gender and welfare'. In *Rights, Gender and Family*

Law, edited by Julie Wallbank, Shazia Choudhry and Jonathan Herring, 119–43. New York: Routledge, 2010.

Collier, Richard. *Masculinity, Law and the Family*. London: Routledge, 1996.

Connell, Raewyn. *Masculinities*. Berkeley: University of California Press, 1993.

Connell, Raewyn and James W. Messerschmidt. 'Hegemonic masculinity: Rethinking the concept'. *Gender & Society* 19, no. 6 (2005): 829–59.

Cox, Meredith, Erin Garrett and James A. Graham. 'Death in Disney films: Implications for children's understanding of death'. *Omega: Journal of Death and Dying* 50, no. 4 (2004–5): 267–80.

Crimp, Douglas. *Melancholia and Moralism: Essays on AIDS and Queer Politics*. Cambridge: MIT Press, 2002.

Crowley, Jocelyn E. 'Organizational responses to the fatherhood crisis: The case of fathers' rights groups in the United States'. *Marriage and Family Review* 39, nos 1–2 (2006): 99–120.

Cvetkovich, Ann. *Depression: A Public Feeling*. Durham: Duke University Press, 2012.

Daniels, Cynthia, ed. *Lost Fathers: The Politics of Fatherlessness in America*. New York: St. Martin's Griffin, 1998.

Davies, Jude. 'I'm the bad guy?: *Falling Down* and white masculinity in 1990s Hollywood'. *Journal of Gender Studies* 4, no. 2 (1995): 145–52.

Davies, Jude, and Carol R. Smith. *Gender, Ethnicity and Sexuality in Contemporary American Film*. Edinburgh: Keele University Press, 1997.

De Lauretis, Teresa. *Freud's Drive: Psychoanalysis, Literature and Film*. Basingstoke: Palgrave Macmillan, 2010.

Dennis, Norman, and George Erdos. *Families without Fatherhood*. London: Institute of Economic Affairs, 1992.

Dixon, Wheeler Winston. *Hollywood in Crisis or: The Collapse of the Real*. Basingstoke: Palgrave Macmillan, 2016.

Dixon, Wheeler Winston. 'Twenty-five reasons why it's all over'. In *The End of Cinema as We Know It: American Film in the Nineties*, edited by Jon Lewis, 356–66. New York: New York University Press, 2001.

Dixon, Wheeler Winston. *Visions of the Apocalypse: Spectacles of Destruction in American Cinema*. London: Wallflower, 2003.

Doty, Mark. *Heaven's Coast: A Memoir*. London: Jonathan Cape, 1996.
Dowd, Margaret. 'Of knights and presidents: Race of mythic proportions'. *New York Times*, 10 October 1992.
Dowd, Nancy E. *Redefining Fatherhood*. New York: New York University Press, 2000.
Dragiewicz, Molly. 'Patriarchy reasserted: Fathers' rights and anti-VAWA activism'. *Feminist Criminology* 3, no. 2 (2008): 121–44.
Dreisinger, Baz. 'The queen in shining armor: Safe eroticism and the gay friend'. *Journal of Popular Film and Television* 28, no. 1 (2000): 2–11.
Dugan, Andrew, and Frank Newport. 'Americans rate JFK as top modern president'. Available at https://news.gallup.com/poll/165902/americans-rate-jfk-top-modern-president.aspx (accessed 17 July 2018).
Dundes, Lauren, and Alan Dundes. 'Young hero Simba defeats old villain Scar: Oedipus wrecks the Lyin' King'. *The Social Science Journal* 43 (2006): 479–85.
Easthope, Antony. *What a Man's Gotta Do: The Masculine Myth in Popular Culture*. London: Routledge, 1992.
Ebert, Roger. 'Jack Frost'. *Chicago Sun-Times*, 11 December 1998.
Edelman, Lee. *No Future: Queer Theory and the Death Drive*. Durham: Duke University Press, 2004.
Erera, Pauline Irit, and Nehami Baum. 'Chat-room voices of divorced non-residential fathers'. *The Journal of Sociology and Social Welfare* 36, no. 2 (2009): 63–83.
Faludi, Susan. *Stiffed: The Betrayal of the Modern Man*. London: Chatto & Windus, 1999.
Feasey, Rebecca. *Mothers on Mothers: Maternal Readings of Popular Television*. Oxford: Peter Lang, 2016.
Fineman, Martha. *The Autonomy Myth*. New York: New Press, 2004.
Fineman, Martha. 'The politics of custody and gender: Child advocacy and the transformation of custody decision making in the USA'. In *Child Custody and the Politics of Gender*, edited by Carol Smart and Selma Sevenhuijsen, 27–50. London: Routledge, 1989.
Fischer, Lucy. *Cinematernity: Film, Motherhood, Genre*. Princeton: Princeton University Press, 1996.

Fish, W. C. 'Differences of grief intensity in bereaved parents'. In *Parental Loss of a Child*, edited by Therese A. Rando, 415–28. Illinois: Research Press Company, 1986.

Flood, Michael. 'Separated fathers and the "fathers' rights" movement'. *Journal of Family Studies* 18, nos 2–3 (2012): 235–45.

Foltyn, Jacque Lynn. 'Dead sexy: Why death is the new sex'. In *Making Sense of Death, Dying and Bereavement: An Anthology*, edited by Sarah Earle, Caroline Bartholomew and Carol Komaromy, 47–51. London: Sage, 2009.

Forrest, Jennifer, and Leonards R. Koos. *Dead Ringers: The Remake in Theory and Practice*. Albany: State University of New York Press, 2002.

Foucault, Michel. 'Friendship as a way of life'. In *Foucault Live: Interviews, 1961–1984*, edited by Sylvere Lotringer, 308–12. Translated by Lysa Hochroth and John Johnston. New York: Semiotext(e), 1996.

Freud, Sigmund. *An Outline of Psycho-Analysis*. Translated by James Strachey. London: Hogarth Press, 1979.

Freud, Sigmund. 'Beyond the pleasure principle'. In *The Standard Edition of the Complete Psychological Works of Sigmund Freud*, vol. 18, 7–64. Translated by James Strachey. London: Hogarth Press, 1955.

Freud, Sigmund. 'Mourning and melancholia'. In *The Standard Edition of the Complete Psychological Works of Sigmund Freud*, vol. 14, 243–58. Translated by James Strachey. London: Hogarth Press, 1955.

Freud, Sigmund. 'On narcissism'. In *The Standard Edition of the Complete Psychological Works of Sigmund Freud*, vol. 14, 67–102. Translated by James Strachey. London: Hogarth Press, 1955.

Freud, Sigmund. 'The future of an illusion'. In *The Standard Edition of the Complete Psychological Works of Sigmund Freud*, vol. 21, 3–56. Translated by James Strachey. London: Hogarth Press, 1961.

Freud, Sigmund. 'Totem and taboo'. In *The Standard Edition of the Complete Psychological Works of Sigmund Freud*, vol. 13, 1–162. Translated by James Strachey. London: Hogarth Press, 1955.

Garber, Marjorie. *Vested Interests: Cross-Dressing and Cultural Anxiety*. London: Penguin, 1993.

Gateward, Frances, and Murray Pomerance, eds. *Where the Boys Are: Cinemas of Masculinity and Youth*. Detroit: Wayne State University Press, 2005.

Gliatto, Tom. 'Running away with the box office by staying Home Alone, Macaulay Culkin is Hollywood's newest little big man'. *People*, 17 December 1990.

Gold, Joshua M., and Oluwatoyin Adeyemi. 'Stepfathers and noncustodial fathers: Two men, one role'. *The Family Journal: Counseling and Therapy for Couples and Families* 21, no. 1 (2013): 99–103.

Gorer, Geoffrey. *Death, Grief and Mourning in Contemporary Britain*. London: The Cresset Press, 1965.

Griswold, Robert L. *Fatherhood in America: A History*. New York: Basic Books, 1993.

Grossman, Joanna L., and Lawrence M. Friedman. *Inside the Castle: Law and the Family in 20th Century America*. Princeton: Princeton University Press, 2011.

Hagin, Boaz. *Death in Classical Hollywood Cinema*. Basingstoke: Palgrave Macmillan, 2010.

Halberstam, J. Jack. *In a Queer Time and Place: Transgender Bodies, Subcultural Lives*. New York: New York University Press, 2005.

Hamad, Hannah. *Postfeminism and Paternity in Contemporary U.S. Film*. London: Routledge, 2014.

Harwood, Sarah. *Family Fictions: Representations of the Family in 1980s Hollywood Cinema*. Basingstoke: Macmillan, 1997.

Hellmich, Christina, and Lisa Purse, eds. *Disappearing War: Interdisciplinary Perspectives on Cinema and Erasure in the Post-9/11 World*. Edinburgh: Edinburgh University Press, 2017.

Herring, Jonathan. 'Relational autonomy and family law'. In *Rights, Gender and Family Law*, edited by Julie Wallbank, Shazia Choudhry and Jonathan Herring, 257–75. New York: Routledge, 2010.

Hindmarch, Celia. *On the Death of a Child*. Abingdon: Radcliffe Medical Press, 2000.

Hoberman, J. '*Nashville* contra *Jaws*, or "The Imagination of Disaster" Revisited'. In *The Last Great American Picture Show*, edited by Thomas Elsaesser, Alexander Horwath and Noel King, 195–222. Amsterdam: Amsterdam University Press, 2004.

Hogan, David J. *Dark Romance: Sexuality in the Horror Film*. Jefferson: McFarland, 1997.

Horton, Andrew. 'Is it a wonderful life? Families and laughter in American film comedies'. In *A Family Affair: Cinema Calls Home*, edited by Murray Pomerance, 45–60. London: Wallflower, 2008.

Hughes, Cynthia Bach, and Judith Page-Lieberman. 'Fathers experiencing a perinatal loss'. *Death Studies* 13 (1989): 537–56.

James, P. D. *The Children of Men*. London: Faber and Faber, 1992.

Jeffords, Susan. *Hard Bodies: Hollywood Masculinity in the Reagan Era*. New Brunswick: Rutgers University Press, 1994.

Jenkins, Claire. *Home Movies: The American Family in Contemporary Hollywood*. London: I.B. Tauris, 2015.

Joyrich, Lynne. *Re-Viewing Reception: Television, Gender and Postmodern Culture*. Bloomington: Indiana University Press, 1996.

Kaplan, E. Ann. *Motherhood and Representation: The Mother in Popular Culture and Melodrama*. London: Routledge, 1992.

Keller, James R. *Queer (Un)Friendly Film and Television*. Jefferson, NC: McFarland, 2002.

Kimmel, Michael. *Manhood in America: A Cultural History*. Oxford: Oxford University Press, 2012.

King, Colbert I. 'Where are the fathers?' *Washington Post*, 10 July 1999.

Kirtz, Mary K. 'Canadian book, American film: Shoeless Joe transfigured on a *Field of Dreams*'. *Literature/Film Quarterly* 23 (1995): 26–31.

Klass, Perri. 'A Bambi for the 90s, via Shakespeare'. *New York Times*, 19 June 1994.

Kleinhans, Chuck. '1993: Movies and the new economics of blockbusters and indies'. In *American Cinema of the 1990s: Themes and Variations*, edited by Chris Holmlund, 91–114. New Brunswick: Rutgers University Press, 2008.

Krämer, Peter. 'Would you take your child to see this film? The cultural and social work of the family adventure movie'. In *Contemporary Hollywood Cinema*, edited by Steve Neale and Murray Smith, 294–311. London: Routledge, 1998.

Lang, Ariella, and Laurie Gottlieb. 'Parental grief reactions and marital intimacy in bereaved and non-bereaved couples: A comparative study'. In *Children and Death*, edited by Danai Papadatou and Constantine Papadatos, 267–75. Washington, DC: Hemisphere, 1991.

Lasch, Christopher. *The Culture of Narcissism: American Life in an Age of Diminishing Expectations*. New York: W. W. Norton, 1991.

Lawrence, Amy. *Echo and Narcissus: Women's Voices in Classical Hollywood Cinema*. Berkeley: University of California Press, 1991.

Lebeau, Vicky. *Childhood and Cinema*. London: Reaktion, 2008.

Leclaire, Serge. *A Child Is Being Killed: On Primary Narcissism and the Death Drive*. Translated by Marie-Claude Hays. Stanford: Stanford University Press, 1998.

Lehr, Valerie. *Queer Family Values: Debunking the Myth of the Nuclear Family*. Philadelphia: Temple University Press, 1999.

Lennard, Dominic W. 'All fun and games … Children's culture in the horror film, from *Deep Red* (1975) to *Child's Play* (1988)'. *Continuum: Journal of Media and Cultural Studies* 26, no. 1 (2012): 133–42.

Lerner, Barron H. 'The art of medicine: Complicated lessons: Lorenzo Odone and medical miracles'. *The Lancet* 373, no. 9667 (2002): 888–9.

Lev, Arlene Istar. 'Gay dads: Choosing surrogacy'. *Lesbian and Gay Psychology Review* 7, no. 1 (2006): 72–6.

Lewin, Tamar. 'Father's vanishing act called common drama'. *New York Times*, 4 June 1990.

Mack, Dana. *Assault on Parenthood: How Our Culture Undermines Parenthood*. San Francisco: Encounter, 1997.

Mackey-Kallis, Susan. *The Hero and the Perennial Journey Home in American Film*. Philadelphia: University of Pennsylvania Press, 2001.

Malin, Brenton J. *American Masculinity under Clinton: Popular Media and the Nineties Crisis of Masculinity*. New York: Peter Lang, 2005.

Mandel, Sharona, and Shlomo A. Sharlin. 'The non-custodial father: His involvement in his children's lives and the connection between his role and the ex-wife's, child's and father's perception of that role'. *Journal of Divorce and Remarriage* 45 (2006): 79–95.

Mandell, Frederick, Elizabeth McAnulty and Robert M. Reece. 'Observations of paternal response to sudden unanticipated infant death'. *Pediatrics* 65, no. 2 (1980): 221–5.

Mann, Karen B. 'Lost boys and girls in Spielberg's *Minority Report*'. *Journal of Narrative Theory* 35, no. 2 (2005): 196–217.

Markert, John. *Post-9/11 Cinema: Through a Lens Darkly*. Lanham: Scarecrow Press, 2011.

Mason, Mary Ann. *From Father's Property to Children's Rights: The History of Child Custody in the United States*. New York: Columbia University Press, 1994.

Maupin, Armistead. *Michael Tolliver Lives*. London: Black Swan, 2008.

McSweeney, Terence, ed. *American Cinema in the Shadow of 9/11*. Edinburgh: Edinburgh University Press, 2017.

Melville, Angela, and Rosemary Hunter. '"As everybody knows": Countering myths of gender bias in family law'. *Griffith Law Review* 10 (2001): 124–38.

Modleski, Tania. *Feminism without Women: Culture and Criticism in a 'Postfeminist' Age*. London: Routledge, 1991.

Morris, Dick. *Behind the Oval Office: Winning the Presidency in the Nineties*. New York: Random House, 1997.

Mulvey, Laura. *Death 24x a Second: Stillness and the Moving Image*. London: Reaktion, 2006.

Nadel, Alan. *Flatlining of the Field of Dreams: Cultural Narratives in the Films of President Reagan's America*. New Brunswick: Rutgers University Press, 1997.

Natoli, Joseph. *Hauntings: Popular Film and American Culture 1990–1992*. Albany: State University of New York Press, 1994.

Neale, Steve. 'The big romance or something wild? Romantic comedy today'. *Screen* 33, no. 3 (1992): 284–99.

Neale, Steve, and Murray Smith, eds. *Contemporary Hollywood Cinema*. London: Routledge, 1998.

Norton, Arthur J., and Louisa F. Miller. 'Marriage, divorce and remarriage in the 1990s'. *Current Population Reports (U.S. Bureau of the Census)* 23, no. 180 (1992): 1–13.

O'Connor, Jane. 'From Jackie Coogan to Michael Jackson: What child stars can tell us about ideologies of childhood'. *Journal of Children and Media* 5, no. 3 (2011): 284–97.

Papke, David Ray. 'Peace between the sexes: Law and gender in *Kramer vs. Kramer*'. *University of San Francisco Law Review* 30 (1996): 1199–208.

Parke, Ross D., and Armin A. Brott. *Throwaway Dads: The Myths That Keep Men from Being the Fathers They Want to Be*. Boston: Houghton Mifflin, 1999.

Paul, Robert A. 'Cultural narratives and the succession scenario: *Slumdog Millionaire* and other popular films and fictions'. *The International Journal of Psychoanalysis* 92, no. 2 (2011): 451–70.

Pearl, Monica B. 'Symptoms of AIDS in contemporary film: Mortal anxiety in an age of sexual panic'. In *The Body's Perilous Pleasures: Dangerous Desires and Contemporary Culture*, edited by Michele Aaron, 210–25. Edinburgh: Edinburgh University Press, 1999.

Peberdy, Donna. *Masculinity and Film Performance: Male Angst in Contemporary American Cinema*. Basingstoke: Palgrave Macmillan, 2013.

Peppers, Larry G., and Ronald J. Knapp. *Motherhood and Mourning: Perinatal Death*. London: Praeger, 1980.

Petley, Julian. 'The monstrous child'. In *The Body's Perilous Pleasures: Dangerous Desires and Contemporary Culture*, edited by Michele Aaron, 87–107. Edinburgh: Edinburgh University Press, 1999.

Pettigrew, Jonathan. '"I'll take what I can get": Identity development in the case of a stepfather'. *Journal of Divorce and Remarriage* 51, no. 1 (2013): 25–42.

Pfeil, Fred. *White Guys: Studies in Postmodern Domination and Difference*. London: Verso, 1995.

Polikoff, Nancy D. 'Lesbians choosing children: The personal is political revisited'. In *Politics of the Heart: A Lesbian Parenting Anthology*, edited by Sandra Pollack and Jeanne Vaughn, 48–54. Ithaca: Firebrand, 1987.

Pomerance, Murray, ed. *A Family Affair: Cinema Calls Home*. London: Wallflower, 2008.

Popenoe, David. *Life without Father*. New York: Free Press, 1996.

Quimby, Karin. 'Will & Grace: Negotiating (gay) marriage on prime-time television'. *Journal of Popular Culture* 38, no. 4 (2005): 713–31.

Quinn, Judy. 'The mighty munchkin: Macaulay Culkin'. *Incentive* 166, no. 12 (1992): 13.

Reagan/Bush Campaign. 'Peace through strength', 1980. Available at http://www.livingroomcandidate.org/commercials/1980/peace-republican#4072 (accessed 3 August 2018).

Reagan, Ronald. 'Inaugural address', 20 January 1981. Available at http://www.presidency.ucsb.edu/ws/?pid=43130 (accessed 3 August 2018).

Riley, Glenda. *Divorce: An American Tradition*. Oxford: Oxford University Press, 1991.

Rizzo, William B. 'Lorenzo's oil: Hope and disappointment'. *New England Journal of Medicine* 329, no. 11 (1993): 801–2.

Roberts, Roxanne. '16 Candles for Chelsea'. *Washington Post*, 27 February 1997.

Robinson, Sally. *Marked Men: White Masculinity in Crisis*. New York: Columbia University Press, 2000.

Rosenman, Andrew S. 'Babies Jessica, Richard and Emily: The need for legislative reform of adoption laws'. *Chicago-Kent Law Review* 70, no. 4 (1995): 1851–96.

Roth, Matt. 'The Lion King: A short history of Disney-fascism'. *Jump Cut: A Review of Contemporary Media* 40 (1996): 15–20.

Rotundo, E. Anthony. *American Manhood: Transformations in Masculinity from the Revolution to the Modern Era*. New York: Basic Books, 1993.

Rubin, Peter. 'Family man: Bill Clinton, national dad'. *New Republic*, 27 April 1998.

Savage, Dan. 'Status is … for gay men; the baby'. *New York Times Magazine*, 15 November 1998.

Schober, Adrian, and Debbie Olson. *Children in the Films of Steven Spielberg*. Lanham: Lexington Books, 2016.

Schwab, Reiko. 'Gender differences in parental grief'. *Death Studies* 20 (1996): 103–14.

Sedgwick, Eve Kosofsky. 'How to bring your kids up gay'. In *Fear of a Queer Planet: Queer Politics and Social Theory*, edited by Michael Warner, 69–81. Minneapolis: University of Minnesota Press, 1993.

Seltzer, Judith. 'Relationships between fathers and children who live apart: The father's role after separation'. *Journal of Marriage and Family* 53, no. 1 (1991): 79–101.

Sharrett, Christopher, ed. *Crisis Cinema: The Apocalyptic Idea in Postmodern Narrative Film*. Washington, DC: Maisonneuve Press, 1993.

Shugart, Helene. 'Managing masculinities: The metrosexual moment'. *Communication and Critical/Cultural Studies* 5, no. 3 (2008): 280–300.

Simonds, Wendy, and Barbara Katz Rothman. *Centuries of Solace: Expressions of Maternal Grief in Popular Literature*. Philadelphia: Temple University Press, 1992.

Simpson, Mark. 'Here come the mirror men: Why the future is metrosexual'. *Independent*, 15 November 1994.

Sinyard, Neil. *Children in the Movies*. London: B. T. Batsford, 1992.

Smart, Carol. 'Power and the politics of child custody'. In *Child Custody and the Politics of Gender*, edited by Carol Smart and Selma Sevenhuijsen, 1–26. London: Routledge, 1989.

Smith, Iain Robert, and Constantine Verevis. *Transnational Film Remakes*. Edinburgh: Edinburgh University Press, 2017.

Sontag, Susan. 'The imagination of disaster'. In *Against Interpretation and Other Essays*, 209–25. New York: Picador, 1966.

Spitz, Ellen Handler. *Illuminating Childhood: Portraits in Fiction, Film, and Drama*. Ann Arbor: University of Michigan Press, 2011.

Stanford, Peter. 'Augusto Odone obituary'. *Guardian*, 1 November 2013.

Strick, Philip. 'Contact'. *Sight and Sound* 7, no. 10 (October 1997): 44–6.

Sturken, Marita. *Tangled Memories: The Vietnam War, the AIDS Epidemic, and the Politics of Remembering*. Berkeley: University of California Press, 1997.

Sturken, Marita. '*Affliction*: When paranoid male narratives fail'. In *The End of Cinema as We Know It: American Film in the Nineties*, edited by Jon Lewis, 203–9. New York: New York University Press, 2001.

Sullivan, Andrew. 'When plagues end'. *New York Times Magazine*, 10 November 1996.

Sullivan, Nikki. *A Critical Introduction to Queer Theory*. Edinburgh: Edinburgh University Press, 2003.

Takemoto, Tina. 'The melancholia of AIDS: Interview with Douglas Crimp'. *Art Journal* 62, no. 4 (2003): 80–91.

Talbot, Kay. *What Forever Means after the Death of a Child: Transcending the Trauma, Living with the Loss*. New York: Brunner-Routledge, 2002.

Tasker, Yvonne. 'Practically perfect people: Postfeminism, masculinity and male parenting in contemporary cinema'. In *A Family Affair: Cinema Calls Home*, edited by Murray Pomerance, 175–87. London: Wallflower, 2008.

Thompson, John O. 'Reflexions on dead children in the cinema and why there are not more of them'. In *Representations of Child Death*, edited by Gillian Avery and Kimberley Reynolds, 204–16. Basingstoke: Macmillan, 2003.

Thompson, Kirsten Moana. *Apocalyptic Dread: American Film at the Turn of the Millennium*. Albany: State University of New York Press, 2007.

Toles, George. 'Film death and the failure to signify: The curious case of Warni Hazard'. *New Review of Film and Television Studies* 15, no. 2 (2017): 211–30.

Truffaut, François. *Hitchcock*. London: Simon & Schuster, 1985.

US Census Bureau. *Living Arrangements of Children 1996*. Washington, DC: US Government Printing Office, 2001.

US Census Bureau. *Statistical Abstract of the United States 2012*. Washington, DC: US Government Printing Office, 2011.

US Census Bureau. 'We the American Women'. *We the Americans Report* 8 (1993): 1–10.

Verevis, Constantine. *Film Remakes*. Edinburgh: Edinburgh University Press, 2005.

Waldman, Steven. 'Deadbeat dads'. *Newsweek*, 4 May 1992.

Walsh, Fintan. *Male Trouble: Masculinity and the Performance of Crisis*. Basingstoke: Palgrave Macmillan, 2010.

Walters, Suzanna Danuta. *All the Rage: The Story of Gay Visibility in America*. Chicago: University of Chicago Press, 2001.

Ward, Annalee R. *Mouse Morality: The Rhetoric of Animated Disney Film*. Austin: University of Texas Press, 2002.

Watney, Simon. 'The spectacle of AIDS'. In *AIDS: Cultural Analysis / Cultural Activism*, edited by Douglas Crimp, 71–86. London: MIT/ October Magazine, 1996.

Watney, Simon. *Policing Desire: Pornography, AIDS and the Media*. London: Cassell, 1997.

Weiss, Andrea. 'From the margins: New images of gays in the cinema'. *Cineaste* 15, no. 1 (1986): 4–8.

Weston, Kath. *Families We Choose: Lesbians, Gays, Kinship*. New York: Columbia University Press, 1991.

Westwell, Guy. *Parallel Lines: Post-9/11 American Cinema*. London: Wallflower Press, 2014.

Willis, Sharon. 'Movies and melancholy'. In *American Cinema of the 2000s: Themes and Variations*, edited by Timothy Corrigan, 61–82. New Brunswick: Rutgers University Press, 2012.

Wilson, Emma. *Cinema's Missing Children*. London: Wallflower, 2003.

Wilson, Emma. *Love, Mortality and the Moving Image*. Basingstoke: Palgrave Macmillan, 2012.

Wisensale, Steven K. *Family Leave Policy: The Political Economy of Work and Family in America*. London: Routledge, 2015.

Wood, Robin. *Hollywood from Vietnam to Reagan … and Beyond*. New York: Columbia University Press, 2003.

Woolley, Elena. 'The end of all things: Overcoming the end of the world in American cinema'. *Cineaction* 95 (2015): 26–35.

Index

A.I. Artificial Intelligence 127–9
Allen, Tim 88, 199
apocalypse 7, 154, 199
Armageddon 50, 56–8, 159
Autumn in New York 100

Bersani, Leo 107, 164, 167–8, 187, 189
Birdcage, The 171–2, 175, 180–6, 190
Blankenhorn, David 26–7, 89
Bly, Robert 22, 46
Bush, (President) George H. W. 3, 25, 203–4
Bush, (President) George W. 25, 203–5

Canetti, Elias 16–17, 55, 114, 134–5, 159–60
Cape Fear 19–21, 45, 71–2, 200
Carrey, Jim 80, 199
Carter, (President) Jimmy 2, 23, 51
children
 as saviour 10–11, 83, 108–9, 147
 as symbols of innocence 99–100, 109, 197
 chosen family 168, 171–2, 177–9; *see also* same-sex parenting
Clinton, (President) Bill 3, 16, 21–5, 75, 155
crisis of masculinity; *see* masculinity
Contact 153–7, 159
Culkin, Macaulay 109
Cure, The 118, 120, 123
custody 44, 78–9, 94

Dante's Peak 45–50, 53
death
 of child 97–9, 101, 108, 121–3
 in cinema 100–3, 133–4
 of father 56–8, 131–2, 134–6, 144, 159–60, 206

parental bereavement 99, 106, 110, 119 (*see also* fatherhood; motherhood)
death drive 13, 52, 102, 198
Deep Impact 50, 53, 59, 98, 131
disaster films 50–3, 58, 62–3, 154
divorce 66–8, 76
Don't Look Now 119
Douglas, Michael 76

Edelman, Lee 14–16, 98, 130, 150, 163, 165–6; *see also* reproductive futurism

Falling Down 75–8, 85, 200
Faludi, Susan 112, 115, 121, 134, 150
family courts 67–9, 72, 81–2, 88–9
family film 9, 49, 143
Fatal Attraction 76
father quest 140–1, 144, 155, 162
fatherhood
 absent 26–8, 45, 66, 73, 116–17
 adoptive 29, 169
 biological 28, 168, 170–1
 breadwinner 4, 30, 43–4, 70, 144, 146
 changing definition 28–30
 and daughters 153–9
 deadbeat dad 4, 27, 74–5
 domestication 11–12, 66, 85, 200–1
 fathers' rights movement 26–8, 68, 72, 76–7, 198
 gay fatherhood 29, 161–2, 167–8, 174, 185–6, 190–3 (*see also* same-sex parenting)
 grief 106–7
 legal definition 69, 172
 noncustodial 68, 73
 presidential 21–5

protection 43–4
redemption 11, 21, 111–12, 148, 196–7, 199–200
responsibility 26–7, 43–4, 71–2, 75, 149–50, 199
sacrifice 35–6, 167, 181–2, 185–92
and sons 111–12, 121–2, 125–6, 134–5, 153
stepfathers 29, 68, 89–93, 116–17, 146
transformation 84–7
feminism 10–11, 85
Field of Dreams 132, 143–4, 160
Freud, Sigmund; *see also* death drive; Oedipal complex; narcissism
father substitute 89–90
mastery 60–2, 102–3, 106, 129, 157, 197–8
melancholia 106–7, 110, 150–1
traumatic neurosis 133–5 (*see also* trauma)

gay rights 4, 152, 161, 164, 169–70, 186
Ghost Dad 144
Godfather, The 100
Good Son, The 108–12

heroism 18, 38, 42–3, 202, 208
heteronormativity 17, 157–9, 170–3, 176, 179, 184; *see also* nuclear family
HIV/AIDS
activism 4, 186–7, 189
post-AIDS 165–6, 192
representation 152–3, 188–9
in US 122–3, 161–5, 187–8
Hollywood
high-concept films 59–60
and independent cinema 10, 123
industrial change 9, 196
remakes 19
Home Alone 20, 71

I Am Sam 81
Ice Storm, The 123–7
immortality 13–17, 62–3, 129, 131–2, 137–8, 159–60; *see also* narcissism
In America 100
Independence Day 50, 53, 60
Indiana Jones franchise 41–2

Jack Frost 144–51
Jaws 42–3, 51–2
Junior 18
Jurassic Park 37–45, 48–9, 60–2, 81

Kindergarten Cop 1, 8, 17, 34–5, 43, 200
Kramer vs. Kramer 68–9

Liar Liar 78, 80–4, 91–2
Lion King, The 132–43, 150–1
Lorenzo's Oil 103–7, 129

masculinity
anxiety 6–7, 12, 32, 112, 121–2, 134
boyhood 99–100, 115
as construction 5–6, 174
crisis of masculinity 2, 5–7, 121–2, 153, 162, 195–9
disenfranchisement 76, 187
hard-bodied 8, 38, 208
and heterosexuality 174–5
and homosexuality 174–6, 184
new man 7, 11, 85–6, 160
pluralization 7, 12, 22–3
whiteness 5–7, 76, 121–2, 137, 195
Mighty, The 109, 118, 120
motherhood
breadwinner 70, 145–6
in family law 77–8
grief 106–7, 110–11, 113–15, 119
lesbian motherhood 161–2, 186 (*see also* same-sex parenting)
marginalization 12, 154
rejection of 184

Mrs. Doubtfire 69–74, 78–80, 90–2, 206
My Girl 109, 120–2

narcissism
  cultural 142, 145
  and immortality 13–17, 145 (*see also* immortality)
  and reproduction 56–7, 132, 150–1, 165–6, 190–1
neoliberalism 72–3, 104, 199
new man; *see* masculinity
Next Best Thing, The 69, 92, 170–2, 174–6, 179–80, 188
Nine Months 35–6, 200
9/11; *see* September 11, 2001
Nixon, (President) Richard 51, 126
non-reproduction 15, 123, 129, 139, 172, 201
nuclear family 40, 47, 66, 72–3, 166, 168–9; *see also* heteronormativity

Object of My Affection, The 166–70, 172–80, 187–8, 190
Oedipal complex 14, 134–5, 137–9, 141, 152

Paradise 108, 112–20, 122, 146
Pearl, Monica 152–3
Peck, Gregory 21
Phenomenon 135

queerness 15, 107, 123, 141–2, 163

Reagan, (President) Ronald 23, 42, 51, 75, 90, 186
Regarding Henry 81, 83–4

reincarnation 152–3
reproduction 49–50, 61–2, 118–19, 154, 158, 171–2; *see also* narcissism; reproductive technology
reproductive futurism 14–16, 48, 100, 130, 166–7, 201; *see also* Edelman, Lee
reproductive technology 28, 169

same-sex parenting 28, 161–2, 169–70; *see also* fatherhood; motherhood; chosen family
Santa Clause, The 73–4, 79–81, 84, 86–9, 91, 93, 146
Schwarzenegger, Arnold 17–19, 43
September 11, 2001 12, 201–5
single parenthood 26, 73
Spielberg, Steven 41–3, 127–8, 203

Terminator 2: Judgment Day 18
Three Men and a Baby 66
To Kill a Mockingbird 83
trauma 45, 108, 115, 129, 132–5, 153; *see also* Freud, Sigmund
True Lies 18
Twister 153–4, 157–9

Vietnam War 2, 42, 51
Volcano 53–6

War of the Roses, The 76, 90
War of the Worlds 202–3, 205
Watergate 42, 51, 125–6
Weather Man, The 205–6
Williams, Robin 70, 88, 199
Wood, Elijah 108, 123–4